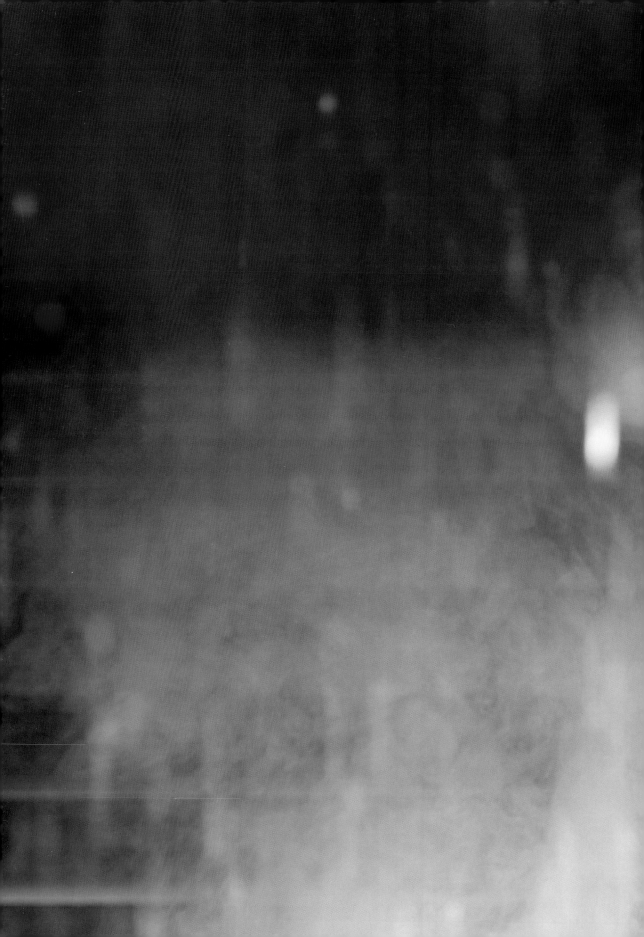

ISBN: 978–981–07–1880–0

Please direct all enquiries to the Publisher:
Singapore Art Museum
71 Bras Basah Road
Singapore 189555
www.singaporeartmuseum.sg

Editors	Tan Boon Hui
	Joyce Toh
Copy Editor	Susie Wong
Writers	Silvia Chan
	David Chew
	Michelle Ho
	Khairuddin Hori
	Tan Siu Li
	Jason Toh
	Joyce Toh
	Naomi Wang Zhenghui
	Susie Wong
Project Management	Silvia Chan
Curatorial Assistants	Linda Lee
	Melissa Tan
	Siti Aimilia Bte Safuan
Design	Muhammad Izdiharuddin
Printed by	Oxford Graphic Printers Pte Ltd

Front Cover:
Jing Quek, *Singapore Idols: Skateboarders* (detail),
2006, Epson inkjet print with ultrachrome K3 ink,
52 x 77.5 cm, Singapore Art Museum collection

Front inside cover:
Ho Tzu Nyen, *The Cloud of Unknowing* (detail),
2011, Installation with single-channel HD video
projection, multi-channel audio, lighting, smoke
machines and show control system, duration 28:00 mins,
Singapore Art Museum collection

Back inside cover:
Suzann Victor, *Expense of Spirit in a Waste of
Shame*, 1994, mixed media: light bulbs, cables, control
unit, broken glass, motors, aluminium rods, mirrors,
dimensions variable, Singapore Art Museum collection

TOMORROW

TOMORROW, TODAY

**CONTEMPORARY ART
FROM THE
SINGAPORE ART MUSEUM
(2009 – 2011)**

sam
singapore**art**museum

Contents

FOREWORD: WHY SAM COLLECTS?

Tan Boon Hui
Director
Singapore Art Museum

Collections define museums. A museum's collection is the spine or focus around which curatorial, programming and communication activities take reference from, and in fact, justify the existence of the museum. This is especially critical in our age of spectacle and flash, when art fairs, private art investments and purveyors of the so-called 'edu-tainment', seem to always reduce public perceptions of contemporary art to what it can fetch on the market, rather than what it means to individuals, communities and nations. All the great museums of the world, be it the Metropolitan Museum of Art and the Museum of Modern Art (MOMA) in New York, the British Museum in London, the Musée d'Orsay in Paris, or the two Palace Museums in Beijing and Taipei, have built their reputations and attractiveness around their incredible collections. Permanent collections are aesthetic statements of what is valuable and worth preserving beyond the changing fashions of art styles and materials. For a contemporary art museum like SAM, the works in the collection represent a record of the creative possibilities pursued by artists in our time. It shows the paths taken, how they respond not only to

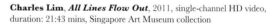

art but to the pressing social contexts of our time. This latter point is particularly vital in the contemporary art of our region and separate SAM from its sister museum, the National Art Gallery, Singapore.

As a relatively young nation in a very old region, Singapore does not have the long accretions of historical time to build the comprehensive and deep collections that these other museums have built up. While this may be a constraining factor for museums of antiquity or modern art museums, as a museum focused wholly on the contemporary or current moment, SAM has the benefit of building its collection in tandem with its artists. Since 2009, SAM has refocused its energies on the possibilities for the creation of art in the present moment, ceding the modern and its antecedents to the newly established National Art Gallery, Singapore.

This publication celebrates the fruits of the re-imagined SAM's new focus on living artists and art practices of our era. Right from the museum's inception in 1996, SAM has been one of the few institutions in the region actively collecting, researching and exhibiting the art of Southeast Asia and the Asian region, particularly

China and India. The contemporary art collection of SAM therefore mirrors the production of art in Singapore, Southeast Asia and the Asian region in current times.

This publication featuring more than 300 works from 180 artists provides the best and most defining snapshot of the main trajectories of current artistic practice in the region, the concerns of its artists and their use of mediums and materials. The curatorial texts accompanying each work attempts to link the art to its social context and its relation to artistic practice. The reader will hopefully discern a clear sense of the richness and distinctive poetics of the art of this region. We hope that all curators, educators, art students, gallerists, collectors, artists and everyone interested in the region's contemporary art will find knowledge and inspiration through reading this publication.

Most of all, this publication is for all the talented artists from Southeast Asia and Asia. Without their passion and creativity, the rich cultural legacy embodied by the art in this book would not have been realised.

SINGAPORE

Ang Song Nian	Kumari Nahappan
Song-Ming Ang	Francis Ng
David Chan	Dawn Ng
Cheo Chai Hiang	Om Mee Ai
Choy Ka Fai	Donna Ong
Genevieve Chua	Sherman Ong
Chua Chye Teck	PHUNK
Chun Kai Feng	PHUNK & Keiichi Tanaami
John Clang	Milenko Prvacki
Safaruddin Dyn	Jing Quek
Eng Joo Heng	Sai Hua Kuan
Amanda Heng	Sima Salehi Rahni
Ho Tzu Nyen	Jeremy Sharma
Hong Sek Chern	Tang Da Wu
Lucas Jodogne	Tang Mun Kit
Zai Kuning	Tang Ling Nah
Jane Lee	Vertical Submarine
Justin Lee	Suzann Victor
Sean Lee	Jason Wee
Lee Wen	Ming Wong
Vincent Leow	Ian Woo
Charles Lim	Joel Yuen
Jessie Lim	ZERO
Jovian Lim	Robert Zhao Renhui
Gilles Massot	Ryf Zaini

Ang Song Nian

And Now,
Like Sleeping Flowers

2009–2010
Archival inkjet on photo paper
Set of 4, edition 1/3
108 x 85 cm (each)

Singapore Art Museum
collection

And Now, Like Sleeping Flowers is an allegorical work about humanity's complex relationship with nature. The work depicts a wild and exuberant jungle-like environment, proffering a contrast to the notion of the Garden City, which Singapore has been famously known as, especially in the 1980s. From a distance, the white flakes in the foreground appear like early winter snow, yet it is an anomaly given the background which shows a tropical green. Reality sometimes challenges our desires to see our world in a specific way. On closer inspection, one realises that the flakes are actually paper confetti that simulate the Chinese practice of *fang lu qian* (or scattering road money). In a Chinese funeral procession, a man precedes the coffin to scatter pieces of offering paper along the road, a practice undertaken to buy the goodwill of malicious spirits in the afterlife. This work is coloured by double meaning. On the one hand, it suggests that man can never bend nature to his will completely, just like the garden city constantly needs to be guarded against the encroachment of wild greenery. On the other hand, it is also a reminder of how human culture and belief have altered the our view on nature and what is natural.

Ang Song Nian (b. 1983, Singapore) lives and works in London. His works have been part of several major art exhibitions like the Singapore International Photography Festival (2010), Singapore Art Exhibition (2009), Singapore Art Show (2005) and Philip Morris Singapore Arts Award (2005). He was also a finalist for the Sovereign Asian Art Prize 2012.

(TJ)

Song-Ming Ang

Be True To Your School

2010
5-channel video, edition 1/5
Duration 3:00 mins (each)

Singapore Art Museum
collection

The video installation, ***Be True To Your School*** was completed during an artist-in-residence programme with the ARCUS (or Residency for Artists, Experiments for Locals) Project, Japan. The residency took place within the Manabi-no-sato Building, which the Oisawa Elementary School occupied until 1995 before it moved out to a larger building. Ang invited former students from Oisawa Elementary School to sing what they remembered of their school song. They were first recorded on video individually–many of them pausing, repeating, and struggling to remember the lyrics. After the individual recordings were completed, he then invited the former students to come during his residency Open Studio to sing the song as a group, somewhat like a school reunion. Having listened to the school song sung by the individuals, he created an accompaniment on *glockenspiel* (a percussion instrument) and performed with the participants.

All the videos are first-take recordings, capturing the singers in their 'unrehearsed' state. The work examines questions of people's sense of belonging, how it is linked to memory and how they identify with different groups of people in the society they inhabit.

Song-Ming Ang (b. 1980, Singapore) is a sound artist and musician exploring various intersections between the avant-garde and the popular. In recent years, his works have spanned audiovisual screenings, DJ sets, interactive installations, laptop improvisations, and listening parties. He graduated from the Goldsmiths College, London with a Master (Distinction) in Aural and Visual Cultures in 2008. In 2011, he participated in exhibitions such as the 3rd Singapore Biennale, the Singapore Arts Festival, Wunderblock, Grimmuseum, Berlin, and in 2012, had a solo exhibition at Künstlerhaus Bethanien, Berlin.

(TJ)

...bear a long history and tradition.

David Chan

Androgenie – Baby Cat
2009
Mixed media, edition 1/2
115 x 95 x 28 cm

Androgenie – Baby Rabbit
2009
Mixed media, edition 1/2
115 x 95 x 28 cm

Singapore Art Museum
collection

Each of these two sculptures, *Androgenie – Baby Cat* and *Androgenie – Baby Rabbit*, is a depiction of a toddler's body combined with the head of an animal which is a common pet in the modern household. Rendered with notable technical skill, the baby cat and rabbit are also accompanied here by small reproductions of objects of domestic life, such as a hairdryer and stovetop – as well as instruments associated with violence, like a machine gun, pistol and knife. Yet any real threat of bloodshed is neutralised as the objects associated with war have become highly aestheticised as 'cute', and art here comes deliberately packaged as oversized toys.

Through his depictions of hybrid human-animal figures, David Chan has probed the issues and questions thrown up by rapid scientific advancements and their impact on society. These are imagined projections of a world living with the consequences of eugenics and genetic engineering, as well as scientific experimentation gone awry. Chan's humanoid creatures become metaphors of humanity, as it adopt animal traits and instincts, prowling the urban jungle as denizens of the modern world.

David Chan (b. 1979, Singapore) graduated from LASALLE College of the Arts in 2003, and Royal Melbourne Institute of Technology in 2004. Chan was the winner of the 23rd UOB (United Overseas Bank) Painting of the Year Exhibition (Representational Medium category) in 2004. In 2009, he took part in the 2nd Animamix Biennial in Taipei, Shanghai and Beijing. He has exhibited widely in Beijing, New York, Shanghai, Korea, Indonesia and Singapore.

(JT)

Androgenie – Baby Cat   *Androgenie – Baby Rabbit*

David Chan

Schizophrenia:
The Bone-Chewing Rat
The Wheel-Cycling Cat
The Cheese-Eating Dog

2004
Oil on canvas, set of three
50 x 50 cm (each)

Seibo Goes to Heaven

2005
Oil on canvas
150 x 150 cm

Singapore Art Museum
collection

Seibo Goes to Heaven hypothesises the possible outcomes of genetic engineering. Seibo the dog, part-mechanical and part-organic, reflects the current debate on transgenics development. In this work, Chan approaches topics of cybernetics, genetic and humanism from a detached yet witty and light-hearted point of view. Seibo is depicted with an air of innocence, with the ruffled collar of a French Harlequin, or an *Arlecchino* as it is known in Italian. The etymology of 'Arlecchino' is linked to one of the devils in Dante's *Inferno*. At the same time, Seibo is portrayed against a cerulean heavenly blue sky and shown with an angel's halo, and the juxtaposition suggests the divine entwined with pervasive evils, especially in relation to the ethical arguments regarding modern-day science.

In ***Schizophrenia: The Bone-Chewing Rat***, ***The Wheel-Cycling Cat***, ***The Cheese-Eating Dog***, an action is untenably associated with each animal, as each creature is paired with an apparatus and a food item not normally associated with it. The normalcy of the image is broken with the cat depicted as running on a hamster's wheel, while the dog eats the cheese and the rat chews the bone. These reversals of roles make the entire scene disconcerting and uncomfortable to view.

David Chan (b. 1979, Singapore) graduated from LASALLE College of the Arts in 2003, and Royal Melbourne Institute of Technology in 2004. Chan was the winner of the 23rd UOB (United Overseas Bank) Painting of the Year Exhibition (Representational Medium category) in 2004. In 2009, he took part in the 2nd Animamix Biennial in Taipei, Shanghai and Beijing. He has exhibited widely in Beijing, New York, Shanghai, Korea, Indonesia and Singapore.

(SC)

Top: *Seibo Goes to Heaven*
Left: *Schizophrenia: The Bone-Chewing Rat,*
The Wheel-Cycling Cat , The Cheese-Eating Dog

Cheo Chai Hiang

Dear Cai Xiong (A Letter From Ho Ho Ying, 1972)

2005
Pencil on unprimed canvas
Set of 4
379 x 257 cm (each)

Singapore Art Museum
collection

A 2005 work which bears a history dating back to more than 32 years ago, ***Dear Cai Xiong (A Letter From Ho Ho Ying, 1972)*** is an important work of art which references events and currents of thought in the artistic circles of the 1970s.

In 1972, Cheo Chai Hiang, then 26, submitted a proposal to the annual Modern Art Society exhibition, of which he was a member, and where he regularly exhibited. The proposed work entitled 'Singapore River', came in the form of written instructions to the exhibition organisers, to draw a square measuring five feet, part on the floor, and part on its adjacent wall. The conceptual piece was rejected by the society, and club founding member Mr Ho Ho Ying, responded to Cheo in a letter which discoursed on the criteria of art in relation to its audiences. Art, he opined, besides being new, also had to resonate with its viewers and possess unique qualities.

The very question of art's purpose, trends in notions of art as tangible objects or pictorially pleasing, and the Singapore art during the 1970s, can be gleaned in this exchange. Cheo's critique of the prevailing forms of representation in Singapore art is evidenced through his proposed conceptual presentation of the Singapore River. In ***Dear Cai Xiong (A Letter From Ho Ho Ying, 1972)***, the said letter, originally written by Mr Ho Ho Ying in Mandarin, is reproduced by Cheo as an installation.

Cheo Chai Hiang (b. 1946, Singapore) studied in the Department of Modern Languages and Literature in the former Nanyang University, Singapore, and went to England in 1971 to pursue art at the Birmingham Polytechnic, and the Royal College of Art, London. From the 1980s, he taught fine art at the University of Western Sydney, Australia. He participated in the Singapore Biennale (2008), and the 6th Asia Pacific Triennial of Contemporary Art (2009).

(MH)

艺术除新之外
总得有可引起共鸣的内涵

才雄兄：

本期的课程于上个星期六结束，现在比较有空，可以和你作长谈。你的信都收到，所设计的 5X5 作品，看你的蓝图与道白说明之后，我有下列的感想：

一、地平面与墙壁空间的利用，固然是一种新派的尝试，环境派画家连整个四方八面的空间都列入作品，比单从地面与墙面空间更具规模。于我看来，问题不在乎多少面的利用，而是在于如何适当地利用。如果美术家发生其内在冲动的内容需要做这种扩展，不妨多利用各面空间，即使两壁的夹角部位，觉得适合作某种的表现，美术家不须征求准证自可应用。

二、你的设计，给观众提示了多面空间的可用性，但缺乏适当应用的说服力。因为两个长方框的不同角度的连接，缺乏令人信服其应用的内涵。观众即使终观全日，也难于从中得到什么满足的振奋。现代若干形而上派的作品，左看右看总不能抹去空虚与呆板的感受。画家尽可以找出十分上乘的理由证明其作品空虚与呆板之必要性，然空虚与呆板原本就对人的思想与心灵无多大作用。直到现在，我个人对现代若干流派，仍然抱著批判接受的态度，可能我个人孤陋寡闻，赶不上时代的前头，也可能我个人思想顽固保守。艺术除新之外，总也得有些可引起共鸣的内涵以及某种特殊性。试想，如果艺术家把一个立方体树立在广场上，八方光秃无他，强曰"这是不折不扣的艺术品"，那观众也可以把一根枯树干树立在公园中，声明是艺术作品，这未免把艺术与非艺术混为一谈。我个人也是相当注重形式，但我所强调的艺术形式，并不是一种不加以构思，不加以修饰的随手捡得之物体。

三、画家可以自由发挥，观众当然可以自由观赏，取其所乐，弃去所恶。若画家要公开展览作品，那观众的心理反应，应受多少得考虑，东西是要给人看，要影响人，如不想考虑这些，当然画家可以自

Cheo Chai Hiang

Li Bo Xue

2009
Mixed media, set of 3
35 x 35 x 5 cm (each)

Singapore Art Museum
collection

The use of language in contemporary artmaking can be a powerful tool, as artists engage with wordplay and multiple allusions. The work, *Li Bo Xue* (利剥削), appears as a set of knife tools. By fashioning the tools partially into Chinese characters, Cheo Chai Hiang invites the viewer to participate in the process of meaning-making. By replacing the ' 刂' radicals, meaning 'knife', with actual kitchen knives, the artist shows the different ways the word *Li Bo Xue* can be read, as well as the ways in which the Chinese language can be open to various interpretations. For example, the word "li" (利), when paired with other Chinese words, can connote a variety of meanings. At the same time, the artist explores how meaning may be generated through transmission or translation from one context or language to another. The work was first shown in the exhibition, 'The Air Conditioned Recession: A Singapore Survey', an exhibition at the Valentine Willie Fine Art gallery, which attempted to examine the social and political dynamics of contemporary Singapore society, through the eyes of Singapore artists.

Cheo is known for his conceptual works in the 1970s that actively sought to question the purpose of art amidst the prevailing modernist style of realist art in Singapore.

Cheo Chai Hiang (b. 1946, Singapore) studied in the Department of Modern Languages and Literature in the former Nanyang University, Singapore, and went to England in 1971 to pursue art at the Birmingham Polytechnic, and the Royal College of Art, London. From the 1980s, he taught fine art at the University of Western Sydney, Australia. He participated in the Singapore Biennale (2008), and the 6th Asia Pacific Triennial of Contemporary Art (2009).

(MH)

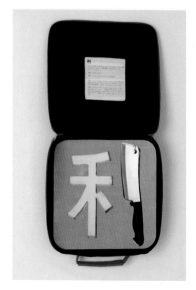 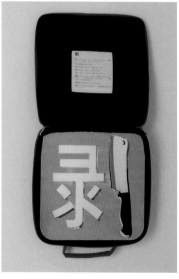 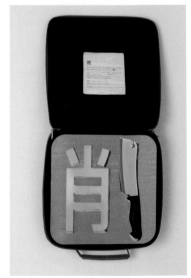

Choy Ka Fai

Rectangular Dreams

2008
Video installation
Duration 22:40 mins

Singapore Art Museum
collection

Originally commissioned by The Arts House to be presented at 'Spotlight Singapore' (a showcase of Singapore culture in Russia), ***Rectangular Dreams*** is a quasi-documentary which traces the evolution of public housing in Singapore. The work takes its title from the rectangular layout and floor plans of its subject matter – the ubiquitous HDB (Housing Development Board) flats which house the majority of Singaporeans. These HDB flats are iconic markers in Singapore's cityscape as well as in its history of nation-building, concrete dwellings laden with their own socio-political histories and resonances.

In his video installation, Choy Ka Fai traces the history of HDB flats and imbues their prosaic, uniform facades and spaces, which many have come to take for granted, with a visual poetics. The visuals are nonetheless balanced by a critical voice that prompts the audience to assess the aspirational declarations made by urban planners, who envision the HDB as a means to change lives for the better.

Choy is an artist and contemporary performance director whose practice explores the intersections of visual art, dance, and theatre. He is often inspired by 'incidental' or 'forgotten' histories, drawing upon these to illustrate parallels with our contemporary times, for instance in his projects, *Reservoir: Residue* and *The Langfang Chronicles*.

Choy Ka Fai (b. 1979, Singapore) graduated from the Royal College of Art, London, under a National Arts Council Overseas Scholarship, and was the recipient of the Young Artist Award, Singapore, in 2010. Prior to that, he was part of the Singapore artists' collective KYTV (Kill Your Television) and an Associate Artistic Director at TheatreWorks, Singapore. His works have been shown at major international venues and festivals, including the 3rd Fukuoka Asian Art Triennale, Japan (2005), the Edinburgh International Festival, United Kingdom, (2009), and the Haus Der Kulturen Der Welt, Berlin, Germany (2005).

(TSL)

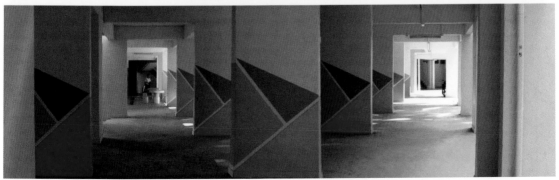

Genevieve Chua

After the Flood #1

2010
Hand-coloured photograph
52 x 77 cm

**After the Flood
#10, #11, #12**

2010
Hand-coloured photograph
52 x 231 cm (triptych)

Singapore Art Museum
collection

The series **After the Flood** consists of 20 photographs depicting the secondary forest found at Kent Ridge, Singapore. After clearance or disturbance by human activity, vegetation will normally recover and revert to its original state only if it is allowed sufficiently time undisturbed. The regrowth initially takes the form of secondary vegetation, such as the *adinandra belukar*. Unlike plants found in primary forests, the species of plants from the secondary forests are more adaptable. According to the artist, **After the Flood** is "hypothesised as a large expanse of space that has settled after the 50th flood. It is an ecosystem that consists of the most resistant of plants in the secondary and tropical rainforest in Singapore."

The pieces shot by the artist along Lornie Road are meticulously hand-painted using the watercolour medium reminiscent of late 19th century hand-painted albumen photographs, an art-form perfected in Japan during the Meiji era. Applied in thin, multiple layers to the photograph, the final effect is haunting and ghostly, taking the image out of the everyday world into another heightened realm of sensation and imagination.

The works of Genevieve Chua (b.1984, Singapore) often explore the fear of the unknown and involve the appropriation of Southeast Asian horror genres, which her works build upon in her attempt to create new narratives. She participated in the Singapore Biennale, 2011, and the M1 Singapore Fringe Festival, 2009. Her works incorporate the use of photography, installation, video, and web-based formats. A recipient of the NAC-Georgette Chen scholarship, Chua graduated from LASALLE College of the Arts, Singapore in 2004.

(TJ)

After the Flood #10, #11, #12

After the Flood #1

Chua Chye Teck

Wonderland

2007
C-prints, set of 500
12.7 x 17.78 cm (each)

Singapore Art Museum
collection

The ephemeral and the metaphorical converge in the artistic practice of Chua Chye Teck who draws inspiration from the everyday objects he finds in his immediate environment. In **Wonderland**, previously 'lost' objects are 'found' by the artist, who bestows upon them a new life in the form of artworks in this suite of 500 photographs. The artist takes on multiple roles as the keeper of the everyday life – history curator, heritage conservator, collections registrar and museum exhibit designer – through the act of locating, cleaning, imaging and presenting these mundane objects sourced from flea markets. These inexpensive and mass-produced objects are given a stylised make-over in the photo studio. Photographed against a deep teal background, they are elevated to the status of museum objects.

Chua Chye Teck (b. 1974, Singapore) specialises in photography. In 2004, he was a participating artist in the exhibition, 'Popular Pleasures through Photography', a visual arts event under the Singapore Arts Festival. In 2009, he undertook a one-year residency at Künstlerhaus Bethanien International studio programme based in Berlin, Germany.

(TJ)

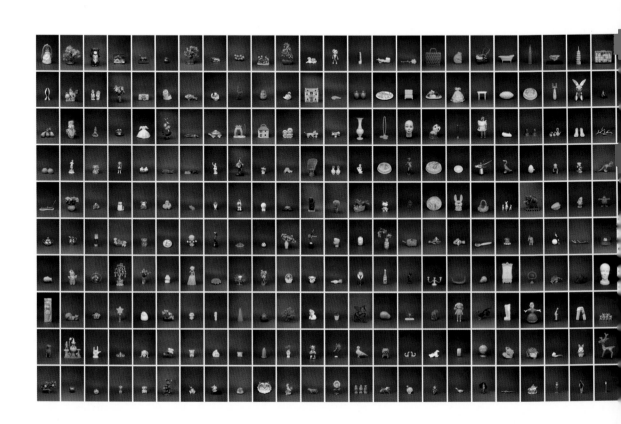

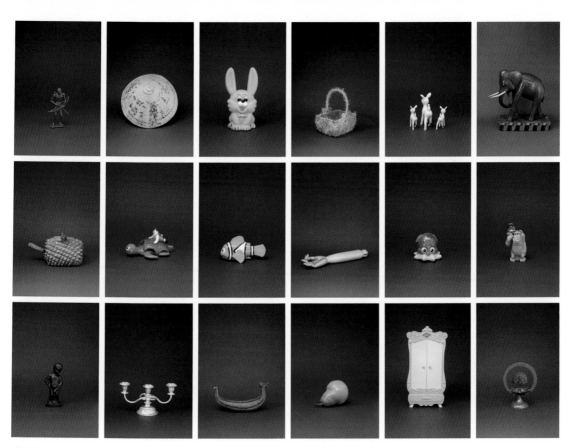

(Detail)

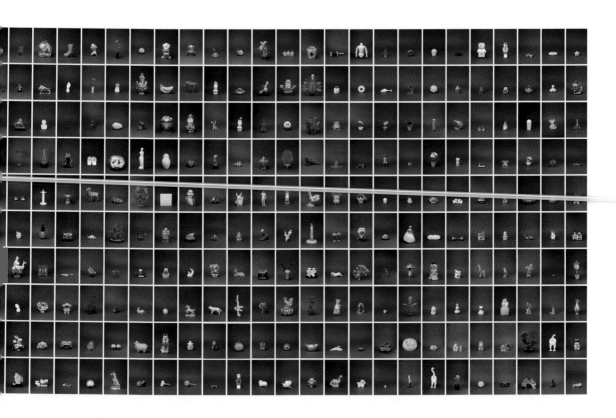

Chun Kai Feng

He's Satisfied from Monday to Friday and on Sunday He Loves to Cry

2009
Mixed media installation
Dimensions variable

Singapore Art Museum
collection

He's Satisfied from Monday to Friday and on Sunday He Loves to Cry was the winning artwork in the Singapore Art Exhibition 2009. In this installation, Chun Kai Feng draws on the convention of the diorama – a three-dimensional or miniature model enclosed in a glass showcase in museums – by presenting what appears to be an office space in an enclosed room. The installation can be viewed through a glass window but is otherwise inaccessible to the viewer. The objects in the installation are rendered in shades of grey, and the clinical and anaesthetised environment presented in the contained space comments on the sterility of working environments and corporate life. At the same time, the installation functions as a kind of psychological space, for interspersed between the everyday objects of office life are items which hint at uncontrollable violence, a reminder of what people are capable of when, or if, pushed to the edge.

The missing human presence in the work suggests the desire of the imaginary occupant of this cheerless space to escape from the boundaries of a seemingly controlled environment. At the same time, the work's title conveys the protagonist's ambivalence and lack of will, suggesting that the office worker perhaps chooses instead the path of least resistance, expressing his/her frustration on Sunday before returning to the same humdrum existence the following work week.

Chun Kai Feng (b. 1982, Singapore) received his Masters in Fine Arts from the Glasgow School of Art in 2010. He was a recipient of the Singapore National Arts Council Bursary in 2009 and the recipient of the Singapore Art Exhibition Prize in 2009.

(TSL)

Chun Kai Feng

Parklife

2008
Mixed media with MDF, perspex, emulsion and acrylic paint
60 x 80 x 50 cm

Singapore Art Museum collection

Chun Kai Feng belongs to an emerging younger generation of Singapore artists who have opted for a more hands-on and crafts-based approach to artmaking, in contrast to the conceptually-driven practices of their predecessors. Eschewing grand gestures, the artist works on a small scale to create monochromatic models of distinctive or iconic structures in Singapore, such as the Singapore Flyer, Marina Bay Sands and HDB flats. His sculptures are reminiscent of toys or playthings – innocuous at first sight – but their details belie sharp social critique.

Parklife depicts a playground and a multi-storey void deck – familiar sights in most HDB (Housing Development Board) estates in Singapore. However this is no innocent cityscape; upon closer inspection, the residential landscape depicted in the work is far from being the family-friendly, cheerful place that it was designed to be. Shades of grey dominate the structures; the playground equipment, which is supposed to provide amusement for children, is warped, dangerous and dysfunctional in its design, creating a sense of discomfort and unease for the viewer taking in the details of this artwork. The loneliness and isolation of the urban landscape is highlighted in *Parklife*, through this model of a fenced-up area designated for living and playing. Instead of a space that is supposed to improve the quality of life for its inhabitants, Chun Kai Feng's colourless model conveys a sense of monotony in a sterile environment.

Chun Kai Feng (b. 1982, Singapore) received his Masters in Fine Arts from the Glasgow School of Art in 2010. He was a recipient of the Singapore National Arts Council Bursary in 2009 and the recipient of the Singapore Art Exhibition Prize in 2009.

(TSL)

Chun Kai Feng

¥ € $

2010
Mixed media with wood, perspex,
weatherproof emulsion paint and
acrylic airbrush paint, custom-
made pedestal, edition 1/2
64 x 42 x 62 cm

Singapore Art Museum
collection

¥ € $ is a model of the newly-opened Marina Bay Sands casino, the latest architectural addition to Singapore's skyline and one in a string of glittering new developments along Marina Bay, designated the country's new entertainment and leisure precinct. The artist has crowned each of the three iconic sloped structures of Marina Bay Sands with a different currency sign; together they spell out an emphatic ¥ € $, a chorus of commercial and capitalist interests chiming in anticipation of all the money to be earned. The backs of these pristine buildings however have been vandalised with large splotches of paint; a literal stain on what would otherwise be an impressive and iconic cityscape. The paint blotches are similar to the 'signature' splotches of paint that Singapore loansharks leave on the doors of their debtors' residences.

Chun Kai Feng's replica of Marina Bay Sands is by no means intended as a straightforward tribute; it is a sharp reminder of the social repercussions of the coming of the casinos in Singapore, an issue which occupied the front pages of the national newspapers for a long period before the casinos were constructed. Much of this active debate and discussion over the consequences the casino would have on Singapore's social fabric have been silenced by the shiny new buildings that have awed many; here, the artist revives these issues with his gleaming stains that mark the cold and colourless models of Marina Bay Sands.

Chun Kai Feng (b. 1982, Singapore) received his Masters in Fine Arts from the Glasgow School of Art in 2010. He was a recipient of the Singapore National Arts Council Bursary in 2009 and the recipient of the Singapore Art Exhibition Prize in 2009.

(TSL)

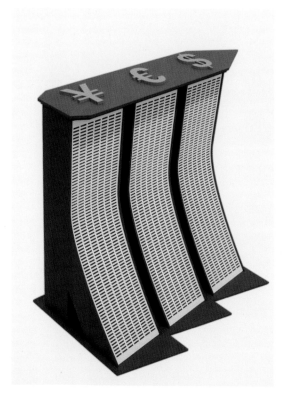

John Clang

The White Book

2007–2009
Interactive photo installation
33.2 x 28.7 x 4.5 cm (book),
220.5 x 85 x 94 cm (booth)

Singapore Art Museum
collection

The ever-changing city life and the sense of displacement entwined with the urban condition inspire the art of John Clang. Seemingly mundane at first glance, the images often solicit an emotional response from the viewer through their casual and intimate approach to portraiture.

The White Book is an installation made up of a white phonebooth-like construction in which a white portfolio embossed with the artist's moniker 'CLANG' is placed. The portfolio contains photographs of selected works from the artist's oeuvre since the early 2000s – *Beijing NYC, Out of Context, Silhouette/ Urban Intervention (Black Tape), Strangers, Time, NYC 64.1°N 21.9°W* and *My Twilight Window*. The intimate telephone box construction to hold the 'white book' is flooded with white light meant to temporarily isolate the viewer, transporting individuals who choose to step into the space to enter into the internal world of the artist.

John Clang's (b. 1973, Singapore) photographs have been exhibited at the Singapore Art Museum, Bank Art Gallery in Los Angeles, United States, and Galerie Collette in Paris. In 2001, he held his first solo exhibition 'Backs by Clang' at the New York studio of Diane von Furstenburg. In 2010, Clang received the President's Designer of the Year Award, Singapore.

(TJ)

Safaruddin Dyn

Maxwell Road
2009
Acrylic on canvas
120 x 150 cm

Ann Siang Hill
2009
Acrylic on canvas
150 x 120 cm

Tiffin Carrier
2009
Acrylic on canvas
150 x 120 cm

Singapore Art Museum
collection

In his work, Safaruddin Dyn strives to push the boundaries of objectivity in his representations of the inanimate objects and places that carry his childhood memories. Utilising images from displaced sites in old photographs, he paints them in a distorted manner that resonates with his hazy memories of these architectural icons in Singapore, referencing ideas of memory and absence. By conscientiously erasing all presence of life, he further highlights the dichotomy between absence and presence.

Maxwell Road and Ann Siang Hill are prominent areas in Singapore that have in recent times undergone tremendous changes. Only a few of these conserved shop-houses with their five-foot ways and Art Déco architecture buildings remain today and many are in peril of being demolished for new urban development.

The iconic tiffin carrier or *tingkat*, as it is locally known, has also slowly faded away into oblivion, replaced by modern conveniences, such as dispensable containers and cutlery. The faded text in ink on the tiffin carrier are the words in Malay, *selamat angkat* and *selamat pakkey* which means "to carry safely" and "to use safely" respectively.

Safaruddin Dyn (b. 1977, Singapore) graduated from LASALLE College of the Arts with a Masters Degree in Fine Arts (2006), and has held solo exhibitions in Singapore and in Hong Kong.

(SC)

Clockwise:
Maxwell Road
Ann Siang Hill
Tiffin Carrier

Eng Joo Heng

Lotus #09, #14, #24

2009
Chinese ink on paper
69 x 70 cm (each)

Singapore Art Museum
collection

In 1986, Eng left Singapore for Paris where he spent the next eight years, and during this sojourn, he was exposed to French impressionism. In *Lotus #9*, *#14* and *#24*, Eng adopts the approach of some of the Impressionist artists, as seen in the rapid application of definitive strokes of unblended colours. Viewed from afar, it shows the transitory effects of light on objects. The lotus in Asian culture is seen as a symbol of purity and resilience. Here, Eng has elected to represent these lotuses using unrestrained organic forms that combine both western and eastern aesthetics of painting.

Eng Joo Heng (b. 1956, Singapore) studied in the Nanyang Academy of Fine Arts, Singapore, before leaving for France in 1986. There, he took up an apprenticeship with a Parisian art studio, Atelier 17, and worked as a printmaker for four years. After returning to Singapore in 2001, he lectured briefly at the Nanyang Academy of Fine Arts before embarking on his current position as a workshop manager and senior printer with the Singapore Tyler Print Institute in 2003.

(SC)

Clockwise:
Lotus #09, #14, #24

Amanda Heng

Another Woman

1996–1997
14 photo prints
Dimensions variable

Singapore Art Museum
collection

Another Woman is Amanda Heng's most seminal work which was executed over a year, involving installation, performance and photography. An exploration of the artist's relationship with her mother, the work can also be seen as an investigation into the domestic realm of women within the traditional Chinese family. The mother and daughter photographs, both clothed and nude, are aimed at exploring the relationship between the two, as well as their identities as independent women. At the same time, it can be seen as the artist's way of reclaiming intimate mother-daughter ties, often unspoken within the traditional Chinese family psyche. The work includes an installation component, where Heng deploys photography and assemblages of objects as a means of investigating memory.

Amanda Heng (b. 1951, Singapore) is one of the founding members of Singapore artists' collective, The Artists Village. She has presented at the 1st Singapore Biennale (2006), the '1st Women's Performance Art Festival' in Osaka, Japan (2001), the 7th Havana Biennial (2000), the 1st Fukuoka Asian Art Triennale, Japan (1999), and the 3rd Asia Pacific Triennial of Contemporary Art, Brisbane, Australia (1999). She was also the 2010 recipient of the prestigious Cultural Medallion award, Singapore.

(MH)

Ho Tzu Nyen

The Cloud of Unknowing

2011
Installation with single-channel
HD video projection, multi-
channel audio, lighting,
smoke machines and show
control system
Duration 28:00 mins

Singapore Art Museum
collection

The Cloud of Unknowing was commissioned for the Singapore Pavilion at the 54th Venice Biennale International Art Exhibition in 2011. In this video installation, Ho Tzu Nyen takes as his central subject, the cloud, and explores its symbolic and aesthetic representation across cultures, history and geography. Shot within a block of public housing in Singapore, *The Cloud of Unknowing* revolves around eight characters and their encounters with a cloud or cloud-like figure. *The Cloud of Unknowing* portrays the characters in a moment of revelation, and their narratives reference a medieval text of the same name about the experience and trials of meditative contemplation upon the divine, where the cloud paradoxically represents both the moment of uncertainty and connection with divinity.

Ho Tzu Nyen (b. 1976, Singapore) has a Master of Arts in Southeast Asian Studies from the National University of Singapore. His practice spans video, painting and theatre. Ho's interest is in deconstructing the media he works in, and in exploiting its slipperiness to question its conventions and applications. More recently, he has focused on video art, which is an apt vehicle for combining his personal interests in film, text, image and music. His recent works such as *Earth* and *The Cloud of Unknowing* are intricately bound up with his personal interest in art history and historiography. His films characteristically comprise elaborate tableaus that refer back to canonical artworks, and condense his multiple, eclectic sources of research and reference. Ho's video works eschew conventional narrative in favour of composing evocative scenes and experiences that are heavily referential and yet completely open to interpretation by the audience, whom Ho regards integral to the 'completion' of his artwork with their reception and response to his work.

(TSL)

Hong Sek Chern

Constructing Old with New

2010
Chinese ink on paper
138 x 138 cm

Singapore Art Museum
collection

Hong Sek Chern works with the traditional medium of Chinese ink on rice paper to portray the architectural features of what she terms as the modern local monuments and icons of Singapore, such as Housing Development Board (HDB) flats, commercial buildings, shop houses and expressways. Hong often fuses multiple perspectives of her subject-matter within a single artwork. Upon closer inspection, one can start to discern clearly the distinctive features of the architectural environment, including interiors and the facades of buildings. In ***Constructing Old with New***, the juxtaposition of all the buildings, old shop-houses and flyovers rotate on an axis and are seen from different angles, but converge in a visual directory to recreate what Hong calls her own "visual fragments of the everyday".

Hong Sek Chern (b. 1967, Singapore) graduated with a Bachelor of Science degree from the National University of Singapore in 1989, and obtained a Diploma in Education from the National Institute of Education in 1990. She graduated from the Nanyang Academy of Fine Arts, Singapore in 1995 and later obtained her Masters degree in Fine Art from Goldsmiths College, the University of London in 1998. She represented Singapore at the Sao Paulo Biennale, 2002, in Brazil where she presented her work entitled *Fragments of a Monument (Once Great)*.

(SC)

Lucas Jodogne

In the Node

2000–2001
Photo, mounted on forex and
framed, set of 8 prints
Edition 1/10
80 x 160 cm (each)

Singapore Art Museum
collection

Technology has made the world smaller with each day. We can literally be at one end of the world one day and the other end the next. The units through which we measure the distance between things such as miles and time zones are no longer barriers but merely numbers.

In the Node depicts, in the artist's words, a "landscape of roads" in the highly charged urban environment of contemporary Asian cities such as Shanghai, Kolkata and Singapore. These landscapes capture the heightened state of connectivity at points or "nodes" that proliferate in each city's transportation system, effectively minimising both physical and experiential distances between the cities' inhabitants and their world-at-large. The virtually sterile landscapes also depict the flip side of seamless global integration – the constant pressure to move on with hardly any space or time for human interaction, unwelcoming of contemplation or reflection.

Lucas Jodogne (b. 1959) studied art photography and cinematography at the Royal Academy of the Arts in Ghent, Belgium. He has made over 160 films commercials, corporate videos, short movies and feature length films, many of which have either won or have been nominated for international awards. Jodogne had his first solo exhibition in 1984 and has showcased his artworks in museums around the world. He is currently a lecturer at Nanyang Technological University's School of Art, Design and Media, Singapore.

(TJ)

Zai Kuning

RIAU

2009
Mixed media installation
(DVD, drawings, map, book,
table and chair)
Dimensions variable

Singapore Art Museum
collection

Since 1999, artist Zai Kuning has been researching on the history of *orang laut* (sea nomads) in the Riau Archipelago in Indonesia. Zai's interest in the nomadic lifestyles of the *orang laut* stem from his critical enquiry into how the politics of geographical boundaries and the formation of nation states re-define personal, cultural and national identities, both self-perceived, and imposed. His film ***RIAU***, completed in 2003, charts his journey and interactions with various sea gypsy communities residing in various islands within the Riau Archipelago, as he seeks to uncover the forgotten histories of this region.

Poetry and story-telling are significant aspects of the multi-disciplinary artist's practice, which traverses the domains of drawing, installation and performance art. The installation ***RIAU***, is a continuation of the artist's meditations and journeys. Presented through the film and four large drawings, the installation also includes a story which the artist wrote, weaving both personal and transmitted memories, in the presentation of a moving account of a sea gypsy's trials and tribulations in search of a place to call home.

Zai Kuning (b.1964, Singapore) was an early member of the artists collective, The Artists Village, Singapore. Trained in ceramics at the Lasalle College of the arts, Zai's earlier forays into cross-disciplinary art forms saw the formation of the Metabolic Theatre Laboratory (MTL), which he founded in 1996, as a platform to experiment with dance and Southeast Asian rituals and performances. Zai has participated in 3rd Fukuoka Asian Art Triennale (2005), as well as numerous international film festivals.

(MH)

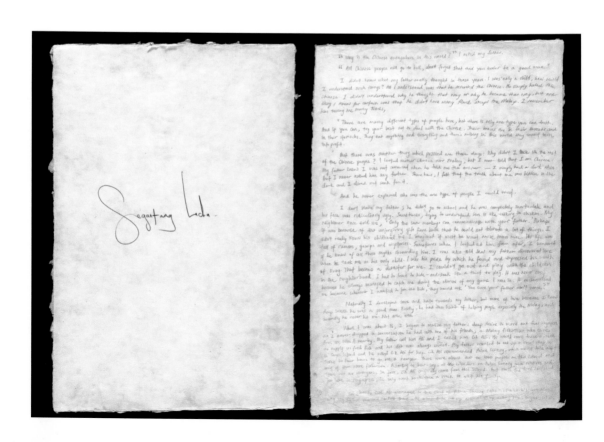

Zai Kuning

Series 1 & 2

2006–2008
Chinese ink on Japanese paper,
sets of 12 and 18
10 x 13 cm (each) and
8 x 11.5 cm (each)

Some Came With Their Soul

2008
Ink on Japanese paper
280 x 150 cm

Singapore Art Museum
collection

Zai Kuning has spent a number of years since 1999 researching the lives of the *orang laut* (sea nomads) in the Riau Archipelago, whose nomadic lifestyle inspired these drawings. Drawing from the shapes of large stones and trees that Zai would come across in Riau, the work is a result of Zai's own personal journey and engagement with the *orang laut* in search of a personal language through the idea of marking. The idea of marking is one inspired by the nomadic lifestyle of the *orang laut* who mark such trees and stones in their travels to denote where they have been – at the same time creating a secret language that only members of their family and tribe can decipher. This secrecy of a personal language, as well as the increasing loss of such languages around the world, inspired Zai to create these series of markings. These markings are created using Chinese ink on handcrafted Japanese paper, in an act of tribute remembering and highlighting the rustic cultures and lifestyles of the *orang laut* today.

Zai Kuning (b.1964, Singapore) was an early member of the artists collective, The Artists Village, Singapore. Trained in ceramics at the Lasalle College of the arts, Zai's earlier forays into cross-disciplinary art forms saw the formation of the Metabolic Theatre Laboratory (MTL), which he founded in 1996, as a platform to experiment with dance and Southeast Asian rituals and performances. Zai has participated in 3rd Fukuoka Asian Art Triennale (2005), as well as numerous international film festivals.

(DC)

Top: *Series 1*
Bottom: *Series 2*

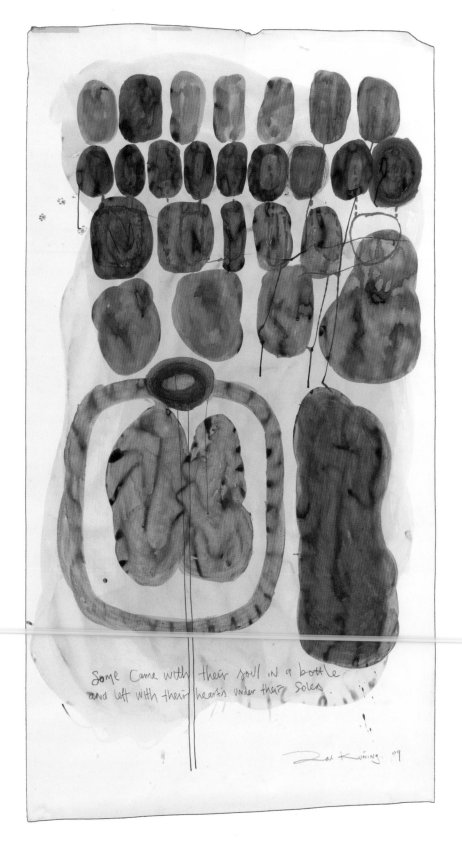

Some came with their soul in a bottle
and left with their hearts under their soles.

Some Came With Their Soul

Jane Lee

Status

2009
Mixed media
480 x 420 x 120 cm

Acquired with the support of
BinjaiTree Foundation in honour
of Chia Yew Kay

Singapore Art Museum
collection

Status is a compelling and contemporary take on the age-old medium of painting. Monumental in scale, this spectacular work problematizes simplistic categorisation of media, as it crosses boundaries of painting, sculpture and installation. No longer just a representational medium in Lee's work, the red paint in *Status* has literally escaped from the conventional canvas to become its own frame, a physical entity in its own right, demanding the viewer to approach it from different angles and perspectives. It is at once sensuous in all its rich colour, viscosity and textural variations, as it is imposingly commanding in its scale. Resembling a doorway, *Status* heralds new ways of approaching and practising painting in this era of art.

Jane Lee (b. 1963, Singapore) has a background in both Fine Arts and Fashion. The recipient of the inaugural Singapore Art Exhibition Prize in 2007, Lee has participated in several notable exhibitions in the region and in Europe, including the Singapore Biennale 2008. In 2009, the artist had her first major solo exhibition at Osage Gallery, Singapore. In 2011, one of Lee's paintings was awarded the Celeste Art Prize, New York, in the Painting category.

(TSL)

(Detail)

Jane Lee

The Object I
2011
Mixed media on wood
165 x 123 x13 cm

The Object II
2011
Mixed media on wood
161 x 125 x 16 cm

Singapore Art Museum
collection

Jane Lee's works are contemporary takes on the age-old practice of painting. Her works challenge simplistic categorisations of media, crossing boundaries of painting, sculpture and installation. No longer just a representational medium in Lee's work, the paint in **The Object I** and **The Object II** has escaped its conventional canvas to become a physical entity in its own right, demanding the viewer to approach it from different angles and perspectives. It is at once sensuous in all its subtle tonalities, viscosity and textural variations. It can be appreciated from several perspectives – whether one chooses to delight in its textures and formal innovation, or more academically, in how it heralds new painting practices in Southeast Asia.

Jane Lee (b. 1963, Singapore) has a background in both Fine Arts and Fashion. The recipient of the inaugural Singapore Art Exhibition Prize in 2007, Lee has participated in several notable exhibitions in the region and in Europe, including the Singapore Biennale 2008. In 2009, the artist had her first major solo exhibition at Osage Gallery, Singapore. In 2011, one of Lee's paintings was awarded the Celeste Art Prize, New York, in the Painting category.

(TSL)

Justin Lee

East & West

2009
Fibreglass
Dimensions variable

Singapore Art Museum
collection

East & West features a small army of terracotta warriors as well as higher-ranking generals, all of whom are adorned with oversized headphones. The work also comprises of three traditional Chinese gentle-ladies who are coiffed and garbed in ancient garments. However, rather than genteel, they are portrayed as modern career-driven women, armed with modern laptops and designer handbags.

Justin Lee's work is witty yet often thoughtful, combining traditional Eastern imagery and with Western iconography. He uses pop art as a playful medium that pits Asian values against 21st century consumerism in an era dominated by capitalism.

Justin Lee (b. 1963, Singapore) received a Diploma in Fine Art from LASALLE College of the Arts in 1999. He held his first solo exhibition in 2003. Since then, he has actively participated in numerous group exhibitions in Singapore; in 2004, these included a group exhibition at the Arts Seasons Gallery, Singapore, and Utterly Art, Singapore. In the same year, he also participated in the Venice Biennale, 9th International Architecture Exhibition, Italy.

(DC)

Justin Lee

Godness Series:
McDonald Kids

2009
Acrylic on canvas
195 x 138 cm

Godness Series:
Mobile Phone Kids

2009
Acrylic on canvas
195 x 138 cm

Singapore Art Museum
collection

Drawn from ancient Chinese iconography, the ***Godness*** series depicts door guardians or spirits who would guard thresholds. In a modern twist, they hold instruments of technology. This effect is used to evoke the jarring relationship between the traditional and the past, and the new and modernised today. An accomplished figurative painter, Lee creates a sense of longing for the nostalgic past by mystifying the paintings with drips and glaze, resulting in less-than-sharp image.

Justin Lee's work is witty yet often thoughtful, combining traditional Eastern imagery and with Western iconography. He uses pop art as a playful medium that pits Asian values against 21st century consumerism in an era dominated by capitalism.

Justin Lee (b. 1963, Singapore) received a Diploma in Fine Art from LASALLE College of the Arts in 1999. He held his first solo exhibition in 2003. Since then, he has actively participated in numerous group exhibitions in Singapore; in 2004, these included a group exhibition at the Arts Seasons Gallery, Singapore, and Utterly Art, Singapore. In the same year, he also participated in the Venice Biennale, 9th International Architecture Exhibition, Italy.

(DC)

Justin Lee

Opera Series: Let's Dance (Female)

2009
Acrylic on canvas
195 x 135 cm

Opera Series: Let's Dance (Male)

2009
Acrylic on canvas
195 x 135 cm

Singapore Art Museum
collection

The **Opera** series continues Justin Lee's exploration of the marriage between eastern and western cultures, between the traditional and the modern, and exploring the ensuing contradictions, conflicts and tensions that arise from the confrontation.

Trying to bring back lost traditional cultures, Lee references a vanishing performative art form, the Chinese opera, but gives it new meaning through a different medium – painting. At the same time, the figures also refer to the old tradition of having a pair of 'door gods' who would stand guard and keep watch over a household. This series of works also harks back to days in the past where such sculptural ornaments and figurines celebrating traditional Chinese arts such as opera were a common sight in well-to-do domestic households.

Justin Lee's work is witty yet often thoughtful, combining traditional Eastern imagery and with Western iconography. He uses pop art as a playful medium that pits Asian values against 21st century consumerism in an era dominated by capitalism.

Justin Lee (b. 1963, Singapore) received a Diploma in Fine Art from LASALLE College of the Arts in 1999. He held his first solo exhibition in 2003. Since then, he has actively participated in numerous group exhibitions in Singapore; in 2004, these included a group exhibition at the Arts Seasons Gallery, Singapore, and Utterly Art, Singapore. In the same year, he also participated in the Venice Biennale, 9th International Architecture Exhibition, Italy.

(DC)

Sean Lee

Everybody Knows You Cried Last Night

2007
Digital prints on archival matt
paper, set of 12, edition 1/5
29.7 x 42 cm, 59.4 x 79.2 cm

HOMEWORK

2011
Digital prints on archival matt
paper, set of 22, edition 3/6
(except for *Soli Deo Gloria*,
edition 3/3)
Dimensions variable

Singapore Art Museum
collection

Everybody Knows You Cried Last Night is presented in a contact sheet format in colour. In *HOMEWORK*, shot four years later, the non-linear impressionistic mode Lee employed previously has evolved into a work that is firmly grounded in a stronger sense of narrative. Both series feature his family members and are at once intimate and voyeuristic portraits of people close to the artist, but staged as fabricated narratives, they also sidestep reality by entering the realm of fiction and illusion. In the artist's words, the works are "short stories within themselves." The artist attributes his stylistic influences to both Antoine d'Agata for his unabridged quality and Nan Goldin for the honesty in her approach to the medium of photography.

Sean Lee (b. 1985, Singapore) is a photographer who has exhibited in Singapore, Paris, Barcelona and New York. In 2007, he won the Special Jury Prize at the Angkor Photo Festival in Siem Reap, Cambodia, as well as the Prix Découverte (Discovery Award) in the 2009 Arles Photo Festival in France. In 2011, Lee won the ICON de Martell Cordon Bleu, the biggest photography prize in Singapore to date.

(TJ)

Everybody Knows You Cried Last Night

It happened when I was around six or seven. He didn't actually punch me, but it felt like he did anyway. The truth is, all parents damage their children at some point.

The Tension Breaker
They started speaking to each other again after this.

HOMEWORK

Lee Wen

Strange Fruit

2003
C-prints, set of 12, edition 1/3
42 x 59.4 cm (each)

Singapore Art Museum
collection

Red lanterns are associated with Chinese ethnicity, as they are commonly found in Chinatown and Chinese restaurants and establishments all over the world. As part of 'Journey of a Yellow Man' – an ongoing body of performance art pieces by Lee Wen that began in the early 1990s in London – *Strange Fruit* sees the artist carrying multiple lanterns at one time. This body of work was motivated by the sweeping assumption he encountered while he was in London, namely that he was from mainland China because of the colour of his skin. This doubly emphasises the stereotyping of ethnicity and identity formations. This performance took place during the Chinese Lantern Festival celebrations in Singapore and for the artist, it was a way to celebrate the festival as a 'one-man lantern procession'. In this 'procession', the lanterns were carried along a route that passes through different landscapes typical of Singapore, from its downtown shop-houses, back alleys, housing estates, a green park, and finally, ending on a beach. The final image is that of the lanterns floating off in the sea as if they are going on another journey beyond.

This performance work had been documented through photographs initiated by the artist himself. Lee Wen (b. 1957, Singapore) is an active proponent of performance art in Singapore and was one of the founders of 'Future of Imagination', a series of international performance art events in Singapore. A member of the artists collectives, The Artists Village and Black Market International, Lee's works have been featured in the 3rd Asia Pacific Triennial of Contemporary Art, Brisbane, Australia, 1999, and the Havana Biennial, Cuba, 1997, amongst numerous other international exhibitions. He was a recipient of Singapore's highest cultural award, the Cultural Medallion, in 2005.

(KH)

Lee Wen

World Class Society

1999
Video installation with survey
forms, badges, jar, stuffed white
globe with wings, stuffed white
star and various media
Edition 1/1
Dimensions variable
Video duration 4:00 mins

Singapore Art Museum
collection

Said to be the first Singapore video installation, this work was shrouded in polemics when first presented at the Nokia Art Singapore exhibition in 1999. A national showcase of the latest trends in Singapore at that time, Lee's work was seen then by some observers as a prescient wake-up call to fellow Singaporeans at the cusp of a new millennium. A former banker, Lee had left the bank to become a member of the artists collective, The Artists Village, a decade earlier, and in this video, he reprises his former profession in a tongue-in-cheek performance. Everything is stark white in Lee's *World Class Society* as the viewer watches the artist – bespectacled and sporting a tie – in a close-up shot of his face as he delivers an emphatic speech questioning the notion of a "world-class" status. Yet through the telescope like cloth apparatus, the viewer is kept at a safe distance from the artist. After the delivery of Lee's speech, viewers are invited to answer a questionnaire on what it takes to be a world-class society, after which they can take home a free 'World-Class Badge'.

Lee Wen (b. 1957, Singapore) is an active proponent of performance art in Singapore and was one of the founders of 'Future of Imagination', a series of international performance art events in Singapore. A member of the artists collectives, The Artists Village and Black Market International, Lee's works have been featured in the 3rd Asia Pacific Triennial of Contemporary Art, Brisbane, Australia, 1999, and the Havana Biennial, Cuba, 1997, amongst numerous other international exhibitions. He was a recipient of Singapore's highest cultural award, the Cultural Medallion, in 2005.

(TJ)

Vincent Leow

Yellow Field

1990
Oil and mixed media on canvas
212 x 249.5 cm

Yellow Field (sketch)

1990
Ink and tempera
22 x 27.8 cm
Gift of the Artist

Singapore Art Museum
collection

Vincent Leow is an early member of The Artists Village which played a pivotal role in the development of performance art in Singapore in the late-1980s. His work **Yellow Field** is a rare and skilfully-executed large scale painting that counters the notion that performance artists in Singapore were not concerned with more traditional art forms like painting during that period.

While the subject-matter of the work appears rather simple – a study of the ubiquitous tee-shirt – the subject morphs into the study of a landscape as well, and the painting, with its textured surface and different colours of light capturing the time of day, speaks volumes for something so deceptively simple. The impact and presence of the painting plays on the possibility of its duality of existence, which on first glance might seem like a representational painting but could also exist as an abstract work. Leow's initial sketch of the work, donated to accompany the painting, shows the artist's intention to explore texture and surface by experimenting with ink and tempera on paper, and was also a means to gauge both composition and colour fields before he started on the painting.

Yellow Field marked a change of direction in Leow's artistic practice, from his foundational training in woodcarving and sculpting to painting. The work is also reminiscent of Seletar airbase, where both Leow and several other members of The Artists Village lived for some time.

Vincent Leow (b. 1961, Singapore) has carved out an important role in Singapore's contemporary art development through three decades of art practice that is rooted in debates over the contemporary Singapore identity. He has exhibited internationally in countries such as Venice, China, Japan, Bangladesh and United States. In 2007, he participated in the 52nd Venice Biennale and had a solo exhibition in Xin Bejing Gallery in China. In 2010, he had a solo exhibition 'Tags and Treats: Works by Vincent Leow', at 8Q, Singapore Art Museum. He is also a prominent figure in the artists collective landscape, as an early member of The Artists Village, founded in 1988, Singapore, and as founder of Plastique Kinetic Worms (PKW).

(DC)

Yellow Field (sketch)

Yellow Field

Charles Lim

All Lines Flow Out

2011
Single-channel HD Video
Duration 21:43 mins

Singapore Art Museum
collection

All Lines Flow Out takes the viewer through the monsoon drains of Singapore, drawing attention to the vast network of *longkangs* (the local term for the massive monsoon drains) which form an unintended map of the country. It is a journey that ends when the rainwater meet and merge with the sea between Singapore and Malaysia. Unfolding along a loose narrative, various individuals are met along the way, each of them has a singular – though not-always pleasant – encounter with the waters. History and personal memory are summoned too, through a brief voice-over from the last inhabitant of Singapore's final remaining house by the sea.

Informed by Lim's own experience as a former national sailor, the work is shaped by what the artist perceives as a paradoxical relationship that Singaporeans often have towards water and the sea. Growing up in a densely populated and highly urbanised environment, few residents on the island show a natural affinity for the very thing that circumscribes its shores. Nonetheless, water sits high on the national consciousness: regarded as a critical resource to ensure national security and survival, it is vigilantly managed and ordered. Yet at times, the human desire for order is upturned when Nature returns with fury in torrential downpours that have caused flash floods in the very heart of the city.

Charles Lim (b. 1973, Singapore) has participated in exhibitions such as Manifesta7, the European Biennial of Contemporary Art, Bolzano, Italy (2008), Documenta 11, Kassel, Germany (2002), as well as film festivals like the Tribeca Film Festival (2011). This work was commissioned by and premiered at the Singapore Biennale 2011, and a version of it garnered a special mention in the Orizzonti Section of the Venice Film Festival 2011.

(JT)

Jessie Lim

Orbs

2005
Black stoneware, set of 4
12 x 17 x 18 cm (two pieces),
13 x 16 x 17 cm, 15 x 18 x 19 cm

Singapore Art Museum
collection

Jessie Lim began her practice by making functional ceramics. Over the years, she has ventured into presenting ceramics as both sculpture and installation. Her accidental foray into this medium came about when she signed up for a pottery workshop in Dartmouth College in Hanover, New Hampshire, where she had received a scholarship to study in the United States in 1982.

In this group of ceramics, Lim has chosen to draw attention to surface and texture while keeping to a simple form emphasised by its minimal palette. Lim's idea of 'accidental imperfection' can be seen here: although there is no symmetry in the ridges and lines found on the orbs, there is overall a sense of order and balance when viewing the work.

Jessie Lim (b. 1954, Brunei) graduated from the University of Singapore in 1976 with a Bachelor of Arts in English Literature. Later, she completed her Diploma of Education from the National Institute of Education, Singapore in 1980. She subsequently took up pottery at Dartmouth College, New Hampshire, United States in 1983. Her works have been exhibited in Singapore, Malaysia, Sweden and Thailand.

(SC)

Jovian Lim

The Voyage to the Ends of the World

2009
K3 chrome ink on Sihl archival
fine art paper, set of 7 prints
89.2 x 118.9 cm (each)

Singapore Art Museum
collection

Jovian Lim is, in his words, inspired by "naturally occurring phenomena that happen in [people's] lives daily", and this work was made using his bathtub as a photographic set.

In this suite of enigmatic images, amorphous forms coalesce to suggest abstracted landscapes and natural undulating hill-locks or alluring bodily figures, depending on the visual imagination of the viewer. The selected photographs from the series take advantage of the camera's ability to transport the viewer to a quiet and contemplative alternate reality where one can reflect on one's psychological and emotional states.

Jovian Lim (b. 1984, Singapore) graduated with a Bachelor of Fine Art (Photography) in Photography at the School of Art, Design and Media, Nanyang Technological University, Singapore, in 2009.

(TJ)

Gilles Massot

Retro Specks Future Pixs

2004
Video and photographic
installation
Dimensions variable

Singapore Art Museum
collection

Singapore-based Gilles Massot's artistic process has evolved over the years to incorporate the idea of the 'space between things', which he often investigates using the deliberate juxtaposition and subsequent interaction, of distinctly different types of visual media. This installation was conceived, according to Massot, as a "video and photo-based time sculpture" inspired by an electrical cable that links mainland Malaysia with island Singapore as part of the train system between the two countries, which he chanced upon during his own journey on this train.

The viewer physically enters this installation, whose various elements are distributed within the physical space of the artwork, along a Cartesian coordinate system. At beginning of the installation are reproductions of the four iconic white marble reliefs that fronted the former Tanjong Pagar Train Station in Singapore. At the other end is a clock-tower 'sculpture' that represents the former Johor Train Station. In between these two elements are photographic stills from a video that depict the train journey between the two sovereign nation-states of Singapore and Malaysia. The viewer walking through this installation is thus also journeying through in an interstitial space between place and time of the two countries and the 'worlds' they exist in.

Gilles Massot (b. 1955, Aix en Provence, France) studied architecture and photography in Marseille, France, and has been based in Singapore since 1981. He has been involved in many arts events in his adopted homeland, including the first edition of the Festival of Arts Fringe (1986), and the Ying Yang Festival (1987). He was also commissioned by the Land Transport Authority, Singapore for a public artwork at the Buona Vista Station in 2007. He currently teaches at the LASALLE College of the Arts, Singapore, and is also a lecturer at the Nanyang Technological University and a member of the artists collective, The Artists Village.

(TJ)

Kumari Nahappan

Om (Aum) Series – Vibration E

1998
Acrylic on linen
128 x 128 cm

Singapore Art Museum
collection

Om (Aum) Series – Vibration E takes its title in part from the word 'Om' (or sometimes spelt as Aum), which is considered of utmost sacred significance in Hindu belief. Signified by the symbol 'ॐ', when intoned, *Om* is believed to be the sound of the infinite. As sheer potential energy, *Om* is the source of creation – omnipotent and universal, it is also ultimately, unknowable. It thus signifies ultimate reality in its manifest as well as unmanifest form, enfolding a complex dualism that courses through much of Hindu philosophy.

Executed during a difficult period during the artist's life, the painting pulsates with dark force and potency. Razor-thin black lines dart across the surface, possessing the disquieting effect like rends in the fabric of reality. The work's captivating power also draws from its synesthetic qualities – its sombre colours and fine tonal graduations translate into the aural realm. When confronted by the actual work, the intonation of sacred Aum can be 'heard' and felt in equal measure. It points to the intricacies of this seemingly understated painting: from a physical object, Nahappan's visual expression finds transformation into the aural, and finally transcendence to the spiritual.

Kumari Nahappan (b. 1953, Malaysia) is the recipient of the UOB (United Overseas Bank) Painting of the Year award (Abstract category) in 1998 and Phillip Morris Group ASEAN Art Award in 1999. In 2006, she exhibited at the Mori Art Museum, Tokyo, as part of 'Spotlight Singapore'. She embarked on a year-long solo exhibition 'Red on the Trail of a Colour' at the Museum of Cultures in Basel, Switzerland (2008) and also exhibited at the Tropenmuseum, Amsterdam (2011). Her public art sculptures can also be seen around Singapore, at the National Museum of Singapore, Changi Airport and ION Orchard shopping mall, Singapore.

(JT)

Kumari Nahappan

Shakti Dimension Two A-B-C

2000
Acrylic on linen (triptych)
119 x 198 cm (each)

Singapore Art Museum
collection

Kumari Nahappan's abstract paintings resist easy identification of content and subject matter, but drawing deeply from Hindu religious belief and practice, the works may be understood as philosophical meditations upon the notions of time, cosmic energy and ritual.

Shakti Dimension Two A-B-C, with its bands of deep red and saturated black, expresses the idea of opposing forces in a potent and fluid co-existence. Similar to Nahappan's other paintings, the colours are produced through a slow and laborious process: she applies thin layers of acrylic paint successively to build up luminous chromatic fields, and in the process, a sliver of a hazy but intense 'in-between' tonality is produced as one colour transits to another. This passage of colour is not just for optical effect, but may be understood as the outcome of opposing energy fields or forces coming into contact with each other, and both sides softly losing definition in the encounter with the 'other'.

In Hindu belief, such a fluid dualism is integral to a dynamic and balanced cosmos, and the work's title is partially derived from the Sanskrit word 'shak', meaning "to be able". *Shakti* is regarded as the divine feminine energy, usually for the purposes of creation/creativity (nurturing and fertile), but also equally capable of destruction. In some aspects of Hinduism, it is personified as the Great Mother Goddess, which is sometimes further embodied in the triple figures of Saraswati, Lakshmi and Parvati (the consorts of the gods Brahma, Vishnu and Shiva respectively). Thus the work's realisation as a triptych takes on an added and spiritual significance, for the 3-in-1 form evokes the holy trinity, either in its male or female expression. Conceptually, this ambiguity is key for *Shakti*, in its unmanifest form, is regarded as pure potential energy – the divine force that permeates the whole universe, its possibilities and their antithesis.

Kumari Nahappan (b. 1953, Malaysia) is the recipient of the UOB (United Overseas Bank) Painting of the Year award (Abstract category) in 1998 and Phillip Morris Group ASEAN Art Award in 1999. In 2006, she exhibited at the Mori Art Museum, Tokyo, as part of 'Spotlight Singapore'. She embarked on a year-long solo exhibition 'Red on the Trail of a Colour' at the Museum of Cultures in Basel, Switzerland (2008) and also exhibited at the Tropenmuseum, Amsterdam (2011). Her public art sculptures can also be seen around Singapore, at the National Museum of Singapore, Changi Airport and ION Orchard shopping mall, Singapore.

(JT)

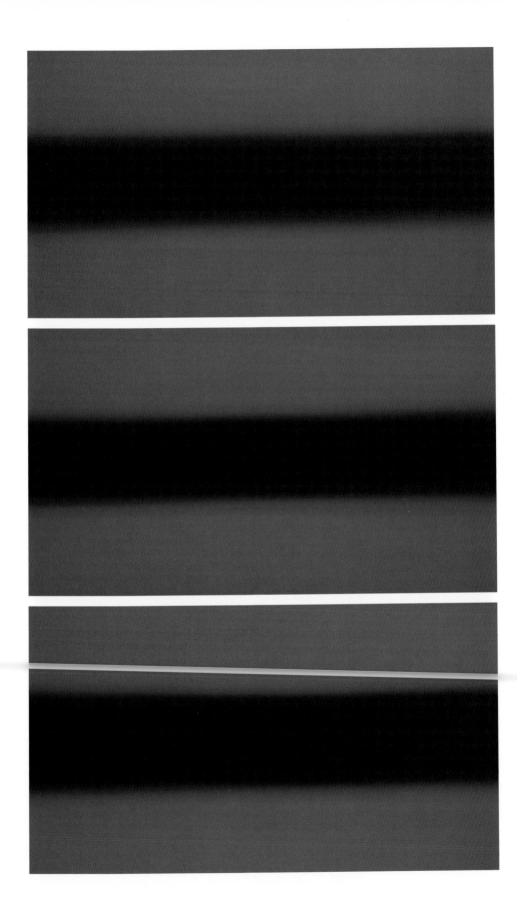

Kumari Nahappan

**Surya Series 99
Number Two**

1999
Acrylic on canvas
88.5 x 88.5 cm

Nine-O-One B

2001
Acrylic on canvas
125 x 125 cm

Singapore Art Museum
collection

Nahappan's transcendental abstract works are informed by the symbolic meaning of colours and numerology in Hindu belief, cosmology and ritual practices, and the artist frequently employs colours as a visual language to examine the connections between rebirth, growth and healing.

In **Surya Series 99 Number Two**, the brilliant hues of yellow and orange suggest the energy and the cyclical life-giving powers of *Surya* (the Sun God in Hinduism). **Nine-O-One B** shows the soft glow of yellow and accents of orange and red behind a swathe of brown tones; the latter evokes the colour of sandalwood which is considered sacred to Hindus as an indispensible item used in religious rituals to purify and heal. In conjunction with employing specific colours, the use of numerology also refers to concepts of the divine in Hindu belief. The number '0' represents Brahman, the creator of beginnings as well as the end of all things. The number '1' symbolises the illuminated realised self, while '9' represents fire or agni, and together they symbolise personal growth and renewal of life.

Kumari Nahappan (b. 1953, Malaysia) is the recipient of the UOB (United Overseas Bank) Painting of the Year award (Abstract category) in 1998 and Phillip Morris Group ASEAN Art Award in 1999. In 2006, she exhibited at the Mori Art Museum, Tokyo, as part of 'Spotlight Singapore'. She embarked on a year-long solo exhibition 'Red on the Trail of a Colour' at the Museum of Cultures in Basel, Switzerland (2008) and also exhibited at the Tropenmuseum, Amsterdam (2011). Her public art sculptures can also be seen around Singapore, at the National Museum of Singapore, Changi Airport and ION Orchard shopping mall, Singapore.

(SC)

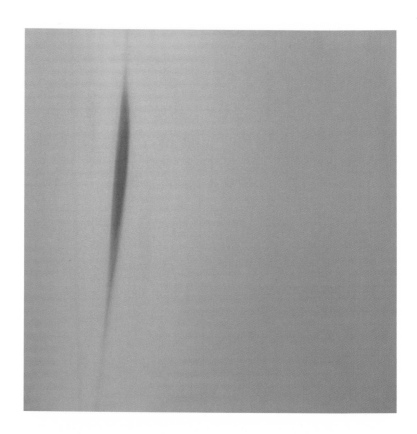

Surya Series 99 Number Two

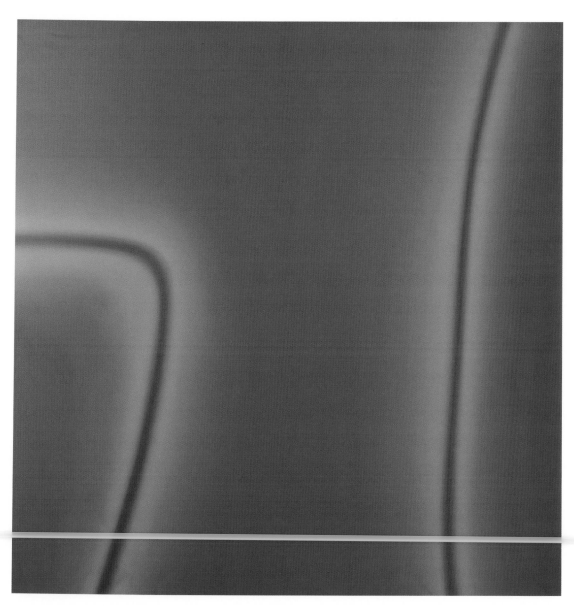

Nine-O-One B

Francis Ng

Displaced (Nos. #1, #2, #3, #4, #5, #8)

2003
C-prints, edition 5/5
126 x 126 cm (each)

Singapore Art Museum
collection

This suite of photographs of the sea shot close-up appears disarmingly simple, but Francis Ng's intense focus on water – and its relationship to the horizon – has resulted in some of the most moving and powerful images that the artist has produced to-date.

Some images capture tranquil waters, others more turbulent, but all exude palpable menace. Keeping the eye fixed on the horizon line is usually a preventive measure against the onslaught of sea-sickness, yet in this instance, the reverse is the effect. The horizon looms and swells, laying bare the unsteady relationship between sea and sky. Ironically, it is the 'tranquil' seas that are most unsettling for the still waters are ominous with foreboding and dead calm, and momentary relief is found only in the breaking of wave and water. The viewer's encounter with the images is a heightened confrontation – in every scene, the water threatens to overwhelm and consume the onlooker. It is an intensity that is reinforced by the crimson that saturates each image. Produced during the process of manually developing the photographs, the red – literally and metaphorically – 'colours' the photographs with symbolism and emotive connotations: passion, love, carnality, desire, danger, Hell.

Photographed at such close-range, the waters reveal no marker of place or location and point to the universal Nowhere/Everywhere, but in actuality, they were shot at very specific sites: the cardinal points of this island-state. Ng went to the sea off the north, south, east and west of Singapore, (Admiralty Road, Marina Bay, East and West Coast respectively) and in a 'baptismal' act, immersed himself bodily in the water to capture each image. Thus the works can be read as an exploration of subjectivity and an extension of Ng's experiential encounters in environments and surroundings, both the known and the less familiar.

Francis Ng (b. 1975, Singapore) is a multi-disciplinary artist whose photographs and installations have strived to examine the dynamics of space, and the relationship between the self and surroundings. He was the winner of both the Jurors' Choice and Grand Prize in the 2001/2002 Philip Morris ASEAN (Association of Southeast Asian Nations) Art Awards for his C-print, *Constructing Construction #1*. Ng also represented Singapore at the 50th Venice Biennale (2003).

(JT)

Facing page:
Clockwise from top left:
Displaced #1, #2, #3, #5, #8, #4

Dawn Ng

Walter

2010
Latex/plastic fibre
600 x 400 x 275 cm

Singapore Art Museum
collection

Walter is Dawn Ng's response and intervention to the landscape of Singapore, where the rapid pace of modernisation has resulted in a city landscape that changes constantly, with the proliferation new apartments and shopping malls, as well as the recent construction of two high-profile casinos. The work questions Singapore's obsession with being "world-class". Ng hopes to illuminate what is truly unique about our landscape – the tapestry of flats, *zhi char* (hawker food) eateries, Hotel 81s, convenience stores and MRT (Mass Rapid Transit) line arteries that, in their own right, are truly local and at times, unapologetically beautiful. *Walter* is a refutation of the oft-heard complaint that Singapore is prosaic and boring, and celebrates the ordinary, by helping us look at this city as children again.

As a curious colossal bunny who pops up across Singapore's standard landscape of flats and heartland enclaves, *Walter* appears and disappears guerrilla fashion, only to be permanently documented in photographs that invite the audience to reminisce over the significance of the spaces it visited. *Walter*'s incongruity to his environment, prompts people to re-examine overlooked and overly familiar places – the 'invisible normal' – by invoking a sense of surprise and wonder.

Dawn Ng (b. 1982, Singapore) graduated from the Slade School of Art at the University College of London and has exhibited widely in Singapore, France, United Kingdom and United States. She is based in Paris.

(KH)

Om Mee Ai

Triptych-W

2010
Oil on canvas
100 x 540 cm (triptych)

Singapore Art Museum
collection

In technique and its visual vocabulary, Om Mee Ai's paintings challenge conventional understanding of paintings. They are meditative in tone and require a perceptual shift from the viewer.

Triptych-W departs in its visual vocabulary from her previous paintings. While her previous works were muted and rather 'flat', *Triptych-W* features clearer grid forms, dominated by layers of white, giving the effect of almost solid shadows that floats. And while previous paintings were square in their dimensions, *Triptych-W* is panoramic, with three canvases joined as one unified composition.

Om's dominating interest is to investigate geometric abstract painting. Her work is shaped by the belief that favours the idea of "art for art's sake".

Om Mee Ai (b. 1959, Korea) graduated from the Open University, United Kingdom in 2006 and has exhibited widely in Singapore and overseas. Mee was the winner for Abstract category at the UOB (United Overseas Bank) Painting of the Year competitions in 2006 and 2007. She is based in Singapore.

(KH)

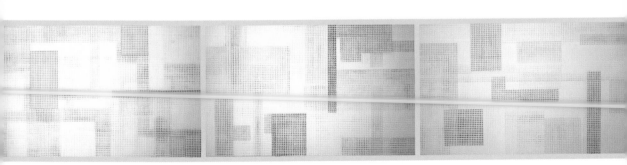

Donna Ong

Crystal City

2009
Glassware
Dimensions variable

Singapore Art Museum
collection

In creating a 'miniature' installation over a life-sized one, Donna Ong believes that seeing with one's eyes alone and entering an illusion is enough to transport the viewer into an alternate psychological reality. The use of glass bottles in *Crystal City* is twofold: arranged quite deliberately to concoct an image of soaring skyscrapers and an urban skyline, they evoke modern buildings that are often clad in sparkling glass. Yet the material of these delicate bottles also suggests that cities exist and are built on the fragile dreams and the hopes of humanity. The work brings out the beauty of everyday objects through the hundreds of common glassware pieces that were individually picked by the artist and the assortment of bottles – now transformed into a breathtaking skyline of a glass city – also pays tribute to the power of the imagination.

Donna Ong (b. 1978, Singapore) is known for her immersive installations which transform found objects into dream-like narratives. Her work has been exhibited extensively both at home and internationally, at platforms such as the inaugural Singapore Biennale (2006), the Kuandu Biennale, Taipei (2008), Jakarta Biennale (2009), and the 11th International Architecture Exhibition, La Biennale di Venezia (2008).

(DC)

Donna Ong

Dissolution

2009
Found Chinese paintings, acrylic,
CCTV cameras,
22 inch TV screens
Set of 3
45 x 100 x 34 cm (each)

Singapore Art Museum
collection

This work was commissioned for the President's Young Talents 2009 exhibition, and subsequently won the People's Choice Award. A departure from the larger-scale, immersive installations that Donna Ong is best known for, this piece furthers the artist's interest in the landscape genre, and develops the directions that Ong first explored in her smaller-scale dioramas created during her residency at the Singapore Tyler Print Institute.

On layered blocks of acrylic, Ong created an imaginary landscape by cutting up the elements of existing (found) Chinese paintings, and rearranging these into a new composition. While her actions appear iconoclastic, even blasphemous, the artist is in fact continuing a practice integral to the conventions of traditional Chinese painting, that of following in the masters' footsteps by patiently and painstakingly copying their works. By sensitively paying attention to every little contour and detail of the trees, shrubbery, figures, mountains and hills that she meticulously cuts out, Ong translates an age-old tradition into a contemporary composition, exploring the representation of perspective and narrative in Chinese landscape pictorial traditions, as well as Western artistic conventions.

Donna Ong (b. 1978, Singapore) is known for her immersive installations which transform found objects into dream-like narratives. Her work has been exhibited extensively both at home and internationally, at platforms such as the inaugural Singapore Biennale (2006), the Kuandu Biennale, Taipei (2008), Jakarta Biennale (2009), and the 11th International Architecture Exhibition, La Biennale di Venezia (2008).

(TSL)

(Detail)

Donna Ong

Dissolution

2009
Found Chinese paintings, acrylic,
CCTV cameras,
22 inch TV screens
Set of 3
45 x 100 x 34 cm (each)

Singapore Art Museum collection

Sherman Ong

Hanoi Haiku

2005
6 prints on archival
semi-gloss paper
75 x 150 cm (each)

Singapore Art Museum
collection

These six photographs, acquired from a series of 17, were made in Hanoi, Vietnam, during Ong's residency at the Goethe Institut's Art Connexions residency project. Witnessing a sudden hailstorm in Hanoi, which was followed by a violent storm, Ong was struck by how the people of the city carried on with their everyday life, and how individuals have their own way of facing what nature may unexpectedly hand them on a daily basis. Seeking to evoke the spirit and form of the Japanese haiku poem, Ong has composed these photographs in a triptych-format with three distinct images that seem to have no discernable narrative. Instead, they are, in his words, "observations in its purest form, distilled into a simple gesture, a moment of reflection, a point in a continuum, touching on the beauty of imperfection, in delicate, quiet, nuanced moments."

Sherman Ong (b. 1971, Malaysia) has received awards in Hong Kong, Greece, Italy, Indonesia and Malaysia. An alumnus of the 1st Berlinale Talent Campus 2003, Ong's works have been premiered at Rotterdam International Film Festival, International Documentary Festival, Amsterdam; Institute of Contemporary Arts, London; International Electronic Art Festival VideoBrasil and the Fukuoka Asian Art Museum, Japan. He has exhibited at 'Ostropicos – Views from the Tropics', Centro Cultural Banco dom Brasil, Brasilia and Rio de Janeiro, Brazil; PhotoQuai Musee du Quai Branly, Paris, and the Singapore Art Show, Singapore Art Museum in 2007. He was the artist-in-residence at the Fukuoka Asian Art Museum, and in 2008, presented a feature film at the Singapore International Film Festival.

(TJ)

Sherman Ong

Life of Imitation,
Ticket Seller

2009
Single-channel video, edition 1/5
Duration 3:26 mins

Life of Imitation,
Mr Neo Chon Teck

2009
Single-channel video, edition 1/5
Duration 3:46 mins

Life of Imitation,
Mr Wong Han Min

2009
Single-channel video, edition 1/5
Duration 5:10 mins

Singapore Art Museum
collection

Sherman Ong's ***Life of Imitation*** consists of three short documentaries of interviews with people whom Ong believes are integral to Singapore's film memory. They are Mr Neo Chon Teck (the last cinema billboard painter in Singapore), Mr Wong Han Min (a collector of cinema archival materials), and a fictional movie ticket seller. The Golden Age of Cinema in Singapore and its cultural significance is accented in the way the production of those films in the 1950s-60s also brought members of the three main ethnic groups closer together during a time when racial tensions were high.

Each documentary clip starts off as an accurate biographical representation of actual events but slowly evolves into fiction as the narrative unfolds. ***Life of Imitation*** combines both archival and recreated materials. Its main theme is the examination and analysis of 1950s and 1960s cinema in Singapore.

Sherman Ong (b. 1971, Malaysia) has received awards in Hong Kong, Greece, Italy, Indonesia and Malaysia. An alumnus of the 1st Berlinale Talent Campus 2003, Ong's works have been premiered at Rotterdam International Film Festival, International Documentary Festival, Amsterdam; Institute of Contemporary Arts, London; International Electronic Art Festival VideoBrasil and the Fukuoka Asian Art Museum, Japan. He has exhibited at 'Ostropicos – Views from the Tropics', Centro Cultural Banco dom Brasil, Brasilia and Rio de Janeiro, Brazil; PhotoQuai Musee du Quai Branly, Paris, and the Singapore Art Show, Singapore Art Museum in 2007. He was the artist-in-residence at the Fukuoka Asian Art Museum, and in 2008, presented a feature film at the Singapore International Film Festival.

(TJ)

Right:
Life of Imitation,
Ticket Seller

Facing page:
Top:
Life of Imitation,
Mr Neo Chon Teck

Bottom:
Life of Imitation,
Mr Wong Han Min

PHUNK &
Keiichi Tanaami

Eccentric City:
Rise And Fall

2010
Tatebanko paper box structures
with video installation
Dimensions variable

Singapore Art Museum
collection

PHUNK is a collective known for its design industry credentials, which heavily influence their approach and aesthetics in artmaking. The works of PHUNK draw on myriad aspects of popular and youth culture, from Japanese manga and anime to British indie music.

Eccentric City: Rise And Fall is PHUNK's collaborative effort with their idol, Japanese artist, Keiichi Tanaami, one of the foremost artists during Japan's countercultural movement of the 1960s. The breadth of Tanaami's creative practice spans fields as diverse as fine art, graphic design, publishing and advertising. *Eccentric City* presents the unique artistic visions and sensibilities of the artists through the age-old Japanese paper craft of tatebanko. A cityscape – a motif cherished by the artists – peopled with PHUNK's and Tanaami's psychedelic and comic-book characters, rises in the air, pulsating with colour and energy, even as its shadow side reminds us of the darker side of urban living. Nearby, a mass of collapsed structures serves as a warning of how the most beautiful and flourishing cities can disintegrate and decay, if their tensions and energies are not reconciled.

PHUNK is a Singapore-based collective formed by artists-designers Alvin Tan (b. 1974, Singapore), Melvin Chee (b. 1974, Singapore), Jackson Tan (b. 1974, Singapore) and William Chan (b. 1973, Singapore). Their practice – which spans art, design, publishing and interactive media – exemplifies the multi-disciplinary approach and diverse cultural influences of a younger generation of Singapore artists. PHUNK's works have received numerous accolades, including the 'Designer Of The Year' award at the 2007 Singapore President's Design Award.

Keiichi Tanaami (b. 1936, Japan) is one of Japan's foremost Pop artists. Closely associated with and inspired by the post-war counterculture movement, Tanaami is best known for his psychedelic graphic style, featuring deformed and /or hybrid beings and creatures rendered in acid colours. Tanaami works across different mediums and disciplines; besides recognition for his art, he has also received critical acclaim for his films, which were presented at the International Short Film Festival, Germany, and the New York Film Festival, United States. He remains active in the pop and youth culture scene today, often collaborating with other creatives. His art is regularly featured in design and lifestyle publications such as 'Wallpaper'. Most recently, his art has been exhibited in the Frieze Art Fair, London, and Art Basel, Switzerland.

(TSL)

PHUNK

Electricity (Neon)

2010
Carbon ink transfer on wood
panels, animated
projection mapping
300 x 830 cm

Singapore Art Museum
collection

Electricity pays homage to the contemporary city, and the artists' longstanding fascination with the architecture and energy that pulses through modern metropolises such as Singapore, Hong Kong and Tokyo. A collage of various urban motifs and distinctive architectural elements drawn from cities all over the world, *Electricity* celebrates the global, cosmopolitan city as it details its diversity, lit up and brought to life by the power of electricity – a reminder of how dependent we are on this essential power source that fuels our contemporary urban lifestyles.

PHUNK is a Singapore-based collective formed by artists-designers Alvin Tan (b. 1974, Singapore), Melvin Chee (b. 1974, Singapore), Jackson Tan (b. 1974, Singapore) and William Chan (b. 1973, Singapore). Their practice – which spans art, design, publishing and interactive media – exemplifies the multi-disciplinary approach and diverse cultural influences of a younger generation of Singapore artists. PHUNK's works have received numerous accolades, including the 'Designer Of The Year' award at the 2007 Singapore President's Design Award.

(TSL)

Milenko Prvacki

Home (red)

1994
Mixed media on paper
58 x 60 cm

Home (blue)

1995
Mixed media on paper
55 x 75 cm

Singapore Art Museum
collection

The ***Home*** series of works by Milenko Prvacki was inspired by his move from Yugoslavia to Singapore in 1992, and spurred by the feelings of dislocation that came with the move. Of this difficult choice, he noted that one had to "intellectually override" nostalgia and emotion in order to execute that move. Nevertheless, Prvacki's ***Home*** series of works are his most emotional. For instance, the constantly recurring image of a church spire in the series is drawn from recollections of his hometown Vojvodina; for the artist, it represents one of the most enduring images that triggers memories of home.

Milenko Prvacki (b. 1951, Ferdin, Vojvodina, Yugoslavia) graduated with a Masters of Fine Arts from the Institute of Fine Arts from Bucharest, Romania. Prvacki was the Dean of Faculty of Fine Arts in LASALLE College of the Arts in Singapore from 2002 to 2011. In 2011, he also participated in group exhibitions at the Museum Van Hedendaagse Kunst Antwerpen in Belgium, and the Torrance Art Museum in Los Angeles. In 1999, he had a solo exhibition at Plastique Kinetic Worms, Singapore. In 2012, he was also awarded the prestigious Cultural Medallion award, Singapore.

(DC)

Home (red)

Home (blue)

Milenko Prvacki

No.1

2009
Oil on canvas
97 x 122 cm

Singapore Art Museum
collection

No. 1 is part of a significant series of works by Prvacki called 'Trophy' that originated in his home country of Yugoslavia. Primarily an abstract painter, Prvacki produced this series as a critique of the socio-political situation in his home country, and as such, it was his first series of works that contained a figurative dimension. Although the 'Trophy' series ostensibly marks the rituals and symbols of heroism, it is also an expression of the disillusionment felt by individuals in a society with class divisions and severe wealth disparity. Feeling disillusioned with the role and lack of power of art to instigate any socio-political change, Prvacki decided to expand the concept of trophies to include the 'prizes' people accumulate and yearn for in life, such as fame and wealth.

After a lapse of 14 years, this particular painting marks the revival of the 'Trophy' series as Prvacki had stopped developing the series in 1995, three years after relocating to Singapore. The painting's muted colour palette therefore marks a return to his earlier works with tonal hues similar to those produced back in Yugoslavia. Prvacki called the work *No. 1* because it is the first of the revived 'Trophy' paintings series. Unlike his previous 'Trophy' paintings done in Yugoslavia which usually had images of dead animals, the 2009 work contains more subdued symbols mixed with other powerful kinds of images, such as the Asian lotus on the left.

Milenko Prvacki (b. 1951, Ferdin, Vojvodina, Yugoslavia) graduated with a Masters of Fine Arts from the Institute of Fine Arts from Bucharest, Romania. Prvacki was the Dean of Faculty of Fine Arts in LASALLE College of the Arts in Singapore from 2002 to 2011. In 2011, he also participated in group exhibitions at the Museum Van Hedendaagse Kunst Antwerpen in Belgium, and the Torrance Art Museum in Los Angeles. In 1999, he had a solo exhibition at Plastique Kinetic Worms, Singapore. In 2012, he was also awarded the prestigious Cultural Medallion award, Singapore.

(DC)

Milenko Prvacki

Tropical Rain

1994
Oil on paper
53 x 83 cm

Singapore Art Museum
collection

Tropical Rain is part of a series Prvacki had developed since his days as a student, being inspired by exotic places around the Adriatic sea, such as islands and volcanoes that he would visit during the summer holidays. Moving to Singapore, he started producing works again for this series.

In this 1994 painting, what was previously regarded as a distant, if 'exotic' tropical ideal, has become an experienced reality. The painting is rendered with heavy brushwork, an abstraction of the land and its natural environment. Moreover, in moving to a foreign land, Prvacki mooted the idea of mental islands – a safe space of isolation for thinking, where one is also forced to develop one's own structures and thoughts. Finally, the power of nature, that of tropical storms, which he newly experienced in Singapore, offers a foil to the politically turbulent situation of Yugoslavia that the artist had just left behind.

Milenko Prvacki (b. 1951, Ferdin, Vojvodina, Yugoslavia) graduated with a Masters of Fine Arts from the Institute of Fine Arts from Bucharest, Romania. Prvacki was the Dean of Faculty of Fine Arts in LASALLE College of the Arts in Singapore from 2002 to 2011. In 2011, he also participated in group exhibitions at the Museum Van Hedendaagse Kunst Antwerpen in Belgium, and the Torrance Art Museum in Los Angeles. In 1999, he had a solo exhibition at Plastique Kinetic Worms, Singapore. In 2012, he was also awarded the prestigious Cultural Medallion award, Singapore.

(DC)

Jing Quek

Singapore Idols: Grasscutters

2006
Epson inkjet print with ultrachrome K3 ink
52 x 77.5 cm

Singapore Idols: Skateboarders

2006
Epson inkjet print with ultrachrome K3 ink
52 x 77.5 cm

Singapore Art Museum collection

The **Singapore Idols** series of photographs is artist Jing Quek's attempt to capture a collective portrait of distinctive communities in Singapore, beyond the commonly used racial divisions that people are familiar with. His brightly-coloured photography celebrates everyday situations and environments, with a stylised take on individual communities that have their own unique sense of culture and identity – a joyful and humorous snapshot of the people who make up the 'face' and landscape of Singapore.

In **Singapore Idols: Skateboarders**, a group of youths typically seen in the shopping malls and skate parks of Orchard Road strut confident poses in a celebrity-style composition, reminiscent of glossy pictures of idols seen in magazines. With their definitive style in fashion apparel and accessories, the collective identity of the group stands out as a distinct community in our urban cityscape. Similarly, a group of foreign workers employed as grasscutters are captured in a playful composition where the subjects, with their unexpected poses, resemble cosplayers or perhaps a group of warriors, rather than grasscutters. Through this, Jing Quek signals the values he ascribes to the individuals featured in his work, in his attempt to address (and subvert) constructions of identity, stereotypes, and communities.

Jing Quek (b. 1983, Singapore) graduated with a Bachelor of Fine Arts in Photography from the School Of Visual Arts, United States. His work has been featured in magazines such as TimeOut Singapore, Newsweek, Surface and Maxim. His photography has also won awards at the 25th UOB Painting Of The Year Competition (Photography section, 2006); the MINInternational Photo Award; and the Pitti Immagine Photo Award. He has exhibited in United States as well as Singapore – some of his recent exhibitions include 'Identity/ Identities', New York (2009) and 'The Air-Conditioned Recession', Singapore (2009).

(TSL)

Sai Hua Kuan

Space Drawing 5

2009
Single-channel video, edition 2/5
Duration 1:02 mins (loop)

Singapore Art Museum
collection

Part of artist Sai Hua Kuan's **Space Drawing** series of videos, **Space Drawing 5** was created at tower Kronpriz in Kaliningrad, Russia, the construction site for the city's new contemporary art centre. Dramatic and compelling, this video captures the journey mapped by a line of rope across a space. Pulled taut, the rope springs into life once released, snapping, ricocheting, bouncing off brick walls, slithering along dusty floors, flying across rooms, and creating a hollow percussion as it weaves in and out between scaffolding and pillars. With high energy and drama, it defines the space it travels through, drawing our attention to the details of the derelict construction site where the artwork was made.

The **Space Drawing** series is a witty reinterpretation of the function of a line (that is, to divide, subtract, and define a space) and the age-old art form of drawing, by extending the conventional two-dimensional practice of drawing (putting lines on paper or onto some other surface) into a three-dimensional spatial intervention, documented not on canvas but on video. **Space Drawing 5** is drawing, video, performance, and a kind of spatial sculpting, all in one, and like much of Sai's work, illustrates the artist's playful approach to conventional categories and forms of art, and his willingness to go beyond these to explore new possibilities that emerge when they combine.

Sai Hua Kuan (b. 1976, Singapore) graduated from the Slade School of Fine Art, University College London (UK) with a Masters in Fine Art. His work has been exhibited in the Singapore Art Exhibition 2009 at the Singapore Art Museum, as well as at several international venues including the International Festival for Arts and Media Yokohama, Japan (2009), EV+A, Ireland (2010), Moscow International Biennale for Young Art, Russia (2010), the 14th Media Art Biennale WRO, Poland (2011) and the Luleå Art Biennale, Sweden (2011). While Sai is perhaps best known for his 'Space Line' series of videos documenting spatial interventions, he also creates installations and mixed-media works which explore interesting and unexpected juxtapositions of objects and interactions.

(TSL)

Sima Salehi Rahni

Circle

2009
3-channel video installation
Duration 8:57 mins

Singapore Art Museum
collection

Filmed in Batam, Indonesia, with actual residents of a village who were engaged to participate, ***Circle*** is a lyrical and allusive work which explores the subjectivity of women in conservative religious communities. The circle is used as a visual motif and metaphor for the boundaries, continuity and repetitive nature of tradition, religion and culture, which for the artist could suggest the subjugation of women, expressed by the despairing wailings of women: sounds likened to mourning. These collective structures and boundaries are deeply embedded in the psyche and perception of women in Iranian society, and consequently, firmly entrenched in its legal, political and economic institutions as well. The well that is featured in the video is the symbolic circle, a metaphor for this endless cycle. Drawing on her personal experiences as an artist originally from Iran, Sima Salehi blends myth with fact in this video to portray this concept of the circle, and the repetitive behaviour that keeps women within its confines.

Sima Salehi Rahni (b. 1967, Iran) graduated with a Masters of Arts Fine Arts degree from LASALLE College of the Arts, Singapore, in 2009. Her work addresses issues of gender through performance, installation, video and drawing, and has been exhibited at the Esplanade and the Singapore Art Museum.

(TSL)

Jeremy Sharma

Cerulean Block

2006
Oil and acrylic on vinyl
100 x 135 cm

Glacier

2006
Oil and acrylic on vinyl
100 x 135 cm

Sea-slab (Rock Bottom)

2006
Oil and acrylic on vinyl
96 x 167 cm

Sea-slab (Tight Bed)

2006
Oil and acrylic on vinyl
122 x 137 cm

Singapore Art Museum
collection

Inspired by a view of the sea while on a trip to Venice, Jeremy Sharma produced these works which are paintings of pure form. The series is a crystallisation of abstraction and figuration, a process of what he calls a "subtraction", which, for the artist, entails *not* creating a likeness of an object from the real world. Nonetheless, the forms also hark back to the prehistoric forms found in the Stone Ages, and also suggest tomb stones. Sharma's unconventional painting techniques involve stamping, scraping, smearing, bandaging, both destroying the pristine canvas surface and creating unusual and interesting surfaces. These works are part of Sharma's series, *The Massive*, which he undertook during his Masters course at LASALLE College of the Arts, Singapore.

Jeremy Sharma (b. 1977, Singapore) graduated with a Masters of Fine Art from LASALLE in 2006. In 2010, he participated in the 14th Asian Art Biennale, Bangladesh. In 2011, he took part in group exhibitions such as 'The Tokyo Book Fair' in Arts Chiyoda, Tokyo, and 'Foris' in Earl Lu Gallery, ICA, Singapore. In the same year, he also held a solo show, 'Variations', at Art Forum Gallery, Singapore.

(DC)

Right:
Cerulean Block

Facing page:
Top:
Glacier

Middle:
Sea-slab (Rock Bottom)

Bottom:
Sea-slab (Tight Bed)

Tang Da Wu

Important Myra

2010
Ink and charcoal on paper
Set of 8 drawings
110 x 80 cm (each)

Singapore Art Museum
collection

Important Myra is a series of ink paintings inspired by philosophical texts of the Chinese philosopher Mencius (372–289 BCE), who declared "老吾老以及人之老，幼吾幼以及人之幼", (*lao wu lao yi ji ren zhi lao, you wu you yi ji ren zhi you*, or when translated means: "Respect the aged of other families as one would, one's own aged; Respect the young of other families as one would, one's own young"). The saying refers to the values of caring for the aged and the young of other families as we would our own. Myra, daughter of fellow Artists Village artist Jeremy Hiah, is featured in this work, together with her artist parents Hiah and Lina Adam. The work can be seen as the artist's dedication to the future generations of Singapore as the nation's hope for the future. ***Important Myra*** depicts the child, emerging from a shell, recalling Italian Renaissance painter Sandro Botticelli's 'Birth of Venus' (1485-86).

One of the first artists in Singapore modern art history to champion experimental artmaking, Tang is known to have spearheaded the beginnings of The Artists Village in 1988, a collective of artists who explored installation practice and performance art. Tang's work is known for its themes of environmental concern as well as critical social issues in Singapore, often using workshops and other artistic strategies that activate audience participation, as part of artmaking. The artist's practice covers a broad range of media: drawing, painting, installation and performance.

Tang Da Wu (b. 1943, Singapore) first obtained his art education from Birmingham Polytechnic and Goldsmiths College, University of London, and participated in the 52nd Venice Biennale (2007), the 3rd Gwangju Biennale (2000), South Korea (2001) and the 1st Fukuoka Asian Art Triennale, Japan (1999).

(MH)

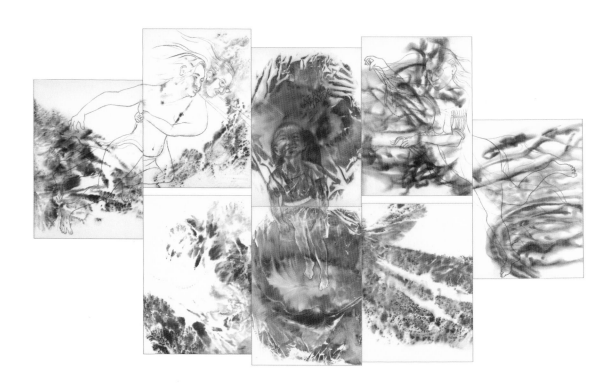

Tang Da Wu

Important Rumi

2010
Ink and charcoal on paper
Set of 7 drawings
110 x 80 cm (each, 6 pieces) and
244 x 154 cm (1 piece)

Singapore Art Museum
collection

Important Rumi is a series of ink paintings inspired by philosophical texts of the Chinese philosopher Mencius (372–289 BCE), who declared "老吾老以及人之老，幼吾幼以及人之幼", (*lao wu lao yi ji ren zhi lao, you wu you yi ji ren zhi you*, or when translated means: "Respect the aged of other families as one would, one's own aged; Respect the young of other families as one would, one's own young"). The saying refers to the values of caring for the aged and the young of other families as we would our own. Rumi, daughter of fellow Artists Village artist Zai Kuning is featured in this work, along with her artist father and his partner Lin Shiyun. In Tang Da Wu's view, Rumi is part of a new generation and society's hope for the future.

Tang portrays Rumi as Saraswati, the Hindu goddess of knowledge, music and the arts. In this work, Rumi is portrayed as one who inherits the traits of her father, fellow Singapore artist Zai Kuning. Zai appears on the left of Rumi playing the guitar – amidst a background rendered in the style of Vincent Van Gogh's Impressionist brushstrokes. This reflects Tang's sentiments of Zai as the Singapore Van Gogh. The rise of a new artistic generation coming into being is being represented by Tang through this metaphor: seen at the bottom left panels of *Important Rumi* is the figure of a dragon returning to soil, and morphing into bones while a phoenix on the right returns to heaven.

Tang Da Wu (b. 1943, Singapore) first obtained his art education from Birmingham Polytechnic and Goldsmiths College, University of London, and participated in the 52nd Venice Biennale (2007), the 3rd Gwangju Biennale (2000), South Korea (2001) and the 1st Fukuoka Asian Art Triennale, Japan (1999).

(MH)

SINGAPORE

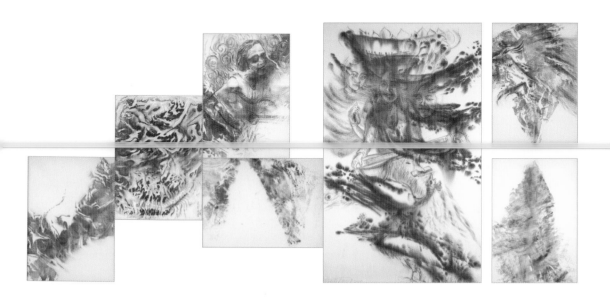

Tang Da Wu

Important Myra

2010
Ink and charcoal on paper
Set of 8 drawings
110 x 80 cm (each)

Singapore Art Museum
collection

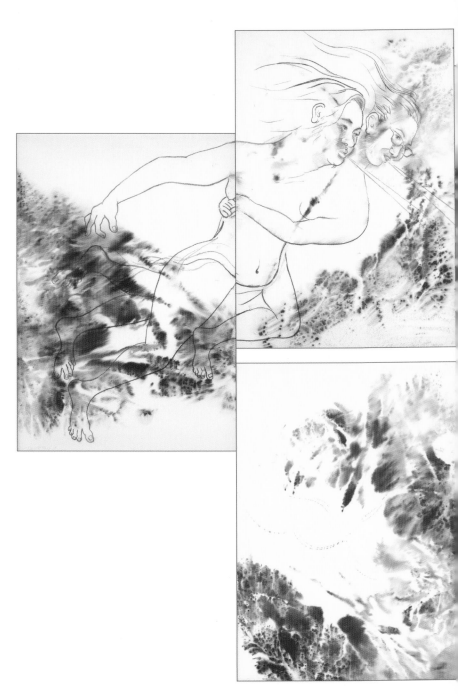

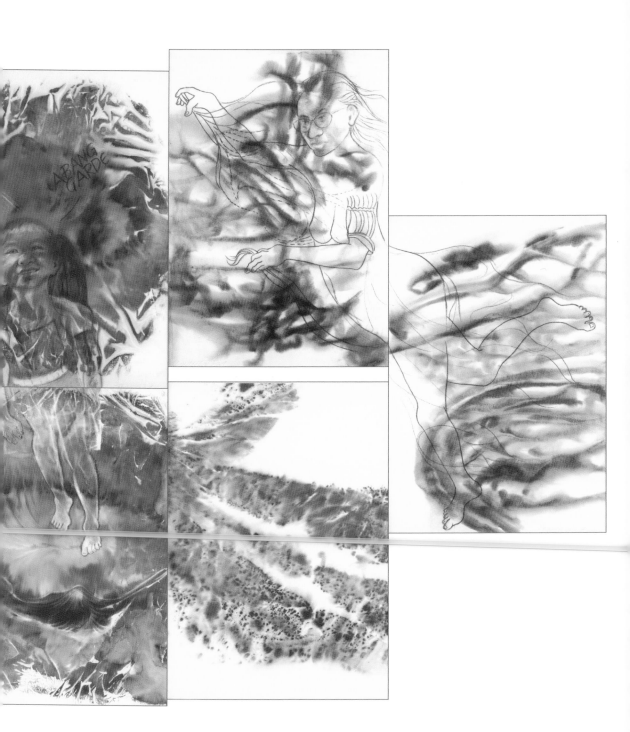

Tang Da Wu

Important Rumi

2010
Ink and charcoal on paper
Set of 7 drawings
110 x 80 cm (each, 6 pieces) and
244 x 154 cm (1 piece)

Singapore Art Museum
collection

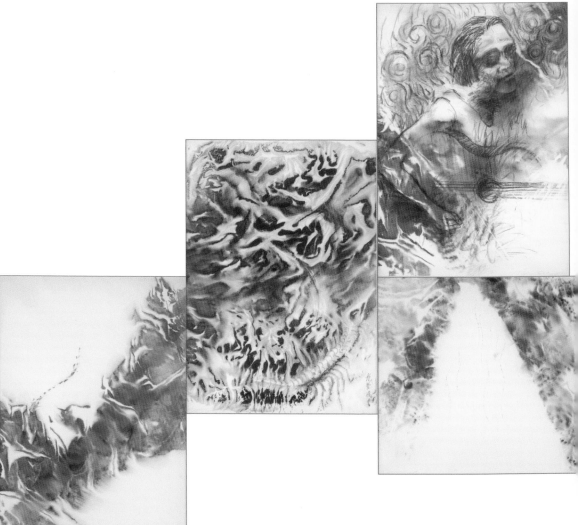

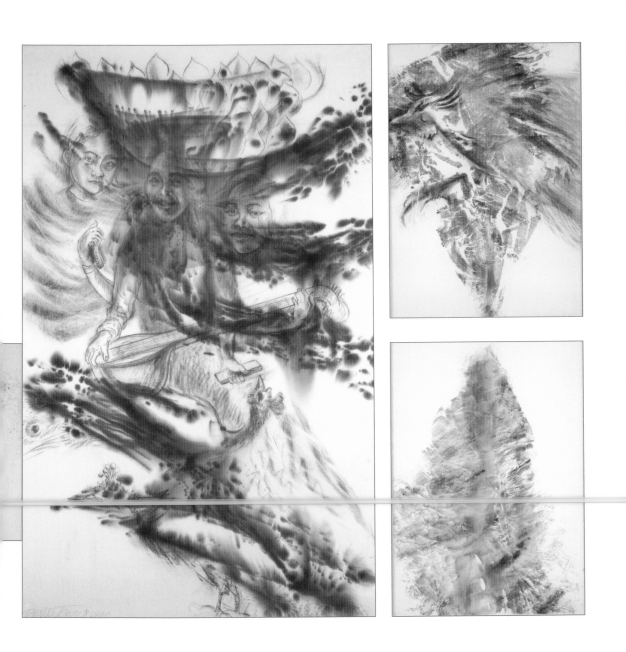

Tang Mun Kit

White Elephant Expostulation

2007
Acrylic, LED lights, found objects
of wood, birdcage casings,
white cloth
Dimensions variable

Singapore Art Museum
collection

White Elephant Expostulation is Tang Mun Kit's response to the Buangkok 'White Elephant affair', an episode in Singapore social history in 2005. On the eve of a Ministerial visit to the neighbourhood in the northern part of Singapore, an anonymous resident planted white elephant cut-outs near the Buangkok train station as a cheeky commentary on the train station's apparent redundancy. Despite the launch of the new subway line, of which the station was part of, it had remained unopened for two years, leading to the public notion that it was literally, a 'white elephant'. To the artist, the incident became a source of inspiration to defining the notion of OB (out-of-bound) markers pertaining to topics that were permissible to be publicly discussed, and Tang referenced the Buangkok white elephant from this incident as a way of questioning these issues.

Tang Mun Kit (b. 1955, Singapore) was actively involved the artists collective, The Artists Village, Singapore, in the late-1980s. Known for his use of found objects, Tang often engages with a wide spectrum of materials in his sculpture and installation that highlight social issues and concerns.

(MH)

Tang Ling Nah

An Other Space Within the House II Scene I

2010
Digital print on archival rag paper, edition 1/5
70 x 105 cm

An Other Space Within the House II Scene II

2010
Digital print on archival rag paper, edition 1/5
70 x 105 cm

Singapore Art Museum collection

An Other Space Within the House is a drawing installation done during Tang's two-month residency at the Kuandu Museum of Fine Arts, Taipei, Taiwan, in 2010. For this work, she used charcoal, paint, paper, masking tape and existing architectural elements in the gallery space to create an illusionary space, taking references from the architecture of the Taipei National University of the Arts. In her work, she 'de-constructs' the original real spaces and 're-constructs' them into imaginary spaces to create a sense of unfamiliar familiarity. Her work resembles *trompe l'oeil* murals. Stairways, doors and windows are important features in her work.

Tang Ling Nah's work is inspired by urban spaces in Singapore, such as the public housing's void decks, alleys, shopping malls and Mass Rapid Transit stations. Tang has long found it important to use a very basic implement (particularly charcoal) and support (paper and/or the wall) to explore buildings and spaces as communicators of stories about human life. In depicting spaces as largely darkened but peppered with glimpses of light, she expresses the paradox of architecture as, in her words, possibly "facilitative and inhibitive of relational development".

Tang Ling Nah (b. 1971, Singapore) has participated in numerous local and overseas group exhibitions, including the Singapore Pavilion at the 11th International Architecture Biennale in Venice (2008); the 2nd Singapore Biennale (2008); Singapore Art Show (2007) and the ASEAN (Association of Southeast Asian Nations) Arts Award Exhibition in Bangkok, Thailand (2004).

(DC)

Vertical Submarine

A View With A Room

2009
Mixed media installation
Dimensions variable

Singapore Art Museum
collection

A View With A Room was created for the President's Young Talents 2009 exhibition, Singapore. It continues Vertical Submarine's interest in the relationship between word and image, the discourse of reading, and the world it evokes.

In this work, the artists are interested in the (mis)translation of text into image, and the degree that social and cultural context play a part in this (mis)translation. How might an Asian reader visualise an archetypal European scene, described by a European writer? What layers of personal meaning or individual agency would a reader bring to bear on his / her own interpretation of a text?

In *A View With A Room*, the artists set about recreating a domestic interior based on descriptive passages extracted from various texts by writers such as Edgar Allan Poe and Georges Perec. The 'image' created by the artists points at the gaps – temporal, spatial and cultural – between the text and the reader (and reality). In keeping with the spirit of Vertical Submarine's works, the work is playfully concealed, waiting to be discovered by an equally playful viewer who will be duly rewarded for his or her sense of adventure and willingness to challenge (gallery-going) conventions.

Vertical Submarine is an art collective comprising members Joshua Yang (b. 1974, Malaysia), Justin Loke (b. 1979, Singapore) and Fiona Koh (b. 1983, Singapore). The artists collective's tongue-in-cheek, mixed media works often incorporate text and wordplay. Their art is a witty, punning critique of contemporary popular culture, strategically employing the visual tropes of the culture or practice they intend to critique, in order to highlight its idiosyncrasies and shortcomings. In 2009, Vertical Submarine received the inaugural President's Young Talents 2009 Credit Suisse Artist Residency Award, Singapore. They were awarded the Celeste Art Prize 2011, New York, in the Installation and Sculpture category for *A View With A Room*. Their other works included *Flirting Point*, Siloso Beach, Singapore and Singapore Art Museum; *Garden of Forking Paths*, Grey Projects, Singapore in 2010.

(TSL)

Vertical Submarine

DeComposition I: Dead Books

2005
Mixed media
Dimensions variable

Singapore Art Museum
collection

Playing on the word 'decompose' which can mean to 'take apart' (the opposite of to 'compose') as well as to 'rot' or 'decay', *DeComposition I: Dead Books* presents a series of books which can no longer fulfil their original functions. There is a book with its pages glued together so that it cannot be opened; a book with its words scratched out; a book with text printed in reverse so that it can only be read in a mirror; a book whose pages are filled with nothing but images of a closed book; an abstracted 'mapping' of one of the essential features of a book – the physical opening and closing of its pages. Through their subversion of the book's essential functions and features, Vertical Submarine liberates the book from its original use-value and proposes new possibilities for this object, which we have come to take for granted.

DeComposition I was presented at the President's Young Talents 2009 exhibition, as a work-within-a-work and part of Vertical Submarine's winning entry.

Vertical Submarine is an art collective comprising members Joshua Yang (b. 1974, Malaysia), Justin Loke (b. 1979, Singapore) and Fiona Koh (b. 1983, Singapore). The artists collective's tongue-in-cheek, mixed media works often incorporate text and wordplay. Their art is a witty, punning critique of contemporary popular culture, strategically employing the visual tropes of the culture or practice they intend to critique, in order to highlight its idiosyncrasies and shortcomings. In 2009, Vertical Submarine received the inaugural President's Young Talents 2009 Credit Suisse Artist Residency Award, Singapore. They were awarded the Celeste Art Prize 2011, New York, in the Installation and Sculpture category for *A View With A Room*. Their other works included *Flirting Point*, Siloso Beach, Singapore and Singapore Art Museum; *Garden of Forking Paths*, Grey Projects, Singapore in 2010.

(TSL)

Vertical Submarine

Fool's Gold

2008
Installation with signboard,
neon lighting
Dimensions variable

Singapore Art Museum
collection

Fool's Gold was created in 2008 for 'ZoukOut', an annual dance music festival, organised by Singapore-based dance club Zouk. In 2008, Zouk commissioned a number of local artists to create artwork for its 'ZoukOut' beach party at Sentosa, based on their theme 'The Gold Experience'.

Vertical Submarine's contribution was an installation featuring a huge arrow-shaped signboard lit up by neon lights. The sign pointed towards the ground, its yellow letters reading: NO GOLD BURIED HERE (此地无藏金). The work alludes to a Chinese idiom about a fool who tried to hide his gold, but made its hiding-place even more conspicuous by erecting a sign on the burial spot disclaiming its existence.

The aesthetics of this work borrows from nightlife culture with its slick graphics, neon lights and pop sensibility. The work is also dependent on its context of a dance / beach party, which is characterised by general inebriation and uninhibited behaviour. In such an environment, party-goers are more liable to attempt what would otherwise seem foolish, and take Vertical Submarine's sign at its word. (In the spirit of fun, the artists collective also included gold-coloured digging implements in their installation, for party-goers who might be inclined to investigate if the organiser had indeed hidden 'mystery' prizes.) Playful and eye-catching, Vertical Submarine's work gently mocks this (youth) culture of getting drunk and making a fool of oneself at such events. In the opinion of the artists, *Fool's Gold* is also an apt project for Sentosa, a designated 'resort' or leisure destination which induces visitors to engage in foolish behaviour, the most vivid example coming from Singapore's history where the British forces defending Singapore during the Second World War pointed their war guns on Sentosa's Fort Siloso in the wrong direction, allowing Japanese troops to capture the island.

Vertical Submarine is an art collective comprising members Joshua Yang (b. 1974, Malaysia), Justin Loke (b. 1979, Singapore) and Fiona Koh (b. 1983, Singapore). The artists collective's tongue-in-cheek, mixed media works often incorporate text and wordplay. Their art is a witty, punning critique of contemporary popular culture, strategically employing the visual tropes of the culture or practice they intend to critique, in order to highlight its idiosyncrasies and shortcomings. In 2009, Vertical Submarine received the inaugural President's Young Talents 2009 Credit Suisse Artist Residency Award, Singapore. They were awarded the Celeste Art Prize 2011, New York, in the Installation and Sculpture category for *A View With A Room*. Their other works included *Flirting Point*, Siloso Beach, Singapore and Singapore Art Museum; *Garden of Forking Paths*, Grey Projects, Singapore in 2010.

(TSL)

Vertical Submarine

Flirting Point

2009
Installation with lightbox and
metal pole
400 x 150 x 150 cm

Singapore Art Museum
collection

Flirting Point was commissioned by local nightclub Zouk for the dance festival 'ZoukOut' 2009, in collaboration with the Singapore Art Museum. It was installed at 'ZoukOut' 2009, and subsequently on the front lawn of SAM from February to April 2010.

The artists of this work created it in response to their own observations of urban situations, where flirtation is often conducted on the pretext of other, 'higher-minded' causes, such as visiting cultural institutions (such as art museums) and pretending to admire art while in actuality admiring other physical forms. Cutting to the chase, the artists have designed a designated "Flirting Point" for all and sundry to indulge unabashedly in this necessary social ritual; ironically and perhaps unsurprisingly, the artwork has achieved the complete opposite of its aim, for by declaring its very purpose and function so explicitly, it has in fact deterred participants from the very activity it was intended to promote. At the same time, this designated 'flirting point' is a sly dig at how behaviour is prescribed, policed and strictly regulated in Singapore.

Vertical Submarine is an art collective comprising members Joshua Yang (b. 1974, Malaysia), Justin Loke (b. 1979, Singapore) and Fiona Koh (b. 1983, Singapore). The artists collective's tongue-in-cheek, mixed media works often incorporate text and wordplay. Their art is a witty, punning critique of contemporary popular culture, strategically employing the visual tropes of the culture or practice they intend to critique, in order to highlight its idiosyncrasies and shortcomings. In 2009, Vertical Submarine received the inaugural President's Young Talents 2009 Credit Suisse Artist Residency Award, Singapore. They were awarded the Celeste Art Prize 2011, New York, in the Installation and Sculpture category for *A View With A Room*. Their other works included *Flirting Point*, Siloso Beach, Singapore and Singapore Art Museum; *Garden of Forking Paths*, Grey Projects, Singapore in 2010.

(TSL)

Vertical Submarine

Paper Room

2003
Installation with paper
Dimensions variable
Image courtest of artist

Singapore Art Museum
collection

Paper Room was Vertical Submarine's first collaborative project. It was conceived as a response to a Land Art workshop that the artists had attended, as a result of which they were required to create a work of Land Art. In thinking through their work, the artists questioned the relevance of Land Art in the highly urbanised environment of Singapore in which they had been brought up, and concluded that filling a room full of paper was more indicative of their contemporary experiences than working with natural elements. Paper is symbolic of the paper chase that Singaporeans subscribe to; it is a symbol of tedious administrative duties, of scholarship and of learning, of work. At the same time, blank sheets of paper are also suggestive of creative endeavour, waiting to be filled with the masterpieces and compositions of writers, poets and composers.

Drawing on these significations, Vertical Submarine covered an entire room with sheets of type-written paper which recorded their conversations about this project. ***Paper Room*** is simultaneously a witty commentary on how overwhelming administration and bureaucracy can be, as it is an evocation of the frustration of creative endeavour, the room-full of crumpled and discarded typewritten papers suggesting the plight of one suffering from writer's block or lack of inspiration.

Vertical Submarine is an art collective comprising members Joshua Yang (b. 1974, Malaysia), Justin Loke (b. 1979, Singapore) and Fiona Koh (b. 1983, Singapore). The artists collective's tongue-in-cheek, mixed media works often incorporate text and wordplay. Their art is a witty, punning critique of contemporary popular culture, strategically employing the visual tropes of the culture or practice they intend to critique, in order to highlight its idiosyncrasies and shortcomings. In 2009, Vertical Submarine received the inaugural President's Young Talents 2009 Credit Suisse Artist Residency Award, Singapore. They were awarded the Celeste Art Prize 2011, New York, in the Installation and Sculpture category for *A View With A Room*. Their other works included *Flirting Point*, Siloso Beach, Singapore and Singapore Art Museum; *Garden of Forking Paths*, Grey Projects, Singapore in 2010.

(TSL)

Vertical Submarine

Shopping For A Personal Letter

2009
Mixed media
site-specific installation
Dimensions variable

Singapore Art Museum
collection

Shopping For A Personal Letter was a site-specific project, created for a temporary glass gallery along Singapore's main shopping stretch, Orchard Road. The installation mimicked the look of a product launch by transforming the rectangular gallery into a product showroom, featuring display cabinets and showcases of letter templates for sale. There were all kinds of personal letters, designed to be despatched, to lovers, family, and friends. Expressions of love, kinship or friendship were imprinted on each letter – all that was lacking was the buyer / sender's signature. Attractively packaged in pseudo-vintage boxed sets and lettered with a flourishing script, these documents presented themselves as an instant, convenient solution to expressing one's feelings to people near and dear, which necessitated little effort on one's part.

Vertical Submarine's work is a commentary on the culture of consumerism in our society today, and how personal items and expressions have become commodified and clichéd. ***Shopping For A Personal Letter*** serves as a reminder to passers-by caught up in the act of conspicuous consumption that – contrary to the advertising slogans of credit card companies – there are certain things that can never really be bought.

Vertical Submarine is an art collective comprising members Joshua Yang (b. 1974, Malaysia), Justin Loke (b. 1979, Singapore) and Fiona Koh (b. 1983, Singapore). The artists collective's tongue-in-cheek, mixed media works often incorporate text and wordplay. Their art is a witty, punning critique of contemporary popular culture, strategically employing the visual tropes of the culture or practice they intend to critique, in order to highlight its idiosyncrasies and shortcomings. In 2009, Vertical Submarine received the inaugural President's Young Talents 2009 Credit Suisse Artist Residency Award, Singapore. They were awarded the Celeste Art Prize 2011, New York, in the Installation and Sculpture category for *A View With A Room*. Their other works included *Flirting Point*, Siloso Beach, Singapore and Singapore Art Museum; *Garden of Forking Paths*, Grey Projects, Singapore in 2010.

(TSL)

Suzann Victor

***Bloodline: Third World
Extra Virgin Dreams***

2011
Mixed media installation:
Glass, Fresnel lens, human blood,
bed, wire
Dimensions variable

Singapore Art Museum
collection

In this dramatic installation, the humble bed – a 'commonplace' object found in every home – transcends its ubiquitous status by taking on the full power of symbol and metaphor. As the site of beginnings and endings – conception, birthing and dying – the bed is also host and witness to each individual's most private worlds of sleep, as well as sexual fantasy/fulfilment, dream and nightmare. Evocative of rest and restlessness, the bed is, in the artist's words, "imprinted with not only the human form but its corporeality." Similarly, the human body is alluded to by way of the quilt, which is used to provide comfort and warmth. Moreover, because it is traditionally stitched together by women using the odds and ends of remnant fabric, the quilt also suggests frugality and poverty. Here, however, running the length of ten meters, it assumes a quality of monumentality that is a compelling contrast to the delicate fragility of the glass slides which make up the individual quilt pieces. Sandwiched in between each pair of glass slides is a mixture of wine and blood, drawn from the artist and occasionally mixed with the blood of another donor.

The installation, ***Third World Extra Virgin Dreams***, was originally commissioned by the 6th Havana Biennial, Cuba (1997), where it was shown in the historic Cabania Fortress. ***Bloodline*** now incorporates elements of the 1997 work – a number of pieces from the original glass quilt containing the blood mixture of the artist and the patriarch of the host Cuban family – while enlarging the quilt through the inclusion of some 3,000 new glass slides and blood from other donors.

Suzann Victor (b. 1959, Singapore) received her PhD in Visual Art in 2009 as well as her Masters of Arts (Honours) in 2000, both from the University of Western Sydney. The former Artistic Director of 5th Passage Ltd. (1991 to 1993), Victor started her practice as an award-winning painter but is now best known for her visually striking, sophisticated installations. Her works often investigate the post-colonial condition, as well as the notion of the abject, the absent body and 'body-machine', as well as the dynamics of female sexuality within patriarchal society. She has exhibited widely at international platforms including 'Thermocline of Art: New Asian Waves' at ZKM Centre for Art & Media, Karlsruhe, Germany (2007), the 6th Gwangju Biennale, Korea (2006), the 49th Venice Biennale (2001) and the 2nd Asia Pacific Triennial of Contemporary Art, Brisbane, Australia (1996). Some of her public works include commissions by the National Museum of Singapore and World Square, Sydney.

(JT)

Right & facing page:
***Third World Extra Virgin
Dreams***, 1997
At the 6th Havana Biennial, Cuba

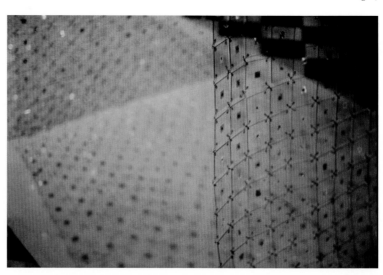

Suzann Victor

Expense of Spirit in a Waste of Shame

1994
Mixed media: light bulbs, cables, control unit, broken glass, motors, aluminum rods, mirrors
Dimensions variable

Singapore Art Museum collection

With its chorus of 'clinks' and mesmerising movement of incandescent lights bulbs caught in an endless dance with mirrors and crushed glass, ***Expense of Spirit in a Waste of Shame*** effortlessly seduces the visual and aural senses. Yet even as it enthrals, the work emanates a sense of unease that can be traced to the ferment of events which have indelibly marked the course of contemporary art in Singapore.

Following a media-incited controversy over a performance art event in Singapore in 1993, and subsequent decade-long proscription on state funding for the art form, Suzann Victor sought alternative strategies to conjure the naked human body as well exploring its attendant associations, such as romantic/sexual desire, fantasy, fulfilment (and the lack thereof), death, and the fraught nature of corporeality. Here, the installation's 'performative' nature can be seen as a reference to the performing (human) body – but one rendered physically absent because of the then-taboo conditions regarding depictions of the naked human form.

Baby rocker motors control each set of light bulbs, driving the light bulbs downwards to their paired elliptical mirrors, and the kinetic work is accompanied by a rhythm of glass clinks each time the bulbs make contact with the mirrors. The work delves into Foucault's theory of the mirror as a heterotopia, a utopia that is, nonetheless, a "placeless place". Like doomed lovers, the bulbs and mirrors are locked in a never-ending cycle of approach and departure – a relationship that is ultimately a futile, narcissist one, for the Other is, in this instance, but a reflection of the Self.

Suzann Victor (b. 1959, Singapore) received her PhD in Visual Art in 2009 as well as her Masters of Arts (Honours) in 2000, both from the University of Western Sydney. The former Artistic Director of 5th Passage Ltd. (1991 to 1993), Victor started her practice as an award-winning painter but is now best known for her visually striking, sophisticated installations. Her works often investigate the post-colonial condition, as well as the notion of the abject, the absent body and 'body-machine', as well as the dynamics of female sexuality within patriarchal society. She has exhibited widely at international platforms including 'Thermocline of Art: New Asian Waves' at ZKM Centre for Art & Media, Karlsruhe, Germany (2007), the 6th Gwangju Biennale, Korea (2006), the 49th Venice Biennale (2001) and the 2nd Asia Pacific Triennial of Contemporary Art, Brisbane, Australia (1996). Some of her public works include commissions by the National Museum of Singapore and World Square, Sydney.

(JT)

Jason Wee

Self-Portrait
(No More Tears Mr Lee)

2009
Installation with shampoo
bottle caps
380 x 324 x 30 cm

Singapore Art Museum
collection

Self-Portrait (No More Tears Mr Lee), is a work made out of 8,000 bottle caps, placed on an angled pedestal. The work alludes to a historical and emotional moment in Singapore's history of independence, while the choice of material used to create this installation is a cheeky reference to a well-known shampoo tagline. The breaking down of the image of the person represents questions of how biographies and histories of historical figures are multifaceted, encouraging the audience to think of these with a multi-perspective approach. This installation is also introspective and self-reflexive in that Jason Wee sees himself represented in this portrait as well, in the way that a person might identify himself or herself with an influential father figure. This work won the People's Choice Award in the Singapore Art Exhibition 2009.

Jason Wee (b. 1978, Singapore) is the recipient of the Lee Foundation Study Grant (2004), and the Shell-NAC Award. He has exhibited in Singapore as well as overseas, including a solo exhibition at Utterly Art, Singapore, and at the Singapore Biennale 2006. Jason Wee is also the founder of Grey Projects, which hosts artist residencies and exhibitions.

(TSL)

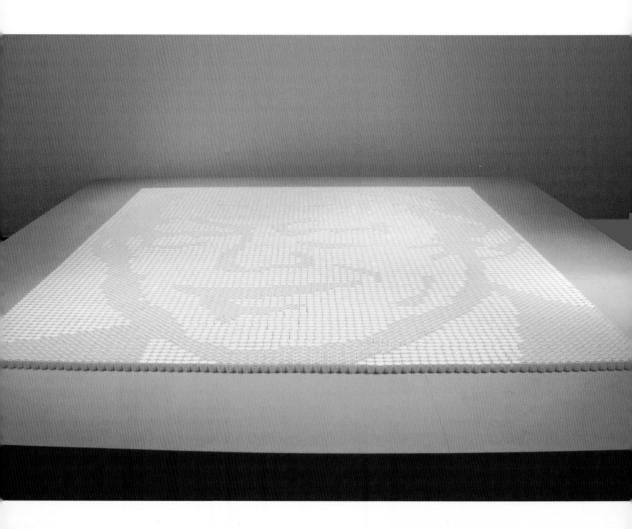

Ming Wong

Filem-Filem-Filem

2008–2010
Polaroid-type photographs,
series of 12 prints
8.5 x 10.8 cm (each)

Singapore Art Museum
collection

Filem-Filem-Filem is a series of digital photographs in 'Polaroid' form that documents Wong's travels throughout Singapore and Malaysia in a quest to uncover the remnants of cinema architecture from the recent past.

Collectively, the prints are an interesting contrast to our era of multiple-screen movie-cum-entertainment complexes in Singapore. Paying tribute to these 'dream palaces', Wong's photographs capture the beauty of these long-lost and forgotten theatres. Some of these old cinemas still retain their signage written in English, Chinese, Tamil and Jawi.

Ming Wong (b. 1971, Singapore) lives and works in Berlin and Singapore. He has had solo shows in Los Angeles, New York, Japan, Italy, Germany and Singapore. He won the Wollita Kulturpreis in Berlin, Germany in 2008, and received Special Mention for 'Expanding Worlds' at the 53rd Venice Biennale in 2009. He completed a year-long residency at Künstlerhaus Bethanien in Berlin from 2007-08 and was awarded the Fire Station Residency and Bursary by ACME Studios in 2005.

(TJ)

Ming Wong

Four Malay Stories

2005
4-channel DV video, in black/
white with audio, edition 2/5
Duration 4:03mins and
25:00 mins (loop)

Four Malay Stories

2009
Acrylic emulsion on canvas,
single cinema billboard
217.5 x 295 cm
Designed by Ming Wong and
hand-painted by Neo Chon Teck

Singapore Art Museum
collection

Bazaar Malay (or pidgin Malay) was the lingua franca spoken and understood by all races in Singapore before its independence in 1965. National language classes in Malay was instituted in schools in anticipation of Singapore joining the peninsula to become part of the Federation of Malaya.

Four Malay Stories shows the artist, a non-Malay speaker, trying to memorise the Malay lines from 16 characters in four films by the late Malay actor-director, P. Ramlee: 'Ibu Mertua Ku /My Mother-in-Law' (1962), 'Labu dan Labi / Labu and Labi '(1962), 'Doktor, Rushdi / Doctor Rushdi' (1971), 'Semerah Padi / The Village of Semerah Padi' (1956). This work charts Wong's efforts in mastering this unfamiliar language, Malay, and incorporating its associated cultural practices into his role. It also includes an English translation as seen in instructional videos for learning foreign languages. Wong re-imagines this legacy so as to re-read 'national cinema' constructed through the performative veneers of language and identity. The mimicry is sly and comic, and the video loops soon expose slippages in acting guises and stances. These imperfections of copying allow for a critical recognition of difference and awareness in such attempts to enter the cultural lives of others who are different from us.

As a form of tribute to 1950s Singaporean cinema, Wong sought to recreate this imagined golden age with Singapore's last surviving cinema billboard painter, Neo Chon Teck, who hand-painted this cinema billboard according to the artist's design.

Ming Wong (b. 1971, Singapore) lives and works in Berlin and Singapore. He has had solo shows in Los Angeles, New York, Japan, Italy, Germany and Singapore. He won the Wollita Kulturpreis in Berlin, Germany in 2008, and received Special Mention for 'Expanding Worlds' at the 53rd Venice Biennale in 2009. He completed a year-long residency at Künstlerhaus Bethanien in Berlin from 2007-08 and was awarded the Fire Station Residency and Bursary by ACME Studios in 2005.

(TJ)

Mana boleh? Ini perempuan saya yang punya!
How can that be? This woman, I'm the owner!

You dah pujuk I. You dah naikkan nafsu I.
You've coaxed me, you've aroused my desire.

Bunulah! Bunulah aku!
Please kill. Please kill me!

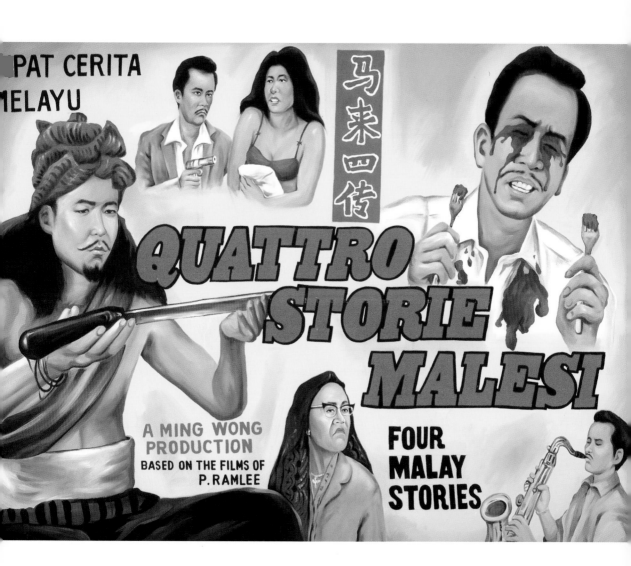

Ming Wong

In Love for the Mood

2009
3-channel HD video, in colour
with audio, edition 1/5
Duration 16:09 mins and
4:00 mins (loop)

In Love for the Mood

2009
Acrylic emulsion on canvas
217.5 x 380 cm
Designed by Ming Wong and
hand-painted by Neo Chon Teck

Singapore Art Museum
collection

The Golden Age of Singapore cinema can be traced to the 1950s and 1960s – two decades of phenomenal cinematic creativity and production that has not been repeated until today. Wong makes a contemporary reconstruction of 1950s Singaporean cinema by collaborating with Singapore's last surviving cinema billboard painter, Neo Chon Teck, who hand-painted this cinema billboard.

A restaging of the famous 2000 Hong Kong film 'In the Mood for Love' by Wong Kar Wai, *In Love for the Mood* substitutes a Caucasian actress for the role of both Chow Mo-Wan and Su Li-Zhen – a man and a woman whose respective spouses were cheating on them with each other. The actress in *In Love for the Mood* is not a native speaker of Cantonese and as a result, recites the lines with difficulty, bordering on exasperation at times, even though the artist Ming Wong, a native Cantonese speaker, is prompting her off-screen. This scene repeats a moment in the source movie whereby Chow helps Su re-enact a future confrontation with her husband about his affair with his wife. A performance primarily about identity, 'Singapore' (Ming) Wong's deliberate miscasting of the main female lead in 'Hong Kong' Wong (Kar Wai)'s tale about the frailty of the human heart and the difficult search for true love elevates the concerns of the film's protagonists to a universal condition encountered by everyone, regardless of race and of language.

Ming Wong (b. 1971, Singapore) lives and works in Berlin and Singapore. He has had solo shows in Los Angeles, New York, Japan, Italy, Germany and Singapore. He won the Wollita Kulturpreis in Berlin, Germany in 2008, and received Special Mention for 'Expanding Worlds' at the 53rd Venice Biennale in 2009. He completed a year-long residency at Künstlerhaus Bethanien in Berlin from 2007-08 and was awarded the Fire Station Residency and Bursary by ACME Studios in 2005.

(TJ)

Ming Wong

Life of Imitation

2009
2-channel HD video, in colour
with audio, edition 1/5
Duration 16:09 mins and
13:00 mins (loop)

Life of Imitation

2009
Acrylic emulsion on canvas, set of
4 cinema billboards
220 x 223 cm, 217 x 165 cm,
215 x 153 cm, 217 x 164 cm
Designed by Ming Wong and
hand-painted by Neo Chon Teck

Singapore Art Museum
collection

Using Singapore's rich history of cinema and a popular national pastime for movie consumption as a starting point, Wong commemorates its milestones and achievements while providing his viewers with a clever and captivating set of billboards that explores shifting notions of identity construction and race relations in contemporary Singapore. Wong makes a contemporary reconstruction of 1950s Singaporean cinema by collaborating with Singapore's last surviving cinema billboard painter, Neo Chon Teck, who hand-painted these cinema billboards according to the artist's design. Revealing the industry's rich ethnic and cultural diversity, Wong also attempts to revisit the past through his contemporaneous take on classic movies.

Douglas Sirk's melodramatic 1959 film titled 'Imitation of Life', serves as the foundation for Wong's *Life of Imitation*. In Wong's localised take on this classic melodrama of familial relationships, he restages the pivotal scene where the character Sarah Jane (a girl of mixed heritage who renounces her African ethnicity to pass off as a white person) sees her African mother for the last time. The tear-jerking moment in the film involves Sarah Jane initially pushing her mother away but eventually holding her in a tight embrace and crying as her emotions overwhelm her. In Wong's reworking of the 1959 American film, he replaces the character of Sarah Jane alternately with three actors – a Chinese, a Malay, an Indian – who each take turns playing the roles of Sarah Jane and her mother. This deliberate casting by the artist highlights the central issues of racial difference and inequality in the original Sirk film.

Ming Wong (b. 1971, Singapore) lives and works in Berlin and Singapore. He has had solo shows in Los Angeles, New York, Japan, Italy, Germany and Singapore. He won the Wollita Kulturpreis in Berlin, Germany in 2008, and received Special Mention for 'Expanding Worlds' at the 53rd Venice Biennale in 2009. He completed a year-long residency at Künstlerhaus Bethanien in Berlin from 2007-08 and was awarded the Fire Station Residency and Bursary by ACME Studios in 2005.

(TJ)

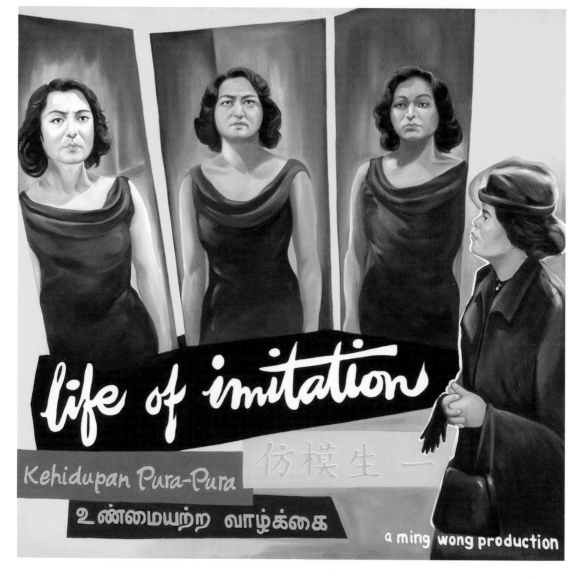

Ian Woo

Lot Sees Salt: First Heart
Lot Sees Salt: Head
Lot Sees Salt: Neck
Lot Sees Salt: Wing
2009
Graphite on paper
210 x 150 cm (each)

Singapore Art Museum
collection

This series is inspired by the Biblical narrative of the character Lot, who was prompted by the angel to flee with his family from the impending destruction of Sodom and Gomorrah. As they left, they were warned not to look back at the city for whoever did so would be transformed into a pillar of salt. Lot's wife, however, ignored the warning and was duly punished. This story inspired Ian Woo to produce these works on paper and the gestural expressions vividly evoke a sense of movement and the effect of transformation.

There are two distinct components evident in his approach: dominant broad strokes and bands of the graphite that suggest a sense of movement and fluidity. Woo skilfully conveys abstract ideas of movement and change, and for the artist, these two components are in a constant and fluid dialogue with each other. However, there is also a suggestion of tension, violence and precarious co-existence as these formal elements push and pull against each other, attempting to dominate and overpower the other.

Ian Woo (b. 1967, Singapore) was awarded a category winner of the Abstract Medium in the 18th UOB (United Overseas Bank) Painting of the Year competition in 1999. In 1999 and 2000, he was also selected for the Jurors' Choice for the Philip Morris ASEAN Art Awards. In 2006, he received his Doctor in Fine Art from the Royal Melbourne Institute of Technology. In 2011, he had a solo show at the Institute of Contemporary Art, LASALLE College of the Arts, Singapore.

(DC)

Facing page:
Clockwise from top left:

Lot Sees Salt: First Heart
Lot Sees Salt: Head
Lot Sees Salt: Neck
Lot Sees Salt: Wing

Joel Yuen

The Human Condition

2010
3 Italian marble sculptures and
3 corresponding photographs
50 x 50 x 15 cm (each)

Singapore Art Museum
collection

Joel Yuen's exposure to contemporary art practices while interning at the 2007 Venice Biennale and his personal interest in Renaissance art led him to combine both experiences into a work that sought to link conceptually two separate art media – photography and sculpture. *The Human Condition* is the artist's personal response to issues of health, spirituality and human suffering.

Focusing on the human attributes such as touching, seeing, learning, this work sets out to question what constitutes reality. Using the technique of *trompe l'œil*, Yuen placed photographic prints of a fake shadow under each sculpted hand to create the illusion of 'reality'. More than just an aesthetic exercise, there are also specific personal references behind the three sculptures. The sculpted hand holding the spine recalls the artist's childhood battle with sclerosis and the two hands holding the heart represents the struggles in life one has to go through. In the final piece, a left hand is shown in a hand-shake pose. Although the right hand is commonly used for the gesture of shaking hands, and the use of the left hand may be interpreted as being rude, more blood circulation flows through the body when the left hand is used to shake hands. For the artist, this gesture actually links one's own heart closer to another human being.

Joel Yuen (b. 1983, Singapore) graduated with a Bachelors of Fine Art from Nanyang Technological University's School of Art, Media and Design, majoring in photography and digital imaging. He was the recipient of the 27th United Overseas Bank Painting of the Year award in 2008 and won a merit prize in the Ngee Ann Distinguished Sculpture awards in 2010.

(TJ)

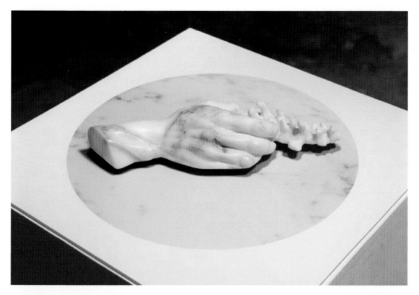

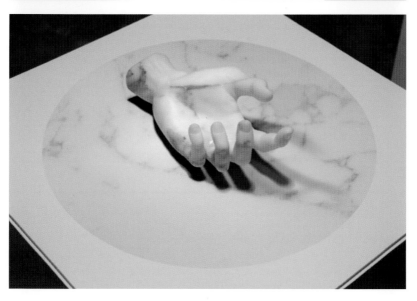

ZERO

Agent Provocateur

2010
Digital print on canvas
102 x 128 cm

Monogram

2010
Digital print on canvas
102 x 128 cm

CMYK Soft Sculptures

2010
Cotton cushion cover,
printed iron-on, set of 5
150 x 100 x 120 cm (each)

Singapore Art Museum
collection

Using an abstract humanoid character in his prints, ZERO's work playfully highlights the legal boundaries of vandalism in Singapore that also co-exist with the obvious fascination that mainstream media has with graffiti art.

The representation of a nude form in *Agent Provocateur*, which is also pixelated, suggests the fluctuating boundaries that are constantly provoked and explored by the artist and his medium. In Singapore, graffiti artists have to carefully negotiate the blurring lines of legality and legitimacy when making their art, and this constant negotiation is part of their mode of art production. At the same time, this 'illegal' production is today appropriated by commercial businesses and galleries, transforming an otherwise ephemeral, temporary art into a commodified art object fuelled by a consumerist culture.

Monogram comments on the heavy usage of icons and imagery incorporated into art today, merging the definition of the artist today and the notion of being a brand name, where the artist's production can become an overt commercial commodity. *Monogram* uses an abstract humanoid figure to playfully refer to one such commissioning by the Louis Vuitton brand, which had engaged artists and designers to come up with limited edition designs for its products.

The seemingly cute, abstract humanoid *CMYK Soft Sculptures* highlight the fascination of mainstream society with graffiti art (which in its original form in Singapore is still considered illegal), thus injecting an element of deviancy into these otherwise innocent plush toys.

ZERO (b. 1979, Singapore) graduated with a Bachelor of Arts (Hons) in Fine Arts from LASALLE College of the Arts in 2008, and was a recipient of the National Arts Council (NAC) Singapore Arts Bursary Award and the Dr. Winston Oh Travelogue Award in 2007.

(DC)

CMYK Soft Sculpture (Cyan)

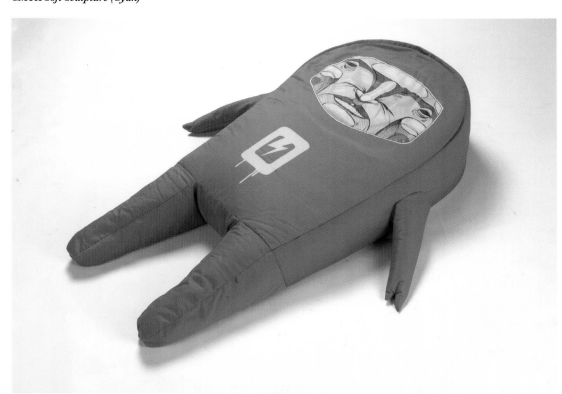

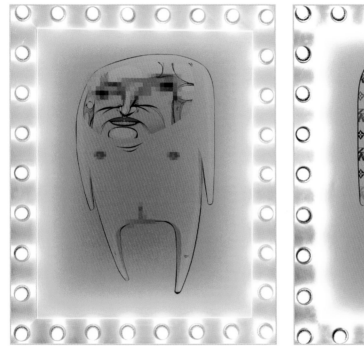

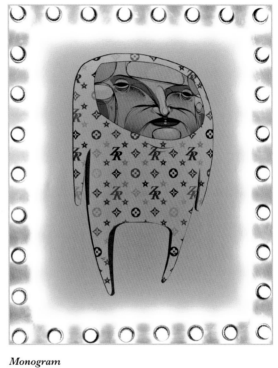

Agent Provocateur

Monogram

Robert Zhao Renhui

If A Tree Falls In The Forest

2009
Mixed media installation
Dimensions variable

Singapore Art Museum
collection

Art and science come together in this faux-scientific display of photographs of exotic endangered or extinct animals, animal specimens, ingenious animal traps and documents. This compelling installation is presented as the outcome of a research expedition and project undertaken by the Institute of Critical Zoologists – which, according to its mission statement, "aims to develop a critical approach to the zoological gaze, or how humans view animals" – as well as the work of zoologist and taxidermist Soon Bo.

Yet the work also questions our faith in empirical science for its title alludes to something else being at play. "If a tree falls in the forest and no one is around to hear it, does it make a sound?" is a philosophical thought experiment about the nature of reality. In actuality, the artist Robert Zhao has fabricated a complex work of fiction. By employing photography, text, sculpture and supposed animal specimens, he probes the certainty of a world 'constructed' by knowledge, and questions in a philosophical manner, the nature of perception (or the taking in of information) and that of judgement (or the organisation of information to coming to conclusions).

Robert Zhao Renhui (b. 1979, Singapore) has had an inexplicable fascination with animals since young. He was awarded a research grant by the Chelsea Arts Club in London, for his photographic research work in Spain in 2007. He has won awards, including the AOP Student Photographer Of The Year award (2007), Emerging Artist Award at the Singapore International Photography Festival (2008), United Overseas Bank Painting of the Year Award, Singapore (2009), and Sotiri International Prize for Emerging Photographers (2009).

(TJ)

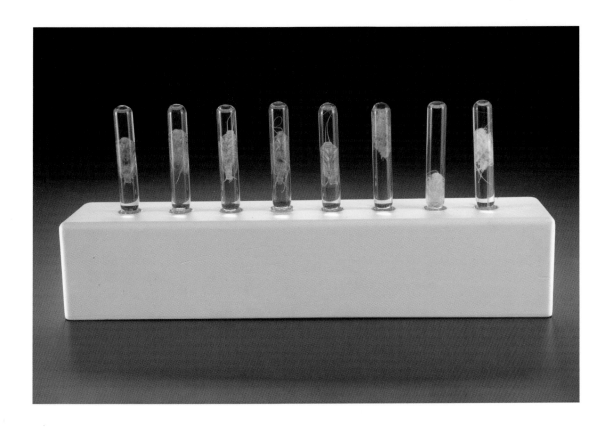

Robert Zhao Renhui

Pulau Pejantan Expedition

2007–2010
Archival piezographic prints,
set of 6 prints
84 x 120 cm (each)

Singapore Art Museum
collection

This suite of visually captivating photographs serves as documentation of the sightings and discoveries made by the Institute of Critical Zoologists (ICZ) during their 2009 expedition to Pulau Pejantan, a remote Indonesia island. Purportedly undiscovered until 2005, the little-known Pulau Pejantan has been a natural paradise, untouched by human contact, which accounts for its unusual and unique bio-diversity, evolutionary oddities and geographical features. That these animals and phenomena are found nowhere else in the world can, however, be explained by another reason: they, like the Institute that discovered them, are entirely fabricated fictions. In so doing, the artist constructs and deconstructs the constitution of 'truth' and questioning how knowledge is produced.

Robert Zhao Renhui (b. 1979, Singapore) has had an inexplicable fascination with animals since young. He was awarded a research grant by the Chelsea Arts Club in London, for his photographic research work in Spain in 2007. He has won awards, including the AOP Student Photographer Of The Year award (2007), Emerging Artist Award at the Singapore International Photography Festival (2008), United Overseas Bank Painting of the Year Award, Singapore (2009), and Sotiri International Prize for Emerging Photographers (2009).

(TJ)

Robert Zhao Renhui

The Blind series

2007-2010
Archival piezographic prints,
set of 10 prints
84 x 120 cm (each)

Singapore Art Museum
collection

Blinds, or nature hides, are used by zoologists to camouflage themselves during the process of observing animals. This suite of photographs demonstrate the effectiveness of 'The Blind', a product launched by the Institute of Critical Zoologists (ICZ) and billed as "the camouflage cloak for contemporary zoologists". This useful and practical device by the ICZ is aimed at meeting the needs of zoologists who have to undertake long hours of fieldwork, and ironically, its existence may be more 'real' than the entirely fictitious Institute.

'The Blind' is based on actual recent development of composite materials, which have the ability to curve electromagnetic light waves, potentially facilitating the invention of "invisibility cloaks". In the photographs, human subjects drape themselves with this futuristic invention, ostensibly for field research that borders on voyeurism, in the natural animal habitats of forests and grasslands. In the process, the artist also questions the concept of "truth" and "objectivity" through the stories he presents to the viewer via the manipulated imagery he has created using the medium of photography.

Robert Zhao Renhui (b. 1979, Singapore) has had an inexplicable fascination with animals since young. He was awarded a research grant by the Chelsea Arts Club in London, for his photographic research work in Spain in 2007. He has won awards, including the AOP Student Photographer Of The Year award (2007), Emerging Artist Award at the Singapore International Photography Festival (2008), United Overseas Bank Painting of the Year Award, Singapore (2009), and Sotiri International Prize for Emerging Photographers (2009).

(TJ)

Ryf Zaini

Disarming the Lion

2011
Metal, electronics, LCD screens
with CD-ROM video footage
250 x 250 x 200 cm

Singapore Art Museum
collection

Disarming the Lion depicts the courageous lion – as represented by its head with proud mane – transformed by artist Ryf Zaini, into a cold, robotic creature clad with a seemingly bleak metal exterior. This robotic representation – in its use of a metal armour to shield itself from the harsh external world – reflects mankind's reliance on technology to achieve the characteristics of a lion: strength, dominance and valour. However, the lion has been decapitated, thus suggesting that such attempts are ultimately futile.

Interactive media and installation artist, Ryf Zaini explores everyday societal issues such as history and technology, using materials and imageries that are at times evocatively curious and also engaging. Using everyday materials, his work speaks to audiences with a familiar yet disarming way.

Ryf Zaini (b. 1980, Singapore) graduated with a Bachelor of Arts (Hons, 1st class), Interactive Media Arts, LASALLE College of the Arts, in 2007. He has exhibited in various venues such as The Esplanade – Theatres on the Bay and the Malay Heritage Centre, in Singapore, and the National Art Gallery of Malaysia. In 2011, he participated in the Busan Biennale Sea Art Festival and the exhibition, 'Hari Raya Standees', at the Singapore Art Museum.

(DC)

SINGAPORE

Southeast Asia

CAMBODIA

Mak Remissa
Meas Sokhorn, Srey Bandol,
Keith Deverell & Sue McCauley
Sopheap Pich
Than Sok
Vandy Rattana

Mak Remissa

***When the Water Rises,
the Fish Eats the Ant;
When the Water Recedes,
the Ant Eats the Fish***

2005–2006
7 photo prints, edition 1/7
50 x 40 cm (each)

Singapore Art Museum
collection

This series is based on a common ancient Khmer proverb: "When the water rises, the fish eats the ant; when the water recedes, the ant eats the fish". It is a proverb that offers an insight into the natural behaviour of two living species when faced with completely changed environments. While fishes are adept at living in water and ants on land, one may dominate the other when the circumstances of nature change. Through this work, the artist expresses his hope for a utopian world where mankind can rise beyond power struggles and the inevitable dictates of a food chain, to live in harmony.

Mak Remissa (b. 1970, Cambodia) graduated in Fine Art and Photography from the Royal Fine Arts School in Phnom Penh and is part of the first generation, Post-90's group of photographers in Cambodia whose main focus lies in journalistic-style photography. Remissa's practice stands apart from that of his peers through the deliberate play on colour and composition. In 1997, Remissa was awarded first and third prize at the National Photo-Journalism Competition organised by the Foreign Correspondents' Club. The artist has exhibited widely abroad in countries such as Singapore, Canada, The Netherlands, France and Switzerland.

(NW)

Meas Sokhorn, Srey Bandol, Keith Deverell & Sue McCauley

The Hawker's Song

2010
Audio-video installation with 8 videos, debris, edition 1/5
Installation dimensions variable
Videos of varying durations

Singapore Art Museum collection

Meas Sokhorn, Srey Bandol & Keith Deverell

The Hawker's Song - Part 2

2010
Multimedia installation in 5 components:

Srey Bandol, **Development 1, 2 and 3**, 2010
Iron, iron netting, aluminium cans, photocopied Cambodian and Korean money, loud speakers, recordings of hawker calls, dimensions variable

Srey Bandol, **Memory**, 2010
Acrylic on canvas and speakers
300 x 100 cm

Keith Deverell, **Hawker's Portraits**, 2010, 4 black-and-white hand prints, printed on Gloss Fibre Base, 40 x 50.5 cm (each) Edition 1/2

Keith Deverell, **The Tapestry of Poverty** 2010
Collected money, staples
100 x 150 cm (approx.)

Meas Sokhorn, **Muted**, 2010
Concrete and polish, bike, broom, basket
Dimensions variable

Installation dimensions variable

Singapore Art Museum collection

A Cambodian-Australian collaboration, **The Hawker's Song** is a video installation that focuses on the dying trade of street hawkers in Cambodia. Referencing literally the songs hawkers sing to attract customers, the works centre on the fast-disappearing hawker trade. Set in the context of rapid modernisation, there is a sense of chaos and disarray that is both bewildering and disconcerting to the viewer. This is perhaps best exemplified by the complex layering of voice recordings of Melbourne-based Cambodians over the chaotic street sounds of modern-day Phnom Penh. While the voices of these overseas Cambodians resonate strongly with nostalgia, the bustle of present-day Phnom Penh drowns out their desire to re-connect with memories of the Cambodia they left behind.

Meas Sokhorn (b. 1977, Cambodia) has actively participated in exhibitions including 'Global Hybrid II' at Hancock University in Los Angeles, United States (2010), and the Asia Pacific Breweries Foundation Signature Art Prize at the Singapore Art Museum (2008).

Srey Bandol (b. 1973, Cambodia) participated in exhibitions such as 'IMPACT: An Art Exhibit About Landmines' in Cambodia and New York (2010) and 'Chambuk', Phnom Penh, Cambodia (2005).

Keith Deverell (b. 1976, United Kingdom) currently lives and works in Australia. He participated in the SONE Residency and Performance in Bundanon, Australia (2010), and 'Rear Window', a Melbourne Laneways Commission in Melbourne, Australia (2009).

Sue McCauley (b. 1955, Australia) participated in 're_VISION' (with video and interactive media artist, Olaf Meyer) at the Australian Centre for the Moving Image in Melbourne (2003), and in 'Antarctica: Secrets of the Frozen World', Museum of Victoria, in Melbourne, Australia (1992).

(NW)

The Hawker's Song (video stills)

Sopheap Pich

Cycle

2004–2008
Rattan and wire
420 x 25 x 90 cm

Singapore Art Museum
collection

According to the artist, Sopheap Pich, the image of the stomach embodies specific ideas popularly held by the Cambodian people. The states affecting the stomach such as hunger, sustenance and disease explore the social anxieties that plague the nation. In the depiction of two stomachs joined together, the connection between the two suggests kinship, collaboration and unity. As a positive spin on the dire social circumstance of Cambodia, Pich can be seen as making a commentary on the duality of society. In that, much can be rectified and reversed through collaboration, connection and positive reinforcement.

Sopheap Pich (b. 1969, Cambodia) was first trained in painting at the University of Massachusetts, United States. Feeling that his paintings did not connect with the Cambodian people, he began experimenting with commonplace materials familiar in Cambodia, developing the style of rattan and wire sculptures that now dominate his work. He has exhibited extensively, particularly in Cambodia and the United States. He also participated in the 4th Fukuoka Asian Art Triennale, Japan (2009) and the 6th Asia Pacific Triennial of Contemporary Art, Brisbane, Australia (2009).

(NW)

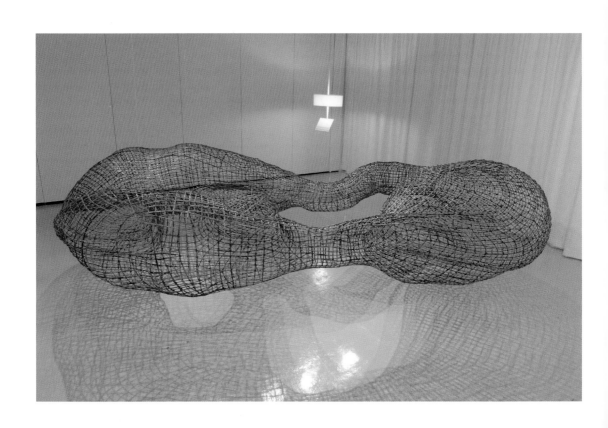

Than Sok

Negligence Leads to Loss; Attention Preserves

2009
Installation with 1 single-channel
DVD video, rattan mat, 7 pillows,
cement spirit house
Dimensions variable
Video duration 9:42 mins

Singapore Art Museum
collection

In Cambodia, the *Neak Ta* is a highly regarded figure of the spirit world and it is believed to hold supernatural influence and power in the Cambodian countryside. Found in the majority of rural Cambodian homes, shrines that resemble wooden huts, or *ktome*, are built as a means of communication, in order for prayers to be answered.

In this work, the artist juxtaposes two different kinds of *ktomes* – one that is elaborately ornate, and likely to belong to the wealthy, and the other, a humbly built structure constructed from incense sticks. In the video, the latter is set ablaze and the ravage of the fire brings to an end the life of the *ktome*. Juxtaposed against each other, the humbly built *ktome* now exists as a heap of ashes, while the other remains tall and magnificent albeit having witnessed the ruin of its kind.

The artist states, "Our religion says things happen purposefully. I see the outside but I do not know the inside. We see people praying, but we do not see their other thoughts and actions. The same person that prays can be the person who burns a house down."

Than Sok (b. 1984, Cambodia) graduated from Reyum Art School in Phnom Penh and has participated in numerous exhibitions such as 'Tragedy' at the Bophana Audiovisual Resource Centre in Phnom Penh, Cambodia (2010), and 'On Site Lab Series-1 + hand' at the Tokyo Wonder Site Aoyama in Tokyo, Japan (2006).

(NW)

CAMBODIA

Vandy Rattana

Fire of the Year

2008
Digital C-prints, set of 9 prints,
edition of 4
74 x 117 cm (each)

Singapore Art Museum
collection

Fire of the Year documents the vicious onslaught of fire in a district on the outskirts of Phnom Penh called Dteuk Tlah, or "clear water", a site where 300 families lived in homes built on stilts by the river. This series of works stands as a grim reminder of the underdeveloped infrastructure in Cambodia and the urban challenges facing its citizens. Amidst the chaos and disarray, a young boy is seen rummaging through the burnt ruins, in search for recyclable materials. An intentional inclusion in this series of works, the young boy embodies the strength and tenacity of the Cambodian spirit, in its ability to endure and bounce back from adversities.

Vandy Rattana (b. 1980, Cambodia) is a self-taught photographer. Rattana began to record the daily activities of his family in 2005 and these works eventually became the subject of his first acclaimed exhibition in Phnom Penh. Notable exhibitions include 'The Bomb Ponds' at the Hessel Museum in New York, United States (2010), 'Fire of the Year' at the 6th Asia Pacific Triennial of Contemporary Art, Brisbane, Australia (2009), and 'TADAIMA: Looking for Sweet Home', Kyushu University, Japan (2009).

(NW)

Vandy Rattana

Bomb Ponds

2009
9 photographic prints and 1
single-channel video, edition 1/5
Photographs: 90 x 105 cm (each)
Video duration: 21:00 mins

Singapore Art Museum
collection

The disturbing blanket of silence on a dark chapter of Cambodia's history drove Vandy Rattana to make *Bomb Ponds*. Initial appearances suggest the photographs capture everyday scenes in the Cambodian countryside, but in actuality, the tranquillity or even non-descript character of the ponds stand in stark contrast to how they came into being.

Known as 'bomb ponds' in the Khmer language, the bodies of water are craters created when the Americans dropped close to three million tons of bombs across the politically-neutral Cambodia during the Vietnam War. Despite the damage, injury and deaths inflicted onto Cambodian civilians who had no knowledge of the war being waged by governments, the bombings were not formally acknowledged for years, and Rattana interviewed several farmers and villagers in the accompanying video, and their anger, sorrow and bewilderment are all too evident.

Like a dark secret kept hidden in plain view, the ponds remain officially invisible, yet are searing, visible reminders to the civilians who lost family and loved ones. Straddling between journalism, historical documentation and art, Rattana's compelling work thus gives voice to a people whose ordeal has been intensified by a second wound of silence.

Vandy Rattana (b. 1980, Cambodia) is a self-taught photographer. Rattana began to record the daily activities of his family in 2005 and these works eventually became the subject of his first acclaimed exhibition in Phnom Penh. Notable exhibitions include 'The Bomb Ponds' at the Hessel Museum in New York, United States (2010), 'Fire of the Year' at the 6th Asia Pacific Triennial of Contemporary Art, Brisbane, Australia (2009), and 'TADAIMA: Looking for Sweet Home', Kyushu University, Japan (2009).

(JT)

INDONESIA

Nindityo Adipurnomo
Apotik Komik
Arahmaiani
Terra Bajraghosa
Wimo Ambala Bayang
Dadang Christanto
FX Harsono
Indieguerillas
Mella Jaarsma
Jompet Kuswidananto
Wiyoga Muhardanto
Nasirun
Eko Nugroho
Erik Muhammad Pauhrizi

Angki Purbandono
Handiwirman Saputra
Yudi Sulistyo
Melati Suryodarmo
Agus Suwage
Agus Suwage & Davy Linggar
Titarubi
Tromarama
Entang Wiharso
I Wayan Sujana (Suklu)
Syagini Ratna Wulan
Tintin Wulia
Albert Yonathan
Muhammad 'Ucup' Yusuf

Nindityo Adipurnomo

Portrait Of Javanese Men (Hong Kong Series)

2005
Digital print on photo paper
Set of 3, edition 3/3
62.8 x 49.8 cm (each)

Portrait Of Javanese Men (Amsterdam Series)

2006
Digital print on etching paper,
set of 3, edition 3/3
68.5 x 52.8 cm (each)

Acquired with support from
KMP Private Ltd.

Singapore Art Museum
collection

Nindityo Adipurnomo's art addresses gender issues as well as questions about the relevance and validity of long-entrenched cultural practices in the contemporary world. A recurrent motif in his art is the konde, a traditional hairpiece worn by Javanese women for ceremonies and special occasions. It is simultaneously part of a woman's allure and femininity as it is a symbol of rigid social hierarchy and gender politics.

In this series of works, Adipurnomo subverts conventions of portraiture by presenting us with portraits of men's faces, all masked by kondes of various shapes and sizes. Normally the male is construed as the 'active' and 'dominant' viewer, while the female is the 'passive' subject of the male gaze. Ironically, the Javanese men in Adipurnomo's portraits have had their vision obscured and obstructed by the very symbol of traditional Javanese femininity. In turn, these men become subjects of the viewer's gaze, which is invited to linger over the sensual coils of the hairpieces which cover the men's faces. This ironic and playful swapping of constructed gender roles and attributes is a reminder of pre-modern notions of gender identity, which were far more fluid and perhaps liberating and empowering than those which have been narrowly defined in recent times.

Nindityo Adipurnomo (b. 1961, Semarang, Indonesia) is a co-founder of Cemeti Art House, one of Indonesia's foremost contemporary art institutions. He is the recipient of the John D. Rockefeller Award (2006), and his work has been presented widely in exhibitions around the world, including the Asia Pacific Triennial of Contemporary Art, Brisbane, Australia (1996), the Havana Biennial (1997), and in 'Contemporary Art in Asia: Traditions/ Tensions', Asia Society, New York (1996).

(TSL)

Facing page:

Top:
**Portrait Of Javanese
Men (Hong Kong Series)**

Bottom:
**Portrait Of Javanese
Men (Amsterdam Series)**

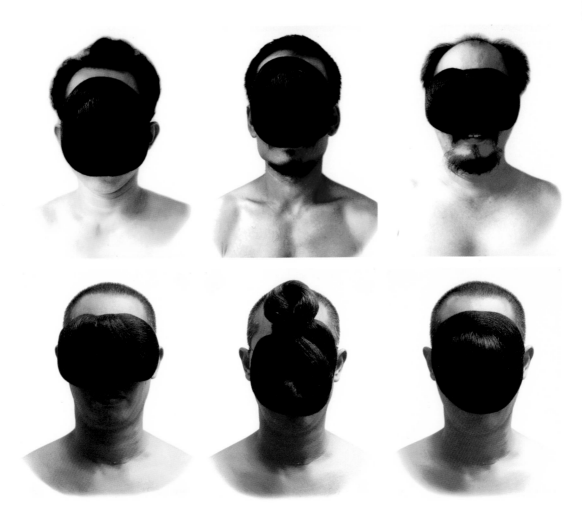

Apotik Komik

Under Estimate

1999
Ink drums, cardboard and paint
500 x 50 x 300 cm

Singapore Art Museum
collection

Under Estimate primarily pokes fun and critiques the sudden 'boom' of Indonesian contemporary art in the mid-1990s. Relationships between artists, curators, collectors and local community/ies are highlighted for contention. Almost echoing traditional dioramas, one segment of the installation depicts a young person flying through stormy clouds on an aeroplane with the words 'international route' inscribed. In the background, the text "young and talented artist" is boldly emblazoned. In their typical bright and comic-like illustrations, with sardonic humour, the works refer to local situations. The installation is primarily made from cut-up ink drums and cardboards, wrapped on the outside with traditional Javanese *batik*. This use of cheap and recycled materials is a common practice in Indonesia, and has been used by other more senior Indonesian contemporary artists such as Heri Dono and Eddie Hara.

Apotik Komik (1997–2005) was an artists collective founded by Samuel Indratma, Bambang 'Toko' Witjaksono, Popok Tri Wahyudi and Ari Diyanto. *Under Estimate* is one of the rare collaborative installation pieces by the now defunct Indonesian artists collective Apotik Komik. The work brings together artists Ari Diyanto, Samuel Indratma, Popok Tri Wahyudi and Bambang Toko Wijaksono, artists recognised today as markers of Indonesian urban art along with Eko Nugroho, Daging Tumbuh, S. Teddy and Taring Padi.

(KH)

(Detail)

Arahmaiani

Crossing Point

2011
Video and fabric
Dimensions variable:
200 x 200 cm each
(flags; 12 pieces)
200 x 300 cm each
(wall hangings; 2 pieces)
Video duration 5:38 mins

Singapore Art Museum
collection

Crossing Point speaks and generates discussions at various levels. It touches on current discussions on religion, semantics and semiotics, tolerance and peace, and ethnology. The artwork demonstrates the artist's awareness, adopted position and opinion, and actions in response to a global phenomenon of fundamentalist beliefs.

In this work, Arahmaiani employs Jawi, a form of writing using the Arabic script that originated in Southeast Asia. It can be written to phonetically reproduce the sounds of any other language. The use of Jawi script is still prevalent today in more traditional parts of Malaysia and Indonesia, particularly for the teaching of Islam. However, Arahmaiani feels that Arabic letters and words have been demonised to suggest terror and inflict fright merely due to its design and correlation with Islam and the Muslim world. Being a Muslim and one from the world's most populous Muslim nation, the artist takes the opportunity to employ Jawi and uses it to 'flag' and 'activate' words or phrases that are relevant to various societies in various parts of the world where she presents her art. This action of mass flag waving in a procession is typical of protests and acts of civil activism but in this case, it is a quiet demonstration of peace albeit odd to passersby. The words such as *akal* (mind), *bakti* (dedication) and *jay* (heart) were used relate to qualities and content found within a museum, they signal the relational quality and site-specificity of the flags and banners which were made especially for a Singapore Art Museum commission.

One of Indonesia's most widely travelled artists, Arahmaiani (b. 1961, Bandung, Indonesia) has participated in the Venice Biennale (2003), Sao Paolo Biennale (2002) and Gwangju Biennale (2002) and the Asia Pacific Triennial of Contemporary Art, Brisbane, Australia (1996), as well as major exhibitions such as 'Cities On the Move', Vienna (1990 onwards), 'Contemporary Art in Asia: Traditions/Tensions', Asia Society, New York (1996) and 'Global Feminism', New York, (2007).

(KH)

Arahmaiani

I Don't Want To Be Part Of Your Legend

2004
Video
Duration 11:00 mins

Singapore Art Museum
collection

Arahmaiani is one of a few women artists from Indonesia whose works actively explore gender issues, often with a strong feminist slant. In this video, Arahmaiani reworks an episode from the epic *Ramayana*. The female protagonist, Sita, is abducted by the evil King Rahwana and subsequently rescued. However court officials doubt her chastity and before her husband Rama can accept her back, Sita has to undergo a test of fire before she can be reunited with him. Arahmaiani's video draws on the aesthetics of traditional *wayang* theatre, as well as the artist's own poetry and haunting vocals, to dramatise Sita's expression of anguish at this test. In this contemporary re-telling, Sita laments: "Is it possible I could make a bargain with fate and not become part of your legend?" The 'legend' refers not just to the Ramayana epic; more pointedly, it questions male attitudes towards women enshrined in traditional stories such as this one.

Arahmaiani (b. 1961, Bandung, Indonesia) is a key figure in the contemporary Indonesian art scene, best known for her socially-orientated performance and installation art. The daughter of an Islamic scholar father and a Javanese mother who practiced Hindu/animist traditions, Arahmaiani has had to navigate between cultures and religions from an early age. As part of her praxis, the artist had chosen to adopt a nomadic lifestyle, encountering and exploring the difficulties of communication across – and even within – cultures. Much of her art reflects these resulting tensions, for instance, between Islamic teachings and Western education. Her work is often provocative and critical of religious as well as political issues, and Arahmaiani has experienced run-ins with fundamentalists as well as authoritarian regimes.

One of Indonesia's most widely travelled artists, Arahmaiani (b. 1961, Bandung, Indonesia) has participated in the Venice Biennale (2003), Sao Paolo Biennale (2002) and Gwangju Biennale (2002) and the Asia Pacific Triennial of Contemporary Art, Brisbane, Australia (1996), as well as major exhibitions such as 'Cities On the Move', Vienna (1990 onwards), 'Contemporary Art in Asia: Traditions/Tensions', Asia Society, New York (1996) and 'Global Feminism', New York, (2007).

(TSL)

Terra Bajraghosa

Liberty Lead the Pixel
2009
Acrylic on canvas
245 x 194 cm

Boom Box Liberty
2009
Acrylic sculpture
170 x 100 x 60 cm

Narcissus Pixelus
2009
Computer game, mixed media
casing, printer, computer
210 x 70 x 70 cm

Acquired with support from
KMP Private Ltd.

Singapore Art Museum
collection

In this suite of works, Terra Bajraghosa revisits and visually revises the iconic 19th century painting, *Liberty Leading the People*, by French artist Eugene Delacroix, a painting which has come to stand for the heroism and ideals associated with the French Revolution. In Delacroix's original painting, Liberty is portrayed as a female figure garbed in yellow, leading her people in the fight for liberty, equality and fraternity - the values represented in France's tri-coloured flag. Terra Bajraghosa updates the spirit of the work with his own playful interpretation set in the present day, where Liberty, presented as a pixelated image, holds a modern-day boom box instead of a rifle as depicted in the original painting. With this re-interpretation, Terra Bajraghosa suggests that the revolution in the streets is still relevant today, only that it is now driven by youth and popular culture fighting for its freedom and independence, as suggested by the symbolism of Liberty's boom box and the pixelated graphics drawn from contemporary digital culture.

Terra Bajraghosa (b. 1981, Yogyakarta, Indonesia) studied Visual Communication Design at the Indonesian Institute of the Arts (ISI), Yogyarkarta, Indonesia. He has held solo exhibitions and has taken part in group exhibitions in countries such as Indonesia, Korea and the United Kingdom. Widely influenced by pop culture, Terra Bajraghosa uses the nostalgic aesthetics of pixel animation and mass communication to comment on the current political and social climate in Indonesia.

(TSL)

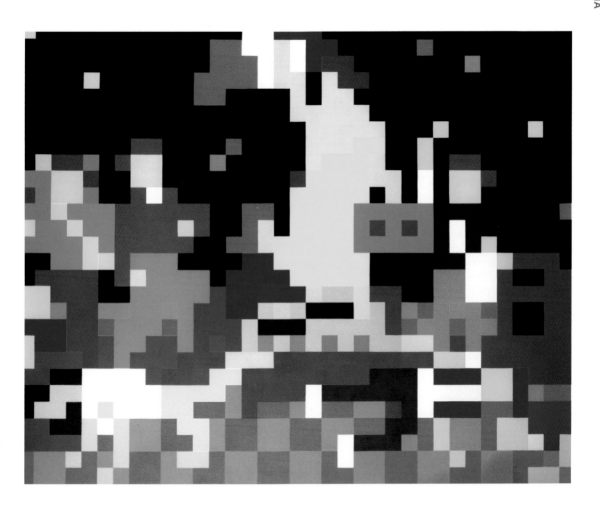

Top:
Liberty Lead the Pixel

Facing page:
Left: *Boom Box Liberty*
Right: *Narcissus Pixelus*

Wimo Ambala Bayang

Angkatan Kedua Belas, Angkatan Kedua Belas (The Twelfth Troop)

2008
Digital C-print on Fuji
professional paper mounted on
aluminium bond
102 x 102 x 3.5 cm

Angkatan Kesembilan (The Ninth Troop)

2008
Digital C-print on Fuji
professional paper mounted on
aluminium bond
102 x 102 x 3.5 cm

Acquired with support from
KMP Private Ltd.

Singapore Art Museum
collection

These works are from a series entitled 'Belanda Sudah Dekat (The Dutch Are Near)', the result of the artist's participation in the Cemeti Art House's residency programme 'Landing Soon'. The interaction with Dutch artists during this residency inspired Wimo Bayang to create a comic visual response towards an old joke reflecting the laid-back culture of Indonesian society, exemplified in a popular idiom: "Be calm, the Dutch are still far away!"

In this quirky and light-hearted series of photographs, Wimo Bayang invited selected groups of people to pose with plastic toy weaponry, alluding to the communist party and military troops from Indonesia's not-too-distant and turbulent post-Independence past. These photographs are humorous snapshots of distinctive micro-communities in Indonesia, but at the same time manifest the artist's unease with what he perceives as the overly complacent and laid-back attitudes found in parts of Indonesian society.

Wimo Ambala Bayang (b. 1976, Indonesia), is a member of Ruang Mes 56, an artists collective in Indonesia dedicated to the development of discourse in contemporary photography. He studied in the Modern School of Design and the Photography Department of the Indonesian Institute of the Arts in Yogyakarta (ISI), Indonesia. Wimo Bayang's photographic series and videos present a playful and unique perspective on cultures and cultural practices. He has exhibited both at home as well as abroad, including presentations at the Jakarta Biennale (2009) and the Yogyakarta Biennale (2011).

(TSL)

Facing page:
Top:
Angkatan Kedua Belas, Angkatan Kedua Belas (The Twelfth Troop)
Bottom:
Angkatan Kesembilan (The Ninth Troop)

Dadang Christanto

Kekerasan I (Violence I)

1995
Terracotta
300 x 300 x 300 cm

Singapore Art Museum
collection

Known as an artist-activist, Dadang Christanto occupies an important place in Indonesian contemporary art history. His works of the 1990s, of which this is a prime example, are powerful and emotive socio-political commentaries on the injustice and bloodletting in his country, in the name of religious, political and ethnic differences. As a child, the artist lost his father in the anti-communist purges that ensued when Suharto assumed power; in his own lifetime, Dadang has witnessed countless instances of social and political oppression.

Kekerasan I was originally exhibited in the artist's 'Perkara Tanah' exhibition in Indonesia, and later shown at the groundbreaking 'Traditions/Tensions' exhibition of contemporary Asian art at the Asia Society, New York. In keeping with the exhibition's title ('Perkara Tanah', or 'The Issue Of Land'), *Kekerasan I* can be read as a sympathetic and moving portrayal of the plight of Indonesia's farmers.

Hundreds of human heads are stacked in a pyramidal shape, recalling the highly stratified power structure of Indonesian society. The heads are sculpted from fired clay – a cheap material readily associated with the land and the humble workers who toil the earth. While they appear similar and uniform from afar, the terracotta heads on closer inspection reveal themselves to be unique individuals, hence endowing each figure with a sense of humanity. Their gaping mouths also suggest the silent screams of victims of violence, and the tower of human heads brings to mind a pile of skulls in the killing-fields, ironically stacked in the shape of a stupa.

Dadang Christanto (b. 1957, Indonesia) is a major figure in Indonesian contemporary art history, having gained international recognition in the 1990s for his works which commented on the socio-political upheavals in his native Indonesia. He has exhibited widely in major exhibitions and biennales, such as the Asia Pacific Triennial of Contemporary Art, Brisbane, Australia, the Sao Paolo Biennale, the Venice Biennale and 'Contemporary Art In Asia: Traditions/Tensions', Asia Society, New York.

(TSL)

(Detail)

FX Harsono

Burned Victims

1998
Installation and
performance video
Dimensions variable
Video duration 8:41 mins

Singapore Art Museum
collection

This work is a powerful installation and performance from a critical turning point in both FX Harsono's art practice as well as the history of Indonesia. Like much of Harsono's earlier works, it makes a strong statement about the horrors of civil violence and the fate of the victimised masses. ***Burned Victims*** was created in response to a tragic episode of the May 1998 riots in Jakarta, during which the rioting mob stormed a shopping mall, sealed off its exits and set it on fire. The motives for such callous brutality remain unknown, but the hundreds of people who were trapped and burnt to death in the shopping mall were all victims of a power struggle that culminated in the downfall of former Indonesian President Suharto.

The performance component of ***Burned Victims*** involved the burning of wooden torsos, during which a placard was displayed to the audience, bearing the word *kerusuhan*, or 'riot'. In the work's installation component, the blackened remains of the wooden torsos are suspended in oblong metal frames, arrangements of regular lines which highlight the agonised contortions of the torsos. Placed before each torso is a pair of burnt footwear, which Harsono retrieved from the site of the 1998 incident. In an almost photo-journalistic fashion, the artist presents to his audience the scorching image of the victims' bodies, to elicit horror and condemnation of civil violence.

FX Harsono (b. 1949, Indonesia) is one of the founding members of the Gerakan Seni Rupa Baru (Indonesian New Art Movement) that initiated the beginnings of contemporary art in Indonesia, and he remains active in the art scene. Harsono's works are remarkable in that they span four tumultuous decades in Indonesian art and history, and have borne witness to a multitude of changes and upheavals in Indonesian politics, society, and culture. Throughout this time, Harsono has continued to question his role as an artist and his position in society, constantly pushing his art and practice to reflect and engage with new social and cultural contexts. His work has been presented widely in Indonesia, the Asia-Pacific region and Europe, at exhibitions including the Asia-Pacific Triennial of Contemporary Art, Brisbane, Australia, and 'Contemporary Art in Asia: Traditions/Tensions', Asia Society, New York.

(TSL)

(Detail)

FX Harsono

Power And The Oppressed

1992
Installation with chair, barbed
wire, lamp, cloth, soil, branches
Dimensions variable

Singapore Art Museum
collection

This work is exemplary of FX Harsono's earlier installations, which offer an insight into the political and social conditions of Indonesia in the 1990s and an artist's response to these issues. The chair – whether in the material form of a throne or the linguistic form, in the term 'chairman' – is a symbol of power and authority. In *Power And The Oppressed*, a lone chair symbolises authoritarian power, its lofty isolation highlighted by a coil of barbed wire. The *keris* (dagger) pinned on the wall behind the chair alludes to the privileging of Javanese culture as Indonesia's national culture while suppressing other cultures during Suharto's authoritarian regime. Symbolic of blood, red-stained pieces of cloth are placed on piles of blackened earth arranged systematically in a grid pattern, as if supplicants to the chair's occupant. The grid-like order brings to mind the central government's obsession with order, in its bureaucratisation of all political and societal organisations. The blood also reminds us of the violent repression of political opponents to the authoritarian regime, particularly the anti-communist purge in 1966 that resulted in the deaths of an estimated half a million Indonesians.

FX Harsono (b. 1949, Indonesia) is one of the founding members of the Gerakan Seni Rupa Baru (Indonesian New Art Movement) that initiated the beginnings of contemporary art in Indonesia, and he remains active in the art scene. Harsono's works are remarkable in that they span four tumultuous decades in Indonesian art and history, and have borne witness to a multitude of changes and upheavals in Indonesian politics, society, and culture. Throughout this time, Harsono has continued to question his role as an artist and his position in society, constantly pushing his art and practice to reflect and engage with new social and cultural contexts. His work has been presented widely in Indonesia, the Asia-Pacific region and Europe, at exhibitions including the Asia-Pacific Triennial of Contemporary Art, Brisbane, Australia, and 'Contemporary Art in Asia: Traditions/Tensions', Asia Society, New York.

(TSL)

FX Harsono

Rewriting The Erased

2009
Installation and 3-channel video
Edition 1/3
Dimensions variable, video
duration 17:18 mins

Gift of the Artist

Singapore Art Museum
collection

In this poignant and meditative performance, FX Harsono seeks to remember - reclaim - that which has been lost or erased. Of Chinese descent in Indonesia, Harsono, like many others, was cut off from his Chinese 'roots' and culture through a series of government policies aimed at fully assimilating Chinese immigrants into Indonesian society. These measures, implemented during Suharto's New Order regime, included requiring all Chinese to change their names to Indonesian-sounding ones, as well as the closure of Chinese schools, press and organisations. The end of Suharto's New Order in 1998 witnessed a lifting of these restrictions, and the Chinese were once again able to use their original names.

During this time, Harsono began to question the seemingly conflicting facets of his identity: Indonesian, Chinese and Catholic. For most of his life, he had to practise a 'politics of denial' in order to feel that he belonged somewhere, and this meant the suppression of his 'Chinese' identity. Now that he is free to reconnect with this forgotten, or repressed, aspect of himself, he seems to question through this work, whether that past still holds any significance for him, or is it the case that, when revisited, simply a series of empty and meaningless gestures, taking shape as ideographs from a language and culture that Harsono can only half-understand? The gestures of the artist are filled with both pathos and power, as he attempts to reclaim a past that is at once intensely personal as it is politically inflected.

FX Harsono (b. 1949, Indonesia) is one of the founding members of the Gerakan Seni Rupa Baru (Indonesian New Art Movement) that initiated the beginnings of contemporary art in Indonesia, and he remains active in the art scene. Harsono's works are remarkable in that they span four tumultuous decades in Indonesian art and history, and have borne witness to a multitude of changes and upheavals in Indonesian politics, society, and culture. Throughout this time, Harsono has continued to question his role as an artist and his position in society, constantly pushing his art and practice to reflect and engage with new social and cultural contexts. His work has been presented widely in Indonesia, the Asia-Pacific region and Europe, at exhibitions including the Asia-Pacific Triennial of Contemporary Art, Brisbane, Australia, and 'Contemporary Art in Asia: Traditions/Tensions', Asia Society, New York.

(TSL)

FX Harsono

Preserving Life, Terminating Life #1

2009
Acrylic and oil on canvas, thread,
200 x 350 cm (diptych)

Preserving Life, Terminating Life #2

2009
Acrylic and oil on canvas, thread
200 x 350 cm (diptych)

Singapore Art Museum
collection

The images in these two works, are drawn from the same source – old albums of black and white photographs that the artist discovered in his family home, and which subsequently inspired his most recent body of work, which investigates personal – as well as political – history.

These two paintings juxtapose images of life and death: images of Harsono's family members are placed side by side with images documenting the exhumation of the mass graves of Chinese murdered in the turbulent years after the Second World War. This contrast poignantly highlights the preciousness and precariousness of life – the lives of those members of the Chinese community and Harsono's family who were lucky to escape the murders, and the lives of generations to come, as intimated by the marriage portrait of the couple in the first painting, and the family portrait in the second painting.

Binding these two disparate halves – family life and cause for celebration on the one hand, murder and death on the other – is a string of words echoing the titles of the works, stitched into the canvases with red thread. For the Chinese, red thread is associated with occasions both auspicious and inauspicious. At weddings and other celebrations, red clothing is worn as a celebratory gesture; at funerals, pieces of red thread are given to guests to bring home when they leave the place of mourning, as a symbol of blessing to ward against unhappy spirits. It is therefore apt that Harsono has chosen to bind the two halves of his canvases with a line of words stitched with red thread – the visual motif of the red line simultaneously suggesting lineage and blood ties, as well as the continuous line of history, all too often stained by bloodshed and violence.

FX Harsono (b. 1949, Indonesia) is one of the founding members of the Gerakan Seni Rupa Baru (Indonesian New Art Movement) that initiated the beginnings of contemporary art in Indonesia, and he remains active in the art scene. Harsono's works are remarkable in that they span four tumultuous decades in Indonesian art and history, and have borne witness to a multitude of changes and upheavals in Indonesian politics, society, and culture. Throughout this time, Harsono has continued to question his role as an artist and his position in society, constantly pushing his art and practice to reflect and engage with new social and cultural contexts. His work has been presented widely in Indonesia, the Asia-Pacific region and Europe, at exhibitions including the Asia-Pacific Triennial of Contemporary Art, Brisbane, Australia, and 'Contemporary Art in Asia: Traditions/Tensions', Asia Society, New York.

(TSL)

Facing page:

Top:
Preserving Life, Terminating Life #1
Bottom:
Preserving Life, Terminating Life #2

perkawinanmeneruskankehidupankematianmenghentikansyapk...santapikematiantakseorangpunmamendiwa.blitar1948

perkawinandibinamembuahkankehidupandanterus...manusi-taksebarusnyamenghentikankehidupan...diriatan...ainblitar1951

POH GOENOENG 21-11-51
6 KORBAN 91 HINGGA 6

FX Harsono

Titik Nyeri (Point Of Pain)

2007
Digital image on lightbox
150 x 150 x 20 cm

Singapore Art Museum
collection

A comparison of *Titik Nyeri* with Harsono's earlier works that dealt with violence and victimisation, makes evident the shift in subject matter and strategies of representation in the artist's practice over the decades. The theme of pain or suffering is revisited in this work, as implied by the butterflies pinned onto the artist's visage. However, the pain here is distinctly different from the kind of pain and violence conveyed in earlier works such as *Burned Victims*. Instead of outright brutality and suffering, the sense of pain and violence in *Titik Nyeri* seems much more aestheticised. The motif of the butterfly immediately evokes associations with beauty and delicacy. The needles too, are much more ambiguous implements or objects of pain and violence. More commonly associated with women's work, craft and domesticity, the pain from the prick of a needle is sharp but fleeting: a momentary 'point of pain' that is inconsequential compared to burning or hacking.

The artist has often remarked that 'violence' in contemporary Indonesia need not take the form of outright brutality; instead, it can manifest itself in subtle and insidious forms such as discrimination. These seemingly minor incidents serve as 'points of pain' – inconsequential on the surface, but when accumulated, slowly wear down their victims.

Another theme explored in Harsono's recent works, as well as in *Titik Nyeri*, is that of self-erasure, or the absence of the self / physical body. The obscuring of the face in this self-portrait suggests a desire to confound expectations of portraiture and its aims, by representing a subject that is difficult to 'pin down', hence conveying that identities are more fluid and shifting than assumed. The second panel of this work makes evident the disappearance of the artist (or the body) from the frame, perhaps – as suggested by the narrative of the two panels – a result of being unable to bear the multiple points of pain. This is a theme explored by Harsono with increasing urgency, in the wake of the post-1998 political and cultural vacuum which saw artists delve into their personal histories in a search for new meaning and subject matter for their art.

FX Harsono (b. 1949, Indonesia) is one of the founding members of the Gerakan Seni Rupa Baru (Indonesian New Art Movement) that initiated the beginnings of contemporary art in Indonesia, and he remains active in the art scene. Harsono's works are remarkable in that they span four tumultuous decades in Indonesian art and history, and have borne witness to a multitude of changes and upheavals in Indonesian politics, society, and culture. Throughout this time, Harsono has continued to question his role as an artist and his position in society, constantly pushing his art and practice to reflect and engage with new social and cultural contexts. His work has been presented widely in Indonesia, the Asia-Pacific region and Europe, at exhibitions including the Asia-Pacific Triennial of Contemporary Art, Brisbane, Australia, and 'Contemporary Art in Asia: Traditions/Tensions', Asia Society, New York.

(TSL)

Indieguerillas

Portable Art is Good For You VI: The Devotee

2010
Digital print on acrylic, vintage suitcase, metal and wood
135.5 x 57 x 32 cm

Singapore Art Museum
collection

This work is from the artists' 'Portable Art' series, which features dioramas in vintage found suitcases. There are only eight such works in this series. In **Portable Art Is Good For You VI**, the artists comment on the burgeoning role of the media through their signature graphic style and medley of characters which borrow freely from pop culture as well as traditional Indonesian symbols and motifs. The form of this artwork is in itself an interesting commentary on the 'globalisation' of art in the face of contemporary market forces and the mushrooming of major art events such as biennales in recent decades, along with its impact on the role and position of the itinerant (contemporary) artist. On another level, the suitcase and its tableau can also be read as a contemporary take on traditional *wayang* (shadow) theatre; the suitcase lights up – making reference to the play of light and shadow in *wayang* theatre – and its cast of characters impart a narrative that is at once entertaining as well as cautionary.

Indieguerillas is a husband and wife duo comprising Miko 'Otom' Bawono (b. 1975, Indonesia) and Santi Ariestyowanti (b. 1977, Indonesia). Both graduated from the Institut Seni Indonesia (ISI, Indonesian Institute of the Arts) in Yogyakarta, majoring in Interior Design and Visual Communication Design respectively. Both artists started off as designers by trade; as such, their works are infused with a graphic, pop sensibility. Their work has been exhibited in Indonesia as well as internationally, including at the exhibition 'Future Pass: From Asia To The World', a parallel event of the Venice Biennale 2011.

Their art is a savvy commentary on humanity's love affair with consumption and capitalism. They draw on the urban aesthetics found in fashion, music and art as well as Javanese motifs, drawing attention to the fact that popular culture is inextricably linked with materialism and the role that the media plays in amplifying our greed and desire for superficial gain, often at the expense of traditional values of community and family.

(TSL)

(Detail)

Wiyoga Muhardanto

Conversation Piece

2010
Installation with sculptures
Dimensions variable

Singapore Art Museum
collection

Conversation Piece comprises a set of sculptures of human legs, installed behind a wall so that only the legs are visible to the viewer, giving the impression that a group of people are having a conversation behind the wall. The wall is meant to be installed at the front of an exhibition space, and covered with the wall text for that respective art exhibition. From the clothing and footwear worn by each pair of legs, one can hazard a guess as to the social status and role(s) of the personages that the legs belong to: the collector, the gallerist, the curator, the *ibu-ibu* (society ladies or wives of collectors) and perhaps even the artist as well. These are personalities often encountered at Indonesian art openings who broker the success of the exhibition and/or the artist whose works are on show. As such, ***Conversation Piece*** is a witty and sharply observant take on the politics and behind-the-scenes negotiations that characterize the highly competitive Indonesian art scene, suggesting that success in this sphere is not as simple or straightforward as merely producing good art, but rather, subject to complex negotiations and relationships which are often concealed from the public eye.

Wiyoga Muhardanto (b. 1984, Jakarta) studied Fine Arts at the Bandung Institute of Technology (Indonesia), majoring in Sculpture. He works exclusively with sculpture, often choosing to replicate objects on a life-sized scale. His realistic sculptures of commodities and objects of desire are playful and acerbic commentaries on contemporary culture. His work has been presented extensively both at home and abroad, including exhibitions at the National Gallery of Indonesia, Jakarta (2007 and 2008), in the Jakarta Biennale (2009), at the Centraal Museum of Utrecht (2009), and at the Saatchi Gallery, United Kingdom (2011).

(TSL)

Nasirun

**Bajaj Pasti Berlalu
(The Bajaj Will Surely
Pass) – Bronze**

2009–2010
Mixed media
294.5 x 140 x 266 cm

**Bajaj Pasti Berlalu
(The Bajaj Will Surely
Pass) – Gold**

2009–2010
Mixed media
310 x 140 cm x 180 cm

**Bajaj Pasti Berlalu
(The Bajaj Will Surely
Pass) – Silver**

2009–2010
Mixed media
344 x 140 x 203 cm

Singapore Art Museum
collection

Bajaj Pasti Berlalu (Bajaj Will Surely Pass) draws on the iconography of traditional Indonesian puppet theatre (*wayang kulit* and *wayang golek*) to make commentary on contemporary conditions. The *bajaj* is a vehicle commonly found on the streets of Jakarta, a mode of transport for the common people that is fast vanishing today, a fact that is alluded to in the artwork's title which conveys not just a sense of movement, but also a certain nostalgia in the 'passing' of a certain way of life. The *bajaj* was imported from India and adapted to local use, just like several aspects of Javanese culture, including the Ramayana and Mahabharata epics, which are constantly retold in *wayang kulit* performances. It is therefore fitting that, in homage to this soon-to-be-outmoded vehicle, Nasirun has embellished the humble *bajaj* with decorative symbols drawn from the Mahabharata epic. The bronze coloured *bajaj* bears the throne of Karna, a powerful Kurava knight, while the gold *bajaj* bears the throne of Baladewa, a renowned knight of the Pandawas. *Bajaj Pasti Berlalu* is a recognisably 'Indonesian' work, in the sense that it projects a distinctively 'Javanese' aesthetic and identity. At the same time, the artist is questioning whether this overarching Javanese identity and ideology – which has for so long dominated Indonesian identity and cultural values, promoted by the Suharto regime as a means for unifying the diverse populations of the Indonesian archipelago – is also losing its hold in our contemporary times, under the onslaught of globalisation and urbanisation. Perhaps these values are, like the *bajaj*, also outmoded, and 'passing' from our time.

Nasirun's approach reflects a renewed interest in recent Indonesian contemporary art to mine native traditions and cultures for artistic material and motifs, and an artistic strategy of syncretism (combining these often disparate motifs and influences), in order to celebrate Indonesia's rich past and cultural and artistic diversity.

Nasirun (b. 1965, Cilacap, Indonesia) graduated from the Indonesian Institute of the Arts (ISI, Institut Seni Indonesia), Yogyakarta. His works have been exhibited extensively in Indonesia, including his solo shows at the Galeri Nasional, Jakarta in 2000 and at Sangkring Art Space, Yogyakarta in 2009. In 2008, his work was presented in Singapore in 'Indonesian Triple Bill', a parallel event of the 2nd Singapore Biennale (2008).

(TSL)

Nasirun

Tanah Airku Indonesia (Indonesia My Motherland)

2009–2010
Mixed media
Dimensions variable

Singapore Art Museum
collection

In this work, the artist's homeland of Indonesia is represented as a strange hybrid that is part-boat, part-mythological creature. While its appearance was inspired by an antique Chinese cannon found in the sultanate of Cirebon (Central Java), that bore a bird's head and a fish's tail, it also references representations of the mythical Garuda, Indonesia's national symbol.

In Nasirun's work, the bird's head is positioned higher than its tail, conveying the impression of the creature soaring in flight. The creature's body is made into a boat-like structure, on which is painted images depicting Indonesia's riches. The curved shape of the boat is typical of the sailing vessels from Madura, where the Madurese have been known as seafarers and merchants.

This work, with its seafaring connotations and symbolisms, makes reference to Indonesia's sprawling archipelago. At the same time, the myriad cultural references in this artwork also pay tribute to the diversity of cultures that has shaped Indonesia into the unique entity that she is today. The hybrid creature of *Tanah Airku Indonesia* is represented as if in mid-flight, soaring majestically on its journey to a destination which is yet unclear. What is evident however is the artist's desire to represent his motherland as a mighty creature of legend, while celebrating and taking pride in its hybridity, in contrast to the fundamentalism and increasingly narrow definition of what it means to be 'Indonesian' that has permeated Indonesian society in recent years.

Nasirun's approach reflects a renewed interest in recent Indonesian contemporary art to mine native traditions and cultures for artistic material and motifs, and an artistic strategy of syncretism (combining these often disparate motifs and influences), in order to celebrate Indonesia's rich past and cultural and artistic diversity.

Nasirun (b. 1965, Cilacap, Indonesia) graduated from the Indonesian Institute of the Arts (ISI, Institut Seni Indonesia), Yogyakarta. His works have been exhibited extensively in Indonesia, including his solo shows at the Galeri Nasional, Jakarta in 2000, and at Sangkring Art Space, Yogyakarta in 2009. His work was also presented in Singapore in the 'Indonesian Triple Bill', a parallel event of the 2nd Singapore Biennale (2008).

(TSL)

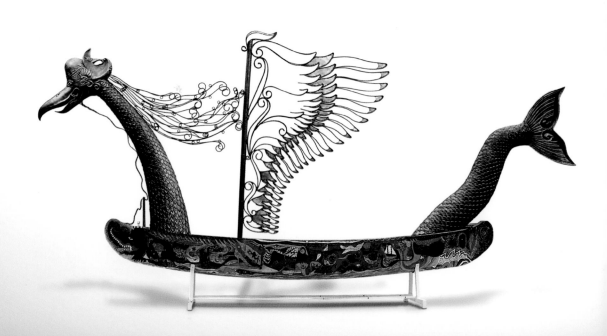

Eko Nugroho

It's All About Coalition

2008
2 bronze figures
190 x 60 x 60 cm (each)

Singapore Art Museum
collection

It's All About Coalition is typical of Eko Nugroho's signature style, which is heavily influenced by popular and comic culture and features strange, hybrid characters. His works are social and political commentaries, peppered with humour, sarcasm and parody. Eko Nugroho believes that art must communicate with people, and sees his work as "a story-telling journey" with different audiences at different sites.

In this work, two figures approach each other, proffering their hands in the universal gesture of a handshake, symbolising friendship or peace. However, the outstretched hand of one character has taken the form of the head of a wolf, its jaws open and ready to snap off the other party's extended hand. The other party is not defenceless either – his other hand, resting by his side, has taken the shape of pincers or claws, ready to retaliate. Both figures are caught in a moment of tension and anticipation – will they attack in mutual distrust, or will there be true coalition between them? The visual, pop appeal of his work is a means for the artist to discuss difficult issues or social causes that are easily overlooked by people.

Eko Nugroho (b. 1977, Indonesia) majored in painting at the Institut Seni Indonesia (ISI, Indonesian Institute of the Arts), Yogyakarta. He has exhibited widely in Asia as well as in Europe, and has participated in major visual art events and exhibitions such as the 5th Asia Pacific Triennial of Contemporary Art, Brisbane, Australia in 2006. Eko Nugroho works in a variety of artistic media, including painting, embroidery and sculpture. Founder of the Daging Tumbuh collective in Indonesia, the artist also often works on collaborative projects with communities and other social creatives in order to bring pressing social issues to the larger community and hopefully, effect change.

(TSL)

Eko Nugroho

Illusion

2007
Embroidery
148 x 296 cm

Singapore Art Museum
collection

Eko Nugroho's *Illusion* illustrates a scene of "crispy crisis" where the environment is depleted of its greenery by monster-like machines in his signature comic / graphic style. With the absence of living forms, what's left of the sterile landscape is a harsh, jagged terrain, exposed to the dangers of over-heating and "crisping" up as a result of environmental destruction.

Often working with thick, dark outlines, Eko Nugroho's style and imagery reflect Indonesia's media-rich and politically-charged environment with its bold colours and bizarre, oftentimes provocative statements. Here, the surrealistic narrative is populated by his characteristic hybrid characters, drawn from comic culture. The hooded figure – who resembles an astronaut, a common 'hero' or figure of wish-fulfilment in boys' comics and cartoons – represents the artist's aversion to depicting stereotypical face-types that could lead to discriminatory thoughts or interpretations of his work, while at the same time, adding a sense of ominous foreboding about the state of the environment depicted here.

Eko Nugroho (b. 1977, Indonesia) majored in painting at the Institut Seni Indonesia (ISI, Indonesian Institute of the Arts), Yogyakarta. He has exhibited widely in Asia as well as in Europe, and has participated in major visual art events and exhibitions such as the 5th Asia Pacific Triennial of Contemporary Art, Brisbane, Australia in 2006. Eko Nugroho works in a variety of artistic media, including painting, embroidery and sculpture. Founder of the Daging Tumbuh collective in Indonesia, the artist also often works on collaborative projects with communities and other social creatives in order to bring pressing social issues to the larger community and hopefully, effect change.

(TSL)

Eko Nugroho

Jembar Negarane, Cupet Pikirane (Big Country, Narrow Mindset)

2007
Acrylic on canvas
200 x 450 x 4.7 cm (triptych)

Singapore Art Museum collection

The title of this work, **Jembar Negarane, Cupet Pikirane**, is a Javanese phrase that loosely translates to "Big Country, Narrow Mindset" in English. It consists of three panels depicting part-man, part-machine characters in a seemingly apocalyptic scene of chaos and terror, with dismembered limbs lying around and a riotous mob threatening to take control. The sense of violence and hostility is further emphasised by the aggressive behaviour of the characters depicted in this triptych and the sharp weapons that they brandish.

The title of this work is critique as well as advice, a reminder to humankind to avoid cannibalising or preying on each other, as illustrated through Eko Nugroho's hybrid robots and monsters. In the foreground, a character distinguished by its red and white colouring turns its back on the scene of violence and chaos. Imprinted on this character's chest is the phrase "Aku Bukan Milikmu" ("I Do Not Belong To You"). This central protagonist serves as a rebel to the status quo; at the same time, by rendering this figure in the colours of the Indonesian flag, the artist could be expressing his wish for his country and countrymen to take heed of the warning in this painting's narrative, and to remember the consequences and dangers of narrow-mindedness that could lead to self-destruction.

Eko Nugroho (b. 1977, Indonesia) majored in painting at the Institut Seni Indonesia (ISI, Indonesian Institute of the Arts), Yogyakarta. He has exhibited widely in Asia as well as in Europe, and has participated in major visual art events and exhibitions such as the 5th Asia Pacific Triennial of Contemporary Art, Brisbane, Australia in 2006. Eko Nugroho works in a variety of artistic media, including painting, embroidery and sculpture. Founder of the Daging Tumbuh collective in Indonesia, the artist also often works on collaborative projects with communities and other social creatives in order to bring pressing social issues to the larger community and hopefully, effect change.

(TSL)

Eko Nugroho

Negeri Yang Kaya Tapi
Miskin Moral
(Rich Country But
Poor In Morals)

2007
Embroidery, set of 5 panels
Various dimensions:
40.9 x 58.7 cm, 36 x 54 cm,
40.2 x 58.2 cm, 39 x 58 cm,
39.9 x 58 cm

Singapore Art Museum
collection

Often working with thick dark outlines in his graphic technique, Eko Nugroho creates imagery that reflects Indonesia's media-rich and politically charged environment. His part-man part-machine characters are often accompanied by bizarre, ironic and oftentimes provocative statements in thought balloons or speech bubbles saying, for instance, "please shoot me from the back", or in the case of this series of work, "Rich Country But Poor In Morals" (as approximately translated). This series of embroidery panels encapsulates the artist's signature techniques, artistic style, and stock characters.

Eko Nugroho (b. 1977, Indonesia) majored in painting at the Institut Seni Indonesia (ISI, Indonesian Institute of the Arts), Yogyakarta. He has exhibited widely in Asia as well as in Europe, and has participated in major visual art events and exhibitions such as the 5th Asia Pacific Triennial of Contemporary Art, Brisbane, Australia in 2006. Eko Nugroho works in a variety of artistic media, including painting, embroidery and sculpture. Founder of the Daging Tumbuh collective in Indonesia, the artist also often works on collaborative projects with communities and other social creatives in order to bring pressing social issues to the larger community and hopefully, effect change.

(TSL)

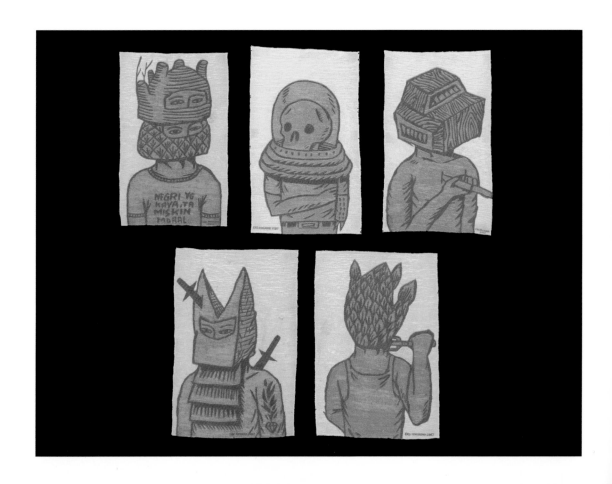

Eko Nugroho

Presiden Siap Berjanji (The President Gets Ready To Make Promises)

2009
Embroidery (machine embroidered rayon thread on fabric backing)
175 x 195 cm

Singapore Art Museum collection

In this embroidery work, the artist lampoons the motions that political candidates go through while campaigning for presidency, revealing their promises and thought processes to be farcical. The artwork is meant to be installed with a pile of gold coins on the floor below it, on the one hand serving as a visual parallel with the gold tones of the embroidery, and on the other, indicating the large sums of money expensed during political campaigns and also suggesting corruption.

Eko Nugroho (b. 1977, Indonesia) majored in painting at the Institut Seni Indonesia (ISI, Indonesian Institute of the Arts), Yogyakarta. He has exhibited widely in Asia as well as in Europe, and has participated in major visual art events and exhibitions such as the 5th Asia Pacific Triennial of Contemporary Art, Brisbane, Australia in 2006. Eko Nugroho works in a variety of artistic media, including painting, embroidery and sculpture. Founder of the Daging Tumbuh collective in Indonesia, the artist also often works on collaborative projects with communities and other social creatives in order to bring pressing social issues to the larger community and hopefully, effect change.

(TSL)

Erik Muhammad Pauhrizi

Replicating Memories – Emil
2009
Oil on canvas
150 x 190 cm

Modern Memory – Adika
2009
Mixed media: digital print and
oil on canvas
217 x 145 cm

Singapore Art Museum
collection

Erik Pauhrizi's works revisit the portrait genre with a contemporary approach. Instead of straightforward representations of his sitters, his portraits are clouded by memory and subjectivity. In a portrait, it is usually the face that is the key to recognition and identifying the sitter and his/her psychological state and status. Pauhrizi's portraits are deliberately vague and filled with uncertainty – the features of his subjects are blurred and hazy, often hidden in shadow or by washes of paint over a digital print, a visual metaphor for the layers of memory that collectively make up our impression of a person.

In *Replicating Memories – Emil*, the Cubist treatment of the sitter's facial features frustrates attempts to easily recognise or identify the subject. In *Modern Memory – Adika*, the monochromatic palette and evocative quality of washes of paint, which in turn allow areas of unpainted digital print to show through, contribute a brooding atmosphere – testament perhaps, to the fragility of memory and the transience of human life. Portraits are a means for us to remember certain people by; Pauhrizi's works are very much about memory as well, but on a more personal and intimate level, coloured by subjective impressions and imperfect recollections.

Erik Muhammad Pauhrizi (b. 1981, Indonesia) graduated with a Bachelor of Arts from the Faculty of Art and Design, Institut Teknologi Bandung (ITB, Bandung Institute of Technology), Indonesia. His work has been presented at several exhibitions in Asia, Europe and America. His earlier works revolve around issues of identity and portraiture; since his move to Berlin however, Pauhrizi has developed an interest in conceptually-driven art and has recently embarked on a series of light-based works where light serves as a metaphor for existential reality and awareness.

(TSL)

Right:
Replicating Memories – Emil

Facing page:
Modern Memory – Adika

Angki Purbandono

Two Small Grenades
2009
Lightbox
151 x 61 x 13 cm

Clown
2009
Lightbox
81 x 121 x 13 cm

Papaya
2009
Lightbox
60.5 x 121 x 13 cm

Football #1
2009
Photograph
111.5 x 111.5 x 4 cm

Football #2
2009
Photograph
111.5 x 111.5 x 4 cm

Acquired with support from
KMP Private Ltd.

Singapore Art Museum
collection

Angki Purbandono is best known for his playful 'scannography' artworks. During an artist residency in Seoul, he experimented with the use of a scanner to record images of objects. By placing his objects in a glaring spotlight, and scanning them at point-blank range; this unexpected technique achieves a visual impact which amplifies the narrativity of his subject-matter.

Angki Purbandono (b. 1971, Indonesia) is one of the founders of Ruang Mes 56, an artists' collective in Indonesia dedicated to the development of discourse in contemporary photography. He studied graphic design at the Modern School of Design, Jogjakarta, and later at Institut Seni Indonesia (Indonesian Institute of the Arts), Yogyakarta, majoring in photography, arts and media recording. Purbandono has exhibited widely in Asia as well as in Europe, including the 4th Fukuoka Asian Art Triennale (2009).

(TSL)

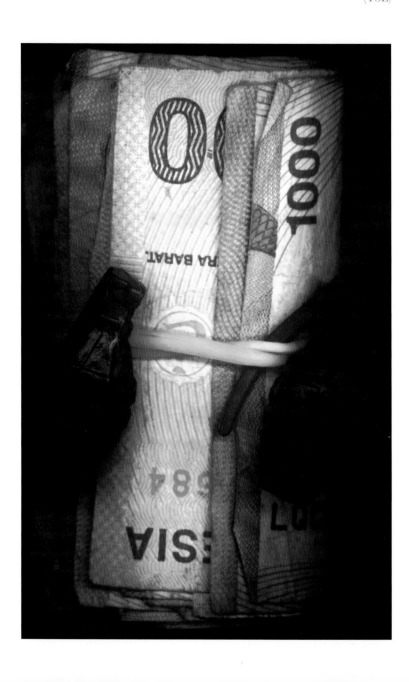

Right:
Two Small Grenades

Facing page:
Top:
Clown

Centre:
Papaya

Bottom:
Football #1
Football #2

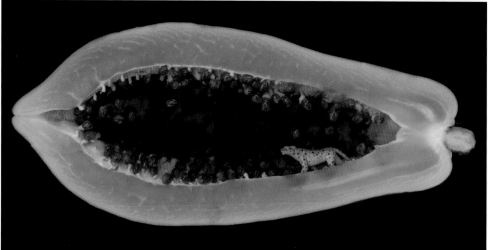

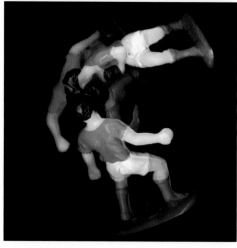

Handiwirman Saputra

Cemani, Telur, Tai Kapur (Chicken, Egg, Chalk Shit)

2008
Mixed media, fibre resin,
Blu-Tack, taxidermied chicken
171 x 110 x 110 cm

Singapore Art Museum
collection

The world of objects is the starting point for Handiwirman Saputra's artistic creation. An adept painter and sculptor, Saputra employs surprising combinations of artistic media and strategies of representation to transform everyday objects. The results are often unusual and startling, as everyday items take on new symbolic or ambiguous meaning. *Cemani, Telur, Tai Kapur* (translated as 'Chicken, Egg, Chalk Shit') skews proportions of scale by presenting a dramatically enlarged egg next to a regular sized, taxidermied chicken. The work playfully overturns our expectations and also functions as an ironic commentary on society's obsession with size. *Cemani, Telur, Tai Kapur* makes fun of the idea that 'bigger is better', for in this case, the only chicken capable of producing such an egg is a dead one.

Handiwirman Saputra (b. 1975, Indonesia) is a member of a major artists collective known as the Jendela Art Group, which became well known in the mid-1990s. While many equate Indonesian art with strong socio-political commentary, the approach of the Jendela Art Group presents a fascinating alternative in their focus on formalist concerns. Their three-dimensional works, of which *Cemani, Telur, Tai Kapur* is a prime example, are often sophisticated and even clinical in finish, and defy easy contextual interpretation. Saputra's art, like that of his fellow Jendela members, has drawn conflicting opinions. On one hand, its formalism has been critiqued as being merely a manipulation of forms in a way that appeals to the sensation-seeking market; on the other hand, this approach to art suggests a contemporary response to the perceived demise of the 'grand narratives' of Indonesian art. In this respect, Saputra and the Jendela Art Group's practice makes an important contribution to contemporary art discourse and debate.

(TSL)

(Detail)

Yudi Sulistyo

Mewujudkan Angan
(Realising Dreams)

2010–2011
Cardboard, plastic pipe, steel,
acrylic and duco paint
160 x 360 x 580 cm

Singapore Art Museum
collection

This piece by Indonesian artist Yudi Sulistyo is a powerful work on several levels. Like the rest of the artist's hyper-realistic war machines, this object is made from cardboard, created from scratch without reference to models nor the use of prototypes and computer software. Its physical presence eschews the conceptual approach to art-making adopted by many artists today, in favour of a return to a more material and hands-on approach which highlights the artist's powers of imagination, as well as his technical skill and craftsmanship in shaping and transforming raw material into an artwork.

Yudi Sulistyo began his series of wrecked war machines in response to a period when Indonesia's military (air force) capabilities were called into question. Various news reports by the Indonesian media highlighted the many setbacks suffered by the Indonesian Air Force, in humiliating contrast to its heyday of the 1960s. At the same time, Indonesia's national carrier, along with other Indonesian airlines, was banned from flying into European airspace because of poor aviation safety records. Hence, the artist's grounded flying machines question our contemporary obsession with and reliance on machines and technology, warning us against our blind faith in the future, and revealing these projections of power and ambition to be hollow and illusory. They are also a symbol of wounded national pride. In this respect, the artist's choice of material to create his work is particularly fortuitous, as these military machines are revealed to be nothing more than 'paper tigers', or simple children's toys masquerading at greatness.

Yudi Sulistyo (b. 1972, Indonesia) graduated from the Institut Seni Indonesia (ISI, Indonesian Institute of the Arts) in 1994 and is best-known for creating life-sized sculptures of war-machines and robots from cardboard. As a child he was fascinated with military machines and weaponry – an interest that has carried over to his adulthood and his artistic practice. His work has been exhibited in Indonesia as well as internationally, with recent presentations at the Singapore Art Museum and in Melbourne, Australia.

(TSL)

Melati Suryodarmo

I Love You I, II, III, IV, V, VI

2007
Lambda print, series of 6
51 x 34 cm (each)

Singapore Art Museum
collection

This series of prints documents a performance by Melati Suryodarmo entitled *I Love You*. Taking as her starting point the three words commonly employed to express deep emotions for another, the artist questions the meaning and significance of this phrase while exploring on a subconscious level the collective psyche of being a woman. The poses captured on these prints may hence be read as abstract metaphors for situations and scenarios in relationships, articulating the fragility and uncertainty of the emotions that humans express verbally.

Melati Suryodarmo (b. 1969, Surakarta, Indonesia) studied under renowned Butoh dancer, Anzu Furukawa, and acclaimed performance artist, Marina Abramovic. She is known for her highly physical, time-based performances, using her body as a theatrical canvas. She has performed widely all over the world, with participation in the Venice Biennale Dance Festival (2007), eBent 07 Festival in Barcelona (2007), Accione 06 in Madrid (2006), 15th International Electronic Art Festival – Video Brasil, Sao Paolo, Brasil (2005), International Performance Art Festival in Toronto (2004), as well as shows in New York, Paris, Bali, Singapore and Sydney.

(TSL)

Melati Suryodarmo

***Exergie – Butter Dance
(Sao Paolo)***

2007
Lambda print, edition 1/5
34 x 51 cm (each)

***Exergie – Butter Dance
(Sao Paolo)***

2000
Video, edition 2/3
Duration 6:23 mins

Singapore Art Museum
collection

In this performance, Melati Suryodarmo, dressed in a black dress and red shoes, dances on pieces of butter that cause her to slip and fall repeatedly. Throughout her performance, she continues to dance, slip, slide and fall unremittingly with increasing intensity. The futility of her actions bordering on absurdity contrasts with the sensuality of her movements and the insistent percussive beat she dances to, capturing the tragicomedy of our contemporary experiences and existence, and offering some form of catharsis through its mingling of fragility, heroism and absurdity.

Melati Suryodarmo (b. 1969, Surakarta, Indonesia) studied under renowned Butoh dancer, Anzu Furukawa, and acclaimed performance artist, Marina Abramovic. She is known for her highly physical, time-based performances, using her body as a theatrical canvas. She has performed widely all over the world, with participation in the Venice Biennale Dance Festival (2007), eBent 07 Festival in Barcelona (2007), Accione 06 in Madrid (2006), 15th International Electronic Art Festival – Video Brasil, Sao Paolo, Brasil (2005), International Performance Art Festival in Toronto (2004), as well as shows in New York, Paris, Bali, Singapore and Sydney.

(TSL)

INDONESIA

Agus Suwage

Curtain

2009
STPI handmade paper, cotton
pulp, pigment
182 x 146.5 x 9.5 cm

Singapore Art Museum
collection

Curtain is part of a series of prints developed during Agus Suwage's residency at the Singapore Tyler Print Institute. This series references two pivotal points in Indonesia's contemporary art and cultural scene: first, the recently passed anti-pornography law which galvanised the Indonesian artistic community in protest against what they perceived to be curbs against artistic freedom of expression by parties insensitive to contemporary art appreciation; and second, the artist's controversial *Pinkswing Park* installation at the 2005 CP Biennale in Jakarta. *Pinkswing Park* included nude images of Indonesian celebrities Anjasmara and Izabel Jahja frolicking in a pastoral paradise suggestive of the Garden of Eden, with only white circles protecting their modesty. The digital images created an uproar amongst conservative Islamic groups, forcing the work to be closed from public view.

As such, *Curtain* addresses issues of censorship; the female nude depicted in this print is partially screened from our view by a curtain of text comprising extracts from the anti-pornography bill. Yet it is possible to read into this work, a gesture of defiance on the part of the artist as well, for the nude in this print is both defiant and languorous in her nudity, stretching back her arms in a classical pose to proudly display her form – after all, the female nude has long been regarded the triumph of the ideals and beauty of art.

Agus Suwage (b. 1959, Indonesia) majored in graphic arts at the Institut Teknologi Bandung (ITB, Bandung Institute of Technology). His works are known for their use of portraiture, the human figure and the technique of appropriation to make playful yet incisive commentary. Themes that run through Suwage's art include those of death, the cult of the celebrity and creative endeavour, and many of his artworks are nuanced commentaries on contemporary social, political and cultural issues, such as the dissemination of images via icons and the mass media. His works are exhibited extensively both at home and abroad, including presentations at the Asia Pacific Triennial of Contemporary Art, Brisbane, Australia; the Havana Biennial, Cuba; the Gwangju Biennale, Korea, and most recently at the MACRO Museum in Rome, Italy, and at the Singapore Art Museum.

(TSL)

Pasal 5 Setiap orang dilarang meminjamkan ata dimaksud dalam Pasal 4 ayat (1). Pasal 6 Seti mempertontonkan, memanfaatkan, memiliki, a sebagaimana dimaksud dalam Pasal 4 ayat (1), perundang-undangan. Pasal 7 Setiap orang dilaran sebagaimana dimaksud dalam Pasal 4. Pasal 8 S atas persetujuan dirinya menjadi objek atau model Pasal 9 Setiap orang dilarang menjadikan orang mengandung muatan pornografi Pasal 10 Setiap or orang lain dalam pertunjukan atau muka umum eksploitasi seksual, persenggamaan atau yang bo Setiap orang dilarang melibatkan anak dalam sebagaimana dimaksud dalam Pasal 4, Pasal 5 pa Pasal 12 Setiap orang dilarang mengajak me menyalahgunakan kekuasaan atau memaksa anak pornografi Pasal 5 Setiap orang dilarang menuhi

Agus Suwage

I Want To Live Another Thousand Years

2005
Tobacco liquid, paper mounted
on canvas
75 x 55 x 2 cm

Singapore Art Museum
collection

I Want To Live Another Thousand Years is a series of celebrity portraits rendered in tobacco liquid. In this work, artist Agus Suwage has cheekily posed various cultural icons and personalities with a hand holding a cigarette in front of their faces. This pose (cigarette held in hand) was a signature pose of trailblazing Indonesian poet Chairil Anwar, who died tragically young. As such, this work serves not only as a tribute to these personalities who have made their mark on history, politics and culture, but also as a kind of *memento mori*, an ironic commentary on the fact that they have all passed on, and their deaths have served to further immortalize their ideas and their personal legends. The vitality of their lives and the significance of these icons' contributions stand in stark contrast to the theme of death which unites these disparate figures; the cigarette in front of each portrait is hence an apt symbol for this dichotomy. For Agus Suwage – himself an avid smoker – the cigarette is what fuels his artistic creativity, but at the same time he is well aware of the detrimental impact of smoking and its links with premature death. The title of the work hence plays on this irony between the immortality of art and great deeds, and the mortality of the physical body. The prominence given to cigarettes, smoking and tobacco in this work also has a particularly piquant resonance, given the inextricable link between tobacco and art in Yogyakarta, where artists rely on wealthy tobacco merchants as patrons of art.

Agus Suwage (b. 1959, Indonesia) majored in graphic arts at the Institut Teknologi Bandung (ITB, Bandung Institute of Technology). His works are known for their use of portraiture, the human figure and the technique of appropriation to make playful yet incisive commentary. Themes that run through Suwage's art include those of death, the cult of the celebrity and creative endeavour, and many of his artworks are nuanced commentaries on contemporary social, political and cultural issues, such as the dissemination of images via icons and the mass media. His works are exhibited extensively both at home and abroad, including presentations at the Asia Pacific Triennial of Contemporary Art, Brisbane, Australia; the Havana Biennial, Cuba; the Gwangju Biennale, Korea, and most recently at the MACRO Museum in Rome, Italy, and at the Singapore Art Museum.

(TSL)

Agus Suwage &
Davy Linggar

Pinkswing Park

2005–2012
Installation with digital print on
canvas mounted on board,
becak swing, resin pebbles
Dimensions variable

Singapore Art Museum
collection

First exhibited in 2005 at the CP Biennale in Jakarta, ***Pinkswing Park*** began a controversy that continues to be a touchstone for discussions of how Indonesian art negotiates the relative freedoms of a society enjoying some degree of democracy after years of authoritarian rule under the Suharto regime. The work was made in response to the exhibition theme 'Urban/Culture', and comprises a room with walls plastered with digital prints depicting two popular Indonesian soap opera stars frolicking in a pastoral idyll. Their poses are a pastiche of various iconic nudes from art history, for instance, Michelangelo's *David*, a sculpture widely considered the epitome of masculine beauty. Unlike classical nudes however, the figures of the two Indonesian celebrities have been playfully censored. In doing so, artists Agus Suwage and Davy Linggar make clear that this is no innocent Garden of Eden; this contemporary 'Adam' and 'Eve' are neither 'pure' nor 'noble' in their nudity, but highly conscious and aware of their state of undress. For instance, Izabel Jahja, the model for the female nude, is photographed cheekily attempting to shield herself from the viewer's gaze. In choosing to represent the models as such, the artists pointedly highlight the gulf between classical ideals – an innocence 'lost' which can never hope to be attained again – and contemporary culture, where beauty is no longer 'natural' but deliberate and 'artificial', and where classical ideals have been filtered through a lens of anxiety about the human body, in particular, what is perceived as its baser instincts and impulses.

Originally intended as a light-hearted dream-garden, a sanctuary for the urban dweller to escape the hustle and bustle of everyday life, this private space of repose became instead an arena for public controversy and contention, with hard-line religious groups protesting against what they perceived as pornographic elements in the work. Under this pressure, the artwork was withdrawn from the exhibition and the entire Biennale closed down eventually, in turn sparking off heated debates and discussions about the nature of contemporary art and its public(s) in Indonesia.

Agus Suwage (b. 1959, Indonesia) majored in graphic arts at the Institut Teknologi Bandung (ITB, Bandung Institute of Technology). His works are known for their use of portraiture, the human figure and the technique of appropriation to make playful yet incisive commentary. Themes that run through Suwage's art include those of death, the cult of the celebrity and creative endeavour, and many of his artworks are nuanced commentaries on contemporary social, political and cultural issues, such as the dissemination of images via icons and the mass media. His works are exhibited extensively both at home and abroad, including presentations at the Asia Pacific Triennial of Contemporary Art, Brisbane, Australia; the Havana Biennial, Cuba; the Gwangju Biennale, Korea, and most recently at the MACRO Museum in Rome, Italy, and at the Singapore Art Museum.

Davy Linggar (b. 1974, Indonesia) studied painting at the Institut Teknologi Bandung (Bandung Institute of Technology) and photography in Germany. Taking everyday objects and events as artistic inspiration, Linggar works across different mediums such as painting and photography. A fashion photographer by trade, Linggar's art is informed by the fertile cross-pollination of the two different cultural and social spheres he inhabits. His work has been exhibited widely in Indonesia as well as in Singapore.

(TSL)

Agus Suwage

Still Crazy After All These Years

2010
Paper and metal (sculpture)

Singapore Art Museum collection

Still Crazy After All These Years is a publication and extensive documentation on the practice of prolific contemporary Indonesian artist, Agus Suwage, from 1985 to 2009. Published with essay contributions by curators and writers such as Hendro Wiyanto, Patrick D. Flores and Seng Yu Jin, this publication edited by Enin Supriyanto was released in May 2010 in two different versions. The 100 copies, limited-edition version, features a glossy, golden hard-boxed cover, with a gold-plated skeleton sculpture embedded within its pages. When first released at an art gallery in Indonesia, these books were stacked to look like actual bars of gold, which quickly depleted as enthusiastic collectors and fans of the artist purchased and immediately took them away.

Agus Suwage (b. 1959, Indonesia) majored in graphic arts at the Institut Teknologi Bandung (ITB, Bandung Institute of Technology). His works are known for their use of portraiture, the human figure and the technique of appropriation to make playful yet incisive commentary. Themes that run through Suwage's art include those of death, the cult of the celebrity and creative endeavour, and many of his artworks are nuanced commentaries on contemporary social, political and cultural issues, such as the dissemination of images via icons and the mass media. His works are exhibited extensively both at home and abroad, including presentations at the Asia Pacific Triennial of Contemporary Art, Brisbane, Australia; the Havana Biennial, Cuba; the Gwangju Biennale, Korea, and most recently at the MACRO Museum in Rome, Italy, and at the Singapore Art Museum.

(KH)

Titarubi

Bayang Bayang Maha Kecil #9 (Shadows of the Smallest Kind)

2010
Stoneware, lamp, pedestal, MDF
board and acrylic, set of 3
130 x 40 x 40 cm (each)

Singapore Art Museum
collection

Bayang Bayang Maha Kecil #9 (Shadows of The Smallest Kind) was inspired by the artist's personal experiences, and comprises ceramic busts of a child with its palms turned outwards to face the viewer. These busts were modelled from the body of Titarubi's own young daughter and are inscribed with Arabic text, a reference to the practice of Muslim mothers chanting prayers over their children for protection. As such, the work tenderly captures a mother's protectiveness and love for her child. However, this is also a deeply ambivalent work, and the manner of the hand gesture may suggest a rejection of rote learning of Arabic texts – and by extension, unquestioning acceptance of religious values.

Titarubi (b. 1968, Bandung, Indonesia) graduated in ceramics from the Bandung Institute of Technology (ITB, Institut Teknologi Bandung). One of Indonesia's pioneering female contemporary artists, Titarubi uses the body as her narrative vehicle, tackling thorny issues of gender, religion and culture in a poetic and often visually stunning way. She is well known for her 'wearable art' performance-installations, and sculptures finely detailed with decorative patterns such as batik or Arabic engraving. One of her notable recent works was a commission entitled *Surrounding David* (2008) for the National Museum of Singapore. Her body of work is important for understanding the tensions and concerns of Indonesian society today, expressed through a characteristically feminine idiom.

(TSL)

Titarubi

Bodyscape

2005
Mixed media: 9 figures with
brocade, lamp, translucent
fibreglass, wire
Dimensions variable

Singapore Art Museum
collection

Titarubi challenges prevalent stereotypes and cultural constructions about the role and place of women (and men) in society. Her works blur the boundaries between 'male' and 'female' characteristics, while questioning the double standards that exist in society with regards to cultural practices. In *Bodyscape*, nine fibreglass human figures are suspended in the air, their bodies wrapped with elaborately patterned lace fabric. Brocade is conventionally associated with femininity, and especially so in Indonesia where it is often used to make the traditional *kebaya* blouse worn by women for formal occasions, and often as a gesture of modesty and one's respect for traditional culture and conservative values. Ironically, the *kebaya* blouse often serves to accentuate the sexual attractiveness of its wearer – its body-hugging cut and the transparency of its lace fabric exposes every curve of the body, thereby 'stripping' women under a male gaze. By wrapping the androgynous sculptures in *Bodyscape* with this feminine fabric, Titarubi is challenging entrenched socio-cultural politics of gender, clothing and the gaze. In addition, her work addresses the particularly fraught issue of what is deemed 'proper' or 'morally acceptable' in representations of the body, adding another layer to the ongoing debate in Indonesian contemporary art about the limits of artistic expression in the representation of the human body, and cultural and social mores.

Titarubi (b. 1968, Bandung, Indonesia) graduated in ceramics from the Bandung Institute of Technology (ITB, Institut Teknologi Bandung). One of Indonesia's pioneering female contemporary artists, Titarubi uses the body as her narrative vehicle, tackling thorny issues of gender, religion and culture in a poetic and often visually stunning way. She is well known for her 'wearable art' performance-installations, and sculptures finely detailed with decorative patterns such as batik or Arabic engraving. One of her notable recent works was a commission entitled *Surrounding David* (2008) for the National Museum of Singapore. Her body of work is important for understanding the tensions and concerns of Indonesian society today, expressed through a characteristically feminine idiom.

(TSL)

(Detail)

Tromarama

Zsa Zsa Zsu

2007
Music video (stop-motion
animation), edition 3/5
Music by R.N.R.M
FFWD Records
Duration 4:42 mins

Singapore Art Museum
collection

Zsa Zsa Zsu is a music video produced for the Bandung-based music band Rock N' Roll Mafia (RNRM). The title of the song is a phrase used to describe the electric connection and chemistry experienced when meeting a new love interest, and is taken from the popular television series, 'Sex And The City'. Likewise, the lyrics of the song narrate the anticipation and longing of infatuation, from a male as well as female perspective.

The storyboard of the **Zsa Zsa Zsu** video emphasises this electric connection, depicting members of RNRM performing the song using the stop-motion animation technique. Unexpected objects such as buttons and beads are used to form the images. This combination of a deliberate low-tech technique and the use of everyday materials is characteristic of Tromarama's unique artistic style, contrasting greatly with many mainstream music videos which rely on the use of high-tech special effects and heavy editing in order to achieve slick production values and a polished end product in order to appeal to viewers. The use of buttons and beads in **Zsa Zsa Zsu** results in images that look blurred and pixelated, reminiscent of the days when technology and mass media were not so developed yet, creating a nostalgic and 'indie' feel to the work.

Tromarama is an artists collective formed in 2004 and based in Bandung, Indonesia. Its members are Febie Babyrose (b. 1985, Indonesia), Herbert Hans Maruli (b. 1984, Indonesia) and Ruddy Alexander Hatumena (b. 1984, Bahrain). Tromarama is known for creating video works using low-tech techniques such as classic animation and stop-motion animation, to transform everyday objects and materials into playful and engaging narratives. Their work has been exhibited widely, including at the Singapore Biennale (2008), the 3rd Asian Art Biennial (2011) in Taiwan as well as at the Mori Art Museum in Tokyo, Japan.

(TSL)

Entang Wiharso

Temple Of Hope: Forest Of Eyes

2010–2011
Aluminium plate, stainless steel, resin, pigment, light bulbs, thread, electrical cables, lava stone
330 x 400 x 300 cm

Singapore Art Museum collection

Temple Of Hope: Forest Of Eyes is the third and last installation in Entang Wiharso's 'Temple' series. Wiharso's 'Temple' works bring together several motifs and themes he has been exploring in his art over the past decade: issues of identity, conflict, humanity and human interconnectedness. The hybrid human forms that form a rhythmic frieze on the walls of *Temple Of Hope* recall the stylised figures carved into temple walls in Southeast Asia such as those of the Hindu Prambanan temple in Java, which the artist lives close to, or those of the puppets used in traditional Javanese shadow puppet theatre. These strange, otherworldly, multiple-limbed figures bear narratives of desire, violence, conflict and conciliation, just as many temple carvings and friezes also recount mankind's journey towards spiritual enlightenment, as the central protagonist or hero makes his way through the world and encounters various trials and tribulations.

Apart from its parallels with traditional *wayang kulit* in its use of stylised figures, light and shadow to convey a narrative, *Temple Of Hope* also highlights the artist's favoured motifs of skin and surfaces – porous and borderless – as metaphors for ambiguity, fluidity, hybridity and transformation, themes that are close to Wiharso's heart and born of the artist's experiences of living in the United States as well as in Indonesia, and raising a family with his American wife. Entang Wiharso's *Temple Of Hope* is hence envisioned as a contemporary temple that draws on Indonesia's rich cultural traditions, motifs and structures for its singular power, while addressing pressing issues in contemporary society.

Entang Wiharso (b. 1967, Indonesia) graduated from the Institut Seni Indonesia (ISI, Indonesian Institute of the Arts) Yogyakarta, and has exhibited widely around the world. His art practice spans painting, sculpture, performance and installation. Often surreal and otherwordly in appearance, Entang Wiharso's artworks address universal human issues of conflict, conciliation, desire, loss and longing.

(TSL)

Detail of the interior of **Temple of Hope**

Entang Wiharso

Temple Of Hope: Forest Of Eyes
2010–2011
Aluminium plate, stainless steel, resin, pigment, light bulbs, thread, electrical cables, lava stone
330 x 400 x 300 cm

Singapore Art Museum collection

I Wayan Sujana (Suklu)

Unconscious Visual #007

2009
Charcoal on canvas
129.5 x 129.5 cm

Acquired with support from
KMP Private Ltd.

Singapore Art Museum
collection

The female figure is a repeated motif of Suklu's more recent series of charcoal drawings in a career that spans 20 years. What is expressed here in **Unconscious Visual #007** is the "view beneath consciousness", a phrase taken from the title of another work in the series (*Pemandangan Dibawah Sadar*, 2010) of Suklu's. This 'view' may be attributed to the Balinese conception of space in their way of life, one that does not draw a clear line between the conscious and the unconscious worlds. Whatever appears in a physical form functions symbolically and metaphorically for this world beneath consciousness.

The repetitive layering of the sinuous and intermingled figures, identifiably female, imbues the work with a treatment that suggests movement, or even an introspection that cuts across time/space. This evocation is furthered in the later 'Moving Space' series.

The work is an interesting example of contemporary drawing and figural representation, where forms acquire a psychological charge rather than a purely narrative or descriptive function. Suklu is also considered an artist who has broken away from the Balinese tradition of art solely as representation of its mystical culture. He pursues contemporary issues of locating self-identity in his personal struggle to understand his past, in particular the complex relationship of men and women.

I Wayan Sujana (Suklu) (b. 1967, Lepang, Kungkung, Bali) graduated from Denpasar Academy of Art, now known as ISI (Institut Seni Indonesia) in 1992. In 2010, he graduated from ITB (Institut Teknologi Bandung), Bandung, in West Java.

(SW)

Syagini Ratna Wulan

BiblioTea

2011
Installation with art books, tea,
video, photographs
Dimensions variable

Singapore Art Museum
collection

BiblioTea is an interactive and playfully acerbic work by emerging Bandung artist Syagini Ratna Wulan. Made specifically for Art HK 2011, **BiblioTea** invites viewers into an imaginary bookshop-cum-tea house where various (fictitious) art books and flavoured teas are on display. The concept here is that the content of the instructive art books have been infused into the teas; thus, one can immediately gain this knowledge by consuming the various teas – an idea that draws on Asian scholarly traditions where tea (and its appreciation) is intimately associated with philosophical and aesthetic contemplation, while simultaneously commenting on contemporary consumerist culture where people expect instant gratification and enlightenment with minimal effort.

The art books also present an insight on the personalities and preoccupations of the contemporary Indonesian art scene, with book titles that slyly refer to the occupations and interests of their authors. Hence for instance, the book "Art Market For Dummies" is 'penned' by Amalia Wirjono, an auctions specialist for Christie's Indonesia; Ade Darmawan, an artist and the founder of alternative Jakarta-based art space, ruangrupa, is the 'author' of "The (No) Future Of Alternative Art Space"; and conceptual sculptor Wiyoga Muhardanto is the 'author' of "World's Greatest Conceptual Imposters". Accompanying the installation are photographs of 'satisfied customers' as well as a video of various people giving testimonials for the efficacy of the teas – a comment perhaps on the necessity of aggressive branding and advertisement in the contemporary art world.

Syagini Ratna Wulan (b. 1979, Indonesia) graduated with a Master of Arts in Cultural Studies from Goldsmiths College, London. Her work is conceptually driven and explores issues of human behaviour and social science. **BiblioTea** was a Finalist Artwork in the Installation / Sculpture Category of the Celeste Art Prize 2011, New York.

(TSL)

Tintin Wulia

Nous ne notons pas les fleurs (We Do Not Notice The Flowers)

2010
8-channel video installation
(unsynchronized, loop)

Singapore Art Museum
collection

Much of Tintin Wulia's work revolves around themes of mobility and identity – issues born of the artist's personal experiences. Her artworks examine questions of origin and home, often showing these essentialist concepts to be fluid and complicated. Maps and passports feature as leitmotifs in her works, investigating how identity and sense of self (or nation) are constructed/deconstructed.

Nous ne notons pas les fleurs encapsulates many of Tintin's concerns and the recurrent themes in her art. It takes its name from a line in the children's classic, 'Le Petit Prince (The Little Prince)', where a geographer explains to the eponymous hero, who is looking for a certain flower, that his profession does not "record the flowers" because unlike the earth, they are ephemeral.

Nous ne notons pas les fleurs is a lyrical and participatory work that captures movement, ephemerality and humanity. The genesis of this video installation lies in an earlier work created by the artist during her residency in India, where she made a flower installation of the map of India and invited the audience to recall where they came from and how they had moved from one place to another. The idea grew, as did the work, to encompass not just flowers but also spices and herbs to represent each country's territory on the world map that the artist would create, before inviting audiences to move these components around according to their personal histories, and documenting the 'performance' on video. The displacement of the flowers and spices mirrors the movement of bodies and serves as a metaphor for cultural and commodity exchange, recalling the complex history of spice trading routes which shaped civilisations in the past. At the same time, it provides an opportunity for the audience to realise how they have personally contributed to the formation of a new world.

Tintin Wulia (b. 1972, Bali, Indonesia) undertook her studies in Bandung, before moving to the United States to pursue higher education and finally settling in Australia. She has a background in music and trained as an architect and film composer in Indonesia and the United States. Her works have been exhibited internationally at major platforms such as the Istanbul Biennial (2005), Yokohama Triennale, Japan (2005), the International Film Festival, Rotterdam (2009) and at the Institute of Contemporary Art, London (2005).

(TSL)

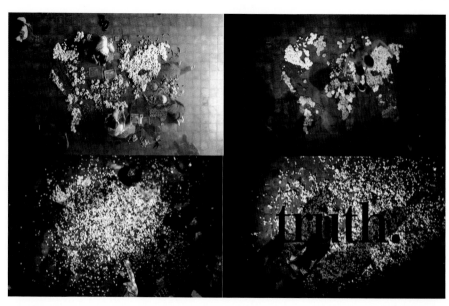

Albert Yonathan

Cosmic Labyrinth

2011
Performance installation with
glazed middle fired ceramic,
slip cast
Dimensions variable

Singapore Art Museum
collection

In ***Cosmic Labyrinth***, Albert Yonathan combines performance with installation. White stupa-shaped ceramic sculptures are arranged in a labyrinthine configuration by the artist during a silent, contemplative performance. The stupa is a motif associated with spirituality; likewise, the act of walking a labyrinth is regarded as a transformative journey of (self) discovery in several cultures. In combining his ceramic sculptures with performance, Yonathan conveys to the audience the importance of the process of artmaking, which, for the artist, is a meditative journey in itself.

Human spirituality is the starting point of his work, and through his artistic creations he attempts to address questions of how mankind relates to the cosmos, by distilling symbolism common across various cultures into minimalist and evocative forms, such as the bird (representing flight, the soul, and the spirit), the pyramid or stupa, and the obelisk. His palette is monochromatic, in order not to detract from the meditative, abstracted forms of his pieces. Repetition (of forms) is also key to Yonathan's work, as it is the cornerstone of rituals and religious practice (the repeated chanting of mantras, for example, or the repetition of motifs in Islamic art). Ceramics is hence a poetic choice as the vessel for Yonathan's spiritual explorations – the process of firing ceramics is one which is not always predictable or able to be controlled by the artist, and accidents in the kiln can result in the destruction of the artwork. Hence, Yonathan's multitude of delicate forms serve to remind us of the human labour that has gone into shaping them, their fragility, and the vagaries of life.

Albert Yonathan (b. 1983, Indonesia) majored in ceramics at Institut Teknologi Bandung (ITB, Bandung Institute of Technology). While he works across different artistic media including painting, drawing and sculpture, he is best known for his minimalist ceramic installations that endeavour to capture a spiritual essence and a sense of (silent) human presence. His work has been presented at numerous exhibitions, including 'Crossroads' (Japan), the first Jakarta Contemporary Ceramics Biennale, and most recently at the 2011 Yogyakarta Biennale. He has also been commissioned to create public art for the Indonesian Exchange in Jakarta.

(TSL)

Albert Yonathan

Silent Union

2011
Installation with glazed middle
fired ceramic, slip cast, and decals
120 x 104 x 16 cm

Singapore Art Museum
collection

Silent Union is a hexagon-shaped installation comprising 61 smaller stacked hexagonal sculptures. Each of these sculptures is green in colour and their topmost tier is decorated with a grid-like pattern on a decal. Although minimalist in form, **Silent Union** conjures up a host of symbolisms spanning several cultures. Its resemblance to a honeycomb as well as its green colour suggest affinities to Islam, where green is regarded a holy colour, often found in mosque interiors, and where the bee is mentioned in the Koran as a metaphor for an ideal devotee. Honey is also regarded in Islam as a universal healing medicine. Honeycomb structures are also commonly found as decorative architectural motifs in mosques, most notably in the Suleimaniye mosque in Istanbul. At the same time, the object-within-an object structure of this installation recalls the *matryoshka* principle of Russian nested dolls, a metaphor for infinity; it also recalls the *mise-en-abyme* motif found in much of medieval art, often as a metaphor for the macrocosmos or larger universe reflected in the microcosmos. The power of this work lies in its apparent visual simplicity, which, through its meditative nature, leads the viewer on a journey of philosophical contemplation.

Human spirituality is the starting point of his work, and through his artistic creations he attempts to address questions of how mankind relates to the cosmos, by distilling symbolism common across various cultures into minimalist and evocative forms, such as the bird (representing flight, the soul, and the spirit), the pyramid or stupa, and the obelisk. His palette is monochromatic, in order not to detract from the meditative, abstracted forms of his pieces. Repetition (of forms) is also key to Yonathan's work, as it is the cornerstone of rituals and religious practice (the repeated chanting of mantras, for example, or the repetition of motifs in Islamic art). Ceramics is hence a poetic choice as the vessel for Yonathan's spiritual explorations – the process of firing ceramics is one which is not always predictable or able to be controlled by the artist, and accidents in the kiln can result in the destruction of the artwork. Hence, Yonathan's multitude of delicate forms serve to remind us of the human labour that has gone into shaping them, their fragility, and the vagaries of life.

Albert Yonathan (b. 1983, Indonesia) majored in ceramics at Institut Teknologi Bandung (ITB, Bandung Institute of Technology). While he works across different artistic media including painting, drawing and sculpture, he is best known for his minimalist ceramic installations that endeavour to capture a spiritual essence and a sense of (silent) human presence. His work has been presented at numerous exhibitions, including *Crossroads* (Japan), the first Jakarta Contemporary Ceramics Biennale, and most recently at the 2011 Yogyakarta Biennale. He has also been commissioned to create public art for the Indonesian Exchange in Jakarta.

(TSL)

Muhammad 'Ucup' Yusuf

Janji Sejahtera / Tepat Janji

2008
Woodcut print on fabric,
woodblocks
240 x 120 cm (each)

Singapore Art Museum
collection

The dense visual tableau of this narrative diptych envisions Ucup's 'ideal' society. In *Janji Sejahtera* (Prosperity Promise), this utopian community is one that is self-sufficient, as proclaimed by the banner "BERDIKARI" ("to stand on one's own feet") on the top of a sheltering tree – the tree often understood in Indonesian art as a metaphor for society and social structure. This is achieved by the spirit of *gotong royong*, where the entire community rallies together to help each other out: those who are able to, impart education to young students; others teach their fellow villagers how to make a living in workshops and small cottage industries (which is paralleled in real life by the artist and his artists collective, Taring Padi's, recovery efforts in Porong, in the wake of a mudslide disaster). This is a community whose members have the land and leisure time to indulge in sports and bonding, and even music jamming sessions (an echo of the camaraderie that characterises the art scene in Yogyakarta, where Taring Padi is based). At the heart of it all is the nuclear family unit, its importance stressed by the central position it occupies in the print. Significantly, Ucup envisions that his utopian society is a multi-religious one coexisting in harmony, as symbolised by the four distinct archetypes of places of worship all lined up on the same roof, on the right of the print.

However, this utopia is not without its threats: at the bottom of the print are images of division and poverty. The companion print *Tepat Janji* is littered with slogans that warn against the all-too-real impediments to this idyllic vision of community that the artist has created: banners warn against corruption and the infiltration of thieves, liars and imposters into the community. This poignantly reflects the chasm between Ucup's utopia and the reality in his homeland; at the same time, the prints brim with hope for a better future, where communities will indeed be able to attain something close to the kind of peace and prosperity envisioned by the artist.

Muhamad 'Ucup' Yusuf (b. 1975, Indonesia) is a founding member of the Indonesian artist-activist collective, Taring Padi. The group – and Ucup's works – centre on Indonesian society and politics, seeking to address social injustices and the rights of minority or marginalised communities. The members of Taring Padi favour woodblock prints because of their ease of production and distribution, enabling the artists to swiftly disseminate their social messages through posters, in hopes of stirring collective awareness and thereby effecting social change.

(KH)

Muhammad 'Ucup' Yusuf

Tak Kunjung Padam

2009
Woodcut print on fabric,
edition 6/6
240 x 120 cm

Singapore Art Museum
collection

Tak Kunjung Padam (Unflagging) is a strong call for justice and social awareness in the wake of the Porong mudslide disaster in East Java, Indonesia. Many hold the opinion that the mudslide was triggered by irresponsible drilling on the part of a private company with connections to the government, and justice has been slow in being meted out. As a result, this disaster has become a rallying cry of the people against unethical corporations and corruption in the government.

Tak Kunjung Padam chronicles the efforts of the victims to get back on their feet, everyone helping out in their own way, in the spirit of *gotong royong* (mutual assistance). Several slogans are prominently etched into the print, calling for justice to be brought to light, and for basic rights to be returned to the victims. In the centre of this densely detailed print, a couple kneels on the ground, and between them a baby's head emerges from a sack, symbolising renewal and regeneration. From the top of the baby's head, a tree-like form sprouts, its branches formed with clenched fists – a universal gesture of protest and assertion of rights. Behind the couple is a steaming crater of mud – a reminder of the tragedy – flanked by two cranes. In the background is a dark silhouette of a cityscape, where grotesque and shadowy figures can be seen engaging in acts of corruption. In contrast, the lower half of the print teems with the activities of the villagers as they attempt to rebuild their community and village, and campaign for heightened awareness about the responsibility of the private company and the suffering of the victims.

Muhamad 'Ucup' Yusuf (b. 1975, Indonesia) is a founding member of the Indonesian artist-activist collective, Taring Padi. The group – and Ucup's works – centre on Indonesian society and politics, seeking to address social injustices and the rights of minority or marginalised communities. The members of Taring Padi favour woodblock prints because of their ease of production and distribution, enabling the artists to swiftly disseminate their social messages through posters, in hopes of stirring collective awareness and thereby effecting social change.

(KH)

(Detail)

Southeast Asia

MALAYSIA

Nadiah Bamadhaj
Eric Chan
Chan Kok Hooi
Chang Yoong Chia
Chong Kim Chiew
Chong Siew Ying
Kow Leong Kiang
Shahrul Jamili Miskon
Justin Lim
Ahmad Fuad Osman
Phuan Thai Meng
Wong Hoy Cheong
Yee I-Lann
Zulkifli Yusoff

Nadiah Bamadhaj

Quiet Rooms

2009
Charcoal on paper
250 x 600 cm (installation size)

Singapore Art Museum
collection

All the components in this wall installation make up an attempt to visually articulate the multifaceted social conundrum in the desire and failure to biologically reproduce. *Quiet Rooms* is a personal departure from Nadiah Bamadhaj's previous work. This installation articulates the diary of a trying time in the life of a married couple attempting to start a family in Yogyakarta's *kampung* (village) context. Both the husband and wife are embroiled in their own personal emotional states. The Medusa-like reference on the male figure is borrowed from previous drawing series, where the snakes act as both writhing emotional demons and, at the same time, a guiding protective force. The idea of surveillance – connoting the uninvited interference of the village inhabitants into her married and personal life – is evoked through the two components on the left of the installation, a reference to a Javanese house with its haughty roof finish and a pair of loudhailers, both suburban elements that imply observation and declaration on the private lives of a *kampung*'s inhabitants. The *Mega Mendung* batik motif on the installation's far right is featured for its cloudy and turbulent implication, within the Javanese context. Finally, the inclusion of the text "doa yaa" ("you should pray") refers to the polite wishes of onlookers, or the aggravating mantra of expensive doctors who are unable to provide answers.

Nadiah Bamadhaj (b. 1968, Malaysia) was trained as a sculptor at the University of Canterbury in New Zealand. She is currently based in Indonesia and now produces work in media ranging from drawings to video and digital images.

(KH)

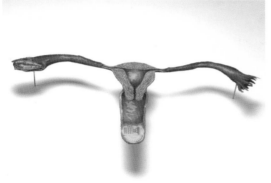

doa yaa

Eric Chan

Flourishing Peony

2009
Oil on linen
150 x 150 cm

Bougainvillea in Crimson

2009
Oil on linen
150 x 150 cm

Lemons & Blooms

2009
Oil on linen
150 x 150 cm

Summer Dahlia in Pink

2009
Oil on linen
136 x 200 cm

Singapore Art Museum
collection

Eric Chan captures the ephemeral by choosing to depict his subjects at their peak of life. Chan paints from images that he photographs, deliberately blurring the details of the object. His work questions the representation of reality and explores the transitory nature of mortality. By painting his subjects at their optimum, he captures a moment of their brief and fleeting life. Chan's voyeuristic photographic eye eliminates all details of the background to draw attention to the beauty of the subject while heightening a sense of alienation and forlornness. The haunting ethereal effect in Chan's work on this set of floral and fauna calls to mind early 18th century Romantic notions of looking towards nature as a way to self-actualisation and to the attainment of spiritual awareness.

Eric Chan (b. 1975, Malaysia) graduated with a Masters of Fine Arts from the Royal Melbourne Institute of Technology (RMIT) administered by LASALLE College of the Arts. Chan was awarded the Philip Morris ASEAN (Association of Southeast Asian Nations) Art Award Jurors' Choice Award in Singapore, 2001/2002. In 2005, he was selected for the Young Artist Programme (Printmaking Residency) by the Singapore Tyler Print Institute. He has held several solo exhibitions since 2000 in Singapore, Malaysia, Philippines, Hong Kong and Dubai.

(SC)

Right:
Flourishing Peony

Facing page:
Top left: **Bougainvillea in Crimson**
Top right: **Lemons & Blooms**
Bottom: **Summer Dahlia in Pink**

Chan Kok Hooi

***Musim Bunga Boleh
(The Season of 'Boleh'
Flower)***

2006–2007
Acrylic on canvas
171 x 209 cm

Singapore Art Museum
collection

Chan Kok Hooi's works are distinctive for their surrealistic and fantastical imagery, often dense with details that combine the banal with the bizarre, imbued with a fascination for the scatological. The motif of the car recurs, as does the theme of familial relations, notably that of mother and child, and this painting – which won the Jurors' Choice in the 2006 Malaysia Young Contemporaries Award – typifies many of those interests. In Chan's world, the quotidian serve to unsettle rather than reassure because they have been so dramatically transformed to a point of an eerie familiarity. Here, the car has morphed into an uncanny, grotesque being: a mother with demure kerchief and multiple breasts, suckling three similar mutant offspring, even as, feline-like, she licks her hand in an inexplicable gesture. In the background, elements of the child's nursery are depicted, but the soft toys too have become semi-automobiles. The title of the work makes reference to a popular slogan in Malaysia – "Malaysia Boleh!" ("Malaysia can do it!"), *boleh* being the Malay word for 'may be able to' or 'can'. The phrase reaffirms and extols triumphant achievement, but when seen in relation to this disconcerting outer space scene, ultimately hints at something darker.

Chan Kok Hooi (b. 1974, Penang, Malaysia) graduated from the Malaysian Institute of Art and is a recipient of the 2006-07 Freeman Foundation Asian Artists Fellowship at the Vermont Studio Centre in United States, the Mayor of Beppu Prize in the Beppu Asia Biennale of Contemporary Art, Japan (2005), the Jurors' Choice in the Philip Morris Malaysia–ASEAN (Association of Southeast Asian Nations) Art Awards (2003), as well as the 2004 and 2007 Malaysia Young Contemporary Award.

(JT)

Chang Yoong Chia

Maiden of the Ba Tree

2007
Oil on ceramic spoons, set of 35
Spoons 13.5 x 5 cm (each)
Installation dimensions variable

Singapore Art Museum
collection

Chang Yoong Chia's *Maiden of the Ba Tree* uses traditional porcelain spoons as objects that reflect his identity as a Malaysian of Chinese descent. As a material, porcelain was originally used amongst the affluent in the past, but today, porcelain utensils are widely used in common households. Adapting the art of traditional storytelling, Chang paints these spoons as if they were frames of a storyboard that takes the viewer on a journey. Here, *Maiden of the Ba Tree* invokes the typical and traditional morality stories found in Asian cultures. It narrates the lament of a mother who assumed that her son had deserted her. Incessantly worried and regretful, growing old and close to the point of death, she later received a revelation that it was she who had failed to acknowledge her son's existence when he was in fact there all along by her side.

Chang Yoong Chia (b. 1975, Malaysia) graduated from the Malaysia Institute of Art in 1996 with a Diploma of Fine Art in painting and since then, he has participated in numerous exhibitions in Malaysia and overseas including 'Art Multiple 2008' at Ke Center for Contemporary Arts, Shanghai, China (2008), 'Parallel Realities' at 3rd Fukuoka Asian Art Triennale, Japan (2005), '3 Young Contemporaries, 1997-2006' at Valentine Willie Fine Art, Malaysia (2006). He held his first solo exhibition at Reka Art Space, Malaysia (2004), where he debuted his 'Flora & Fauna' series. He was awarded the Rimbun Dahan Artist-in-Residency, Kuang, Malaysia, in 2006. Most recently, he participated in the JENESYS Program (2007/2008). Chang is also a founding member of the artists collective, Spacekraft.

(KH)

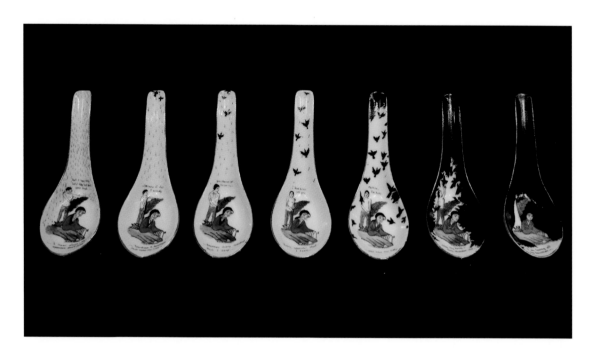

Chong Kim Chiew

The Stamp of Misreading

2005
Acrylic on paper
122 x 91 cm

The Picture of Misreading 2

2006
Acrylic on paper
110 x 91 cm

The Picture of Misreading 3

2006
Acrylic on paper
110 x 91 cm

The Picture of Misreading 4

2006
Acrylic on paper
110 x 91 cm

Singapore Art Museum
collection

In the series of paintings, Chong employs postage stamps from the colonial era as grounds for dialogues on legacies and identities against the realities of today. Once part of a powerful and flourishing British Empire, many important decisions made in imperial territories such as Malaysia have impacted its future, economic and political make-up. In this series, the place and significance of nobility is evoked trough the erasure of the faces of Sultans, the tropical landscape is represented as desolate, and the map of Britain is inserted in place of the Malaysian one; and in so doing, the artist reminds us of the roles colonial masters play in the formation of our destinies and identities.

Designs on stamps often depict the social, political and even geological landscape of its origins. As a result, they are often used in the study of history and anthropology. Chong's paintings explore and question the arbitrary demarcations of national borders and concepts of identity, belonging and nation-building.

Chong Kim Chiew was born in Malaysia in 1975 and graduated from Guangzhou Academy of Fine Art, China in 2001. While at the Academy, Chong majored in oil painting. Presently based in Kuala Lumpur, Malaysia, Chong's practice is inspired by principles of cartography, their powers of visual representation and how they orientate and inform our understanding of histories, identities and perception of territories.

(KH)

Left:
The Picture of Misreading 2

Centre:
The Picture of Misreading 3

Right:
The Picture of Misreading 4

The Stamp of Misreading

Chong Siew Ying

Pulse

2010
Charcoal and acrylic medium on
paper mounted canvas, 3 panels
201 x 411 cm (triptych)

Singapore Art Museum
collection

Pulse draws upon the idioms of Northern Song and the later Yuan landscape painting in Chinese art, through which the artist gives an impressionistic treatment to natural phenomena in the world. Physical elements of a landscape such as towering mountains, rolling hills and rivers of the countryside are done in faint and mellowed brushstrokes; the landscape is borne out of such subtle manouevres. The work's monochromatic palette continues the Eastern sensibilities of ink and wash, in that every brushstroke and mark must be charged with meaning, to produced harmonic compositions. In so doing, the work expresses the Chinese philosophy of the harmony of man and nature, and how a landscape painting need not depict external reality, but instead, represents the inner landscape of the mind. At the same time, *Pulse* also harnesses Western art techniques such as depth and single-point perspective, in addition to a cinematic vignette, the latter a result of the artist's fascination with old French films. A contrast to Chong's previous oil paintings, this new series of works blends both these stylistic and conceptual sensibilities of East and West, and shows Chong's development as an artist who is channelling both worlds into her work.

Chong Siew Ying (b. 1969, Kuala Lumpur, Malaysia) studied at the L'Atelier 63 Paris, France, from 1994 to 1996. Chong was awarded the Freeman artist in Residency at the Vermont Studio Centre in United States. In 2007, she participated in a few group exhibitions, in Galeri Nasional Indonesia, Jakarta, Indonesia and Rimbun Dahan Gallery, Kluang, Malaysia. In 2006, she had two solo shows in Galerie Deprez-Bellorget, Paris, France and in Valentine Willie Fine Art in Kuala Lumpur, Malaysia.

(DC)

Kow Leong Kiang

Untitled

2007
Oil on canvas
120 x 228.5 cm

Singapore Art Museum
collection

Political posters and buntings in the painting recall a scene from the 2004 Malaysian General Election in a sleepy village in the state of Kelantan. At every election since the country's independence in 1957, two major political parties, Barisan Nasional (National Front) and Parti Islam Semalaysia, PAS (Islamic Party of Malaysia) have fought tooth and nail to win Malay votes and the support of the Malay heartland, each claiming to represent either progress or moral superiority or both. Yet, till today, the typical Malay *kampong*, as depicted in the painting, remains quiet, underdeveloped and neglected. The manner in which life in the village is represented in this painting however defies its romantic allure and attempts to describe much of the opposite. In a sophisticated play of symbols, the two male protagonists represent the two opposing political parties – Barisan Nasional and PAS, the lone and innocent female represents the emerging Malaysian political party, Parti Keadilan Rakyat , PKR (People's Justice Party). The cat that sits in the midst of this 'triangle' represents the citizens who are uncertain about whom to choose.

Kow Leong Kiang (b. 1970, Malaysia) was awarded the Grand Prize at the Philip Morris ASEAN (Association of Southeast Asian Nations) Art Awards in 1998, and he received the Asian Artist Fellowship by the 11th Annual Freeman Foundation in the United States in 2004.

(KH)

Shahrul Jamili Miskon

Making Sense Can Sometimes Get Out of Hand

2009
Cement cast sculptures & acrylic sheets, set of 35
Installation dimensions variable

Singapore Art Museum collection

Shahrul Jamili is amongst a new breed of young, foreign-educated artists to have come onto the Malaysian contemporary art scene in recent times. As a devout Muslim, Shahrul's works are generally filled with meditations on religiosity and the responsibility of the self as a social entity. ***Making Sense Can Sometimes Get Out Of Hand***, for example, came about as a result of the artist's own contemplation over trying to make art that is at once utilitarian and meaningful for both artist and society. Turning to hand signs used by the deaf, Shahrul mimics this silent yet empowering method of communication through hand gestures to produce this witty installation of 35 hand sign alphabets that literally reads "making sense can sometimes get out of hand".

Shahrul Jamili Miskon (b. 1978, Malaysia) was first trained as ceramicist in Central Academy of Arts, Kuala Lumpur and later went on to graduate with a Bachelor in Fine Arts from the Surrey Institute of Arts, United Kingdom, in 2003.

(KH)

Shahrul Jamili Miskon

Making Sense Can Sometimes Get Out of Hand
2009
Cement cast sculptures & acrylic sheets, set of 35
Installation dimensions variable

Singapore Art Museum collection

Justin Lim

The Everlasting Gaze

2011
Acrylic and graphite on paper
and screen-print on Perspex
183 x 152.4 cm

Death and All His Friends

2011
Acrylic and graphite on paper
and screen-print on Perspex
183 x 152.4 cm

The Butcher

2011
Acrylic and graphite on paper
and screen-print on Perspex
183 x 152.4 cm

Singapore Art Museum
collection

The Everlasting Gaze, *Death and All His Friends*, *The Butcher* comprises of three paintings assembled as a triptych, and were made by Malaysian artist Justin Lim when he participated in a residency program in Vermont, USA.

Responding to the multi-cultural and multi-religious situation of his country of origin, Malaysia, where Islam is the predominant religion of its majority Malay population, Lim utilises potent and symbolic icons and visual elements that, if used inappropriately, could cause serious friction within the various communities there. For example, in *The Butcher*, the dog, an animal which is regarded as 'impure' by Muslims, is juxtaposed next to the butcher's hanging meat; in *Death and All His Friends*, icons from various religions mingle with symbols of life and death, such as food, the human skull, dead rodent and surgical apparatus. In *The Everlasting Gaze*, the Islamic requirement for modesty, as portrayed by the local women wearing the *hijab*, is depicted in contrast to westernised and laissez-faire attitudes towards female dress.

These paintings examine the price and place of religious zeal and the precarious balance for cultural harmony within a multicultural society. They solicit responses from a delicate demography that reflects the social environment of Lim's homeland, and the paintings ultimately serve to conjure up more questions than provide answers, and illustrate the potential for various social convulsions and the fragility of multi-cultural harmony.

Justin Lim (b. 1983, Malaysia) first completed a BA (Hons) in Fine Art (Painting) in 2005 before continuing his postgraduate studies under the Open University (UK) at LASALLE College of the Arts in Singapore. Also known as a percussionist recording and playing with various world music ensembles, Lim has exhibited in group and solo exhibitions in Singapore and Malaysia. In 2008, he participaed in the Malaysia-Australia Visual Artist Residency programme at Rimbun Dahan, Malaysia, and in 2011, was a fellow at the Asian Artist Fellowship programme at Vermont Studio in USA.

(KH)

From left: *The Everlasting Gaze*, *Death and All His Friends*, *The Butcher*

Ahmad Fuad Osman

Recollections of Long Lost Memories

2007
Slide projection, 71 slides
Edition 2/3
Dimensions variable

Gift of the Artist as part of the
Asia Pacific Breweries Foundation
Signature Art Prize 2008

Singapore Art Museum
collection

The occasion of the 50th anniversary of Malaysia's independence from British colonial rule prompted Ahmad Fuad Osman to revisit his country's history and to interrogate the slippery nature of memory and remembering. Working with archival photographs, the artist re-presents 71 images in the form of a slide projection, with a contemporary post-modern twist. Using computer digital manipulation, Fuad Osman has inserted a fictional character into each historical scene; at times, the figure appears to blend in unobtrusively, but in other instances, outrageously taking centre-stage. This bearded 'cool dude' persona – replete with sunglasses, rock n' roll shirt and other accoutrements of consumer culture – may be well at home in modern-day Malaysia, but is also a 'foreign intruder' in these historical scenes. His anachronistic intervention jolts the recognition of otherwise familiar images – the iconic photographs which have documented defining moments in Malaysian history.

With humour and irony, **Recollections** also probes a more serious question: because the generation of today has no direct experience of these momentous historical events, how can one truly relate to, 'recall' or ever know the past? The work thus suggests that, like tourists, most will only ever relate to history like visitors to a distant and exotic land.

Ahmad Fuad Osman (b. 1969, Malaysia) received his Bachelor of Fine Art from the University of Technology Mara, Selangor in 1991. Ahmad Fuad Osman has held several solo shows in Malaysia and has been the recipient of many art awards, such as the Jurors' Choice Award winner of the Phillip Morris Malaysia Art Award (2000 and 2003). He is a founding member of the MATAHATI artists collective in Malaysia.

(JT)

Phuan Thai Meng

The WE Project
2010
Mixed media installation
with 9 paintings and 2 videos,
photographs, nets, sweets and
other mixed media
Dimensions variable

Singapore Art Museum
collection

Led by artist Phuan Tai Meng, ***The WE Project*** is a satire on the inefficiencies in local governance on state initiated, urban re-development projects and local urban paradoxes. It represents a frustrated community (or "ordinary people", according to the artists) under such circumstances. As an example, a series of nine painted silhouettes named *Supermodels*, points fingers into blank spaces, representing the perceived apathetic attitudes of civil servants. Sweets, wrapped in colourful plastic are strewn around the installation, suggesting the temptations and bribes that corrupt a society. In another part of the installation, a painting features a screenshot of an online media file titled "Truly Malaysia, Asia", in the process of loading, giving the impression that society seems to be in an eternal limbo, even confused and never whole. The videos were created by the artists Wong Teck Leong and Liew Teck Leong.

Phuan Thai Meng (b. 1974, Malaysia) studied painting at the Malaysian Institute of Art, graduating in 1996. A co-founder of Rumah Air Panas collective in Malaysia, Phuan has mostly exhibited in Malaysia and Singapore.

(KH)

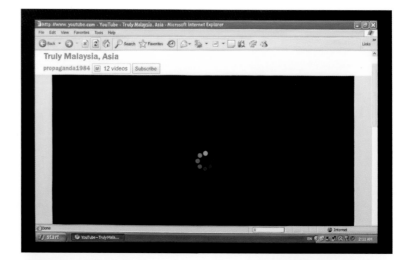

Top:
Truly Malaysia
2010
Oil on canvas
60 x 90 cm

Bottom:
Urban Landscape 2
2010
Oil on canvas
16 x 22 cm

Facing page:
Installation view

Wong Hoy Cheong

The Charity Lady (After Jean-Baptiste Greuze's La Dame de Charite, 1775)

2009
from 'Days of Our Lives' series
Digital print on archival coated
canvas, edition 3/15
83 x 112 cm

Reading (After Henri Fantin-Latour's Le Lecture, 1877)

2009
from 'Days of Our Lives' series
Digital print on archival coated
canvas, edition 5/15
83 x 112 cm

Singapore Art Museum
collection

Malaysian artist Wong Hoy Cheong creates 'local' adaptations of paintings by 18th and 19th century classical French painters that typically depict iconic moments in European culture and histories. By employing this strategy, readings are readjusted to a more familiar context, bringing the various domestic scenes and communities that are close to us today to the forefront.

The works bear layered iconographical meanings: the act of 'reading' references the position of Muslim women, while 'The Charity Lady', touches on the quality of filial piety within the Buddhist Burmese community. Both images speak of matters dear to us today, particularly that of religiosity, the decay of traditional family values and the state of geopolitical affairs. These issues are further reinforced by the imbued heightened sense of melodrama. This is a deliberate ploy, particularly when, the title of this series of works, 'Days of Our Lives', was borrowed from an American television soap opera series.

Today, such television series are arguably regarded as perpetuating undesirable infiltrations of foreign culture and perspectives onto a local audience, and these photographic works by Wong Hoy Cheong become a mirror for their personal reflection of their lives and times.

Wong Hoy Cheong (b. 1960, Malaysia) graduated in English Literature from Brandeis, Massachusetts, and holds a Masters in Education from Harvard University, Cambridge, and a Masters of Fine Arts from University of Massachusetts, Amherst, United States. Wong has participated in various international exhibitions, often representing Malaysia in platforms including the 3rd Liverpool Biennial, United Kingdom (2004), 2nd Guangzhou Triennial, China (2005) and 10th Lyon Biennale, France (2009).

(KH)

Top:
The Charity Lady (After Jean-Baptiste Greuze's La Dame de Charite, 1775)

Bottom:
Reading (After Henri Fantin-Latour's Le Lecture, 1877)

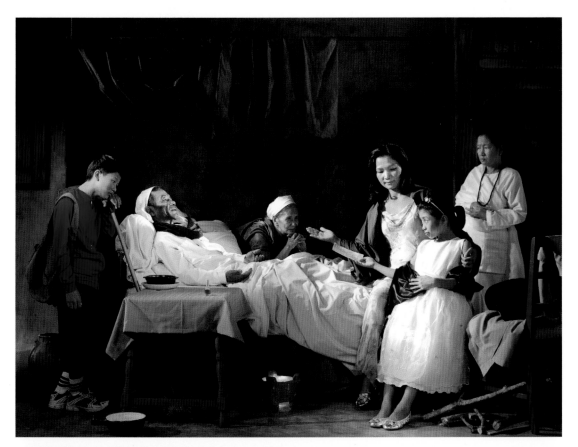

Yee I-Lann

Sulu Stories

2005
Kodak Endura paper, set of 13
prints, edition 2/8
Dimensions variable

Singapore Art Museum
collection

Through the use of archival images and digital manipulation, **Sulu Stories** makes a statement about contemporary identity from the vantage point of Sulu's historical roots. As a maritime region, Sulu's physical horizons are dominated by water and embody the fluid and enigmatic nature of identity and culture in the region. The Sulu zone marks the intersection of two polities – Malaysia and Indonesia. In this way, the seas of the region unite as much as they divide. The artist's experience in the Philippines demonstrates the contested state of an 'authentic' identity, subject to geographic placement; where she writes: "Whilst in the Philippines I was constantly asked, 'Where are you from?' 'I am from Sabah.' I would answer. 'Ah, a Filipina' was the common response. […] But I am welcomed with a knowing embrace, we know we are connected; our histories, fate and horizon line is shared."

Yee I-Lann (b. 1971, Malaysia) was born in Kota Kinabalu, Sabah in East Malaysia, to a New Zealand mother and Sino-Kadazan father. She grew up hearing stories of Sulu and identifies strongly as being Sabahan. She received her Bachelor of Arts in Visual Arts from the University of South Australia, Adelaide, in 1992 and later studied at the Central St Martin School of Arts in London. Working with various media including photography, installation and video, her practice seeks connections between physical landscapes and cultural identity. Yee I-Lann has exhibited widely in Malaysia and internationally; she represented Malaysia at the 3rd Asia Pacific Triennial of Contemporary Art, Brisbane, Australia (1999) and exhibited at ARCO, Madrid (2000).

(NW)

(Detail)

Zulkifli Yusoff

Koleksi Ibu
(Mother's Collection)

2010
Print and acrylic on canvas
mounted on plywood
243 x 243 cm

Singapore Art Museum
collection

Zulkifli Yusoff's **Koleksi Ibu** is a collage of images that recalls the artist's memories of his mother's personal collection of an assortment of paraphernalia. The artist's mother is represented in the work through heart-shaped motifs, scraps of 1960s radio, film and *Wanita* (Woman) magazines, as well as Muslim religious readers and multiple images of Bougainvillea flowers, brought together under the title **Koleksi Ibu**, which translates literally into "Mother's Collection".

In these various motifs, the artist's personal experience meets the objects' broader significance in Malaysian cultural history. For instance, the religious reader referenced in the collage is 'Tafsir al-Azhar', a 5-volume modern Qur'anic exegesis written by prominent Indonesian author, *ulema* (Muslim scholar) and politician, Hamka (1908-1981), which takes into account indigenous experience to explain verses of the Qur'an. Hamka, who was a reformer, also interpreted verses of the Qur'an in the context of his reform ideas in which *bid'ah* and superstition were the main targets. The national unity of Indonesia was another of Hamka's concerns that found its way into the pages of Tafsir al-Azhar. In the 1970s, books and religious texts such as Tafsir al-Azhar became widely used as reference material in Malaysian society. The artist's personal recollection of Tafsir al-Azhar in relation to his mother, references the broader common practice adopted by many mothers at the time, of educating children through Hamka's philosophy. Texts such as Hamka's Tafsir al-Azhar were hence significant in shaping the consciousness of post-independence Malaysian society. The artist juxtaposes these images of the religious reader, whose contents decoded religious teachings and applied them to everyday life, with images of things taken from daily life in the 1970s, such as the entertainment magazine clippings. In so doing, Yusoff recalls his own experience of being brought up on religious teachings amidst popular culture, and thereby, creates a visual layering of the domains of religion and popular culture in the 1970s.

Zulkifli Yusoff (b. 1962, Kedah, Malaysia) is a lecturer at the Sultan Idris Education University, Malaysia, and is regarded as one of the most cutting-edge artists of the contemporary Malaysian generation. His works are in various public collections including those of the Fukuoka Asian Art Museum as well as Hiroshima Art Museum, Japan.

(KH)

Southeast Asia

MYANMAR

Ko Aung
Tun Win Aung & Wah Nu
Nge Lay (Hlaing Yupar Wint)

Ko Aung

Human

2008–2009
Photo installation
Dimensions variable

Singapore Art Museum
collection

Human represents a gateway into the artist's mind and soul. In creating works that are largely ambiguous, Ko Aung's metaphoric references shed light on the conflicting states of human nature. The black-and-white installation consists of a six-panel, photo installation, along with flooring akin to the grids of a chessboard. Viewers approach the photo installation by physically stepping on the 'chessboard' grids. In this way, viewers become part of the artwork. Like the portraits in the photographs, viewers are similarly situated in a particular context. Confronted with giant-sized question marks, viewers are prompted to ponder upon the importance and complexity of our daily decision-making processes. Not unlike a game of chess, the game of life is explored in this series with their primary subjects, male and female, holding an object each, almost as if questioning its presumed utilitarian purpose.

Ko Aung (b. 1973, Myanmar) is a self-taught professional photographer. He has been working with photography since 1993 and has been exhibiting in several countries such as Myanmar, Cambodia, Thailand and Vietnam. Ko Aung currently lives and works in Yangon, Myanmar.

(NW)

Tun Win Aung & Wah Nu

Ke ke ke! Ke ba la ba!
2009–2010
Video installation with 2 DVDs, 1 black-and-white video with sound, projector, and 1 DVD in colour, with sound, edition 1/3
Dimensions variable
Videos duration 3:00 mins (loop) and 15:00 mins (loop)

Singapore Art Museum collection

The work consists of a 2-channel video installation: a black-and-white projection and a coloured video shown on a TV monitor, which are placed directly across from each other. The video tells of an old woman's wish to regain her memories and youthfulness; trapped in an aging and deteriorating body, she is further plagued with feelings of isolation due to the passing of her beloved husband. The projection on the other hand features a series of edited sequences taken from three black-and-white films from the 1970s. The projection makes visible the unfulfilled longings of the old lady in its depiction of images of freedom, youth, joy and hope. Through the confrontation of both video works, the viewer physically straddles both worlds through the negotiation of sight and sound. The title of the work comes from the repeated words of the old woman in the video. "Ke ke ke! Ke ba la ba!" means "It's all right! Please come!" in the Myanmar language.

Tun Win Aung (b. 1975, Myanmar) and Wah Nu (b. 1977, Myanmar) a husband and wife team, have participated in exhibitions that include 'Videozone V' at the 5th International Video Art Biennial, Tel Aviv, Israel (2010) and the 6th Asia Pacific Triennial of Contemporary Art, Brisbane, Australia (2009).

(NW)

MYANMAR

Nge Lay
(Hlaing Yupar Wint)

Me and Another Process

2008–2009
Photographs, set of 5
Unique edition
91.4 x 121.9 cm (each)

Singapore Art Museum
collection

In this series, the artist uses the simple combination of a torchlight and two hands to create the aesthetic for the work. Intimate, close-ups shots of the artist's hands are captured via the simple process of cupping her hands over a torchlight. The process is straightforward yet powerful in its targeted emphasis on the torchlight's source of luminosity. The close-up study of the artist's hands also lends a certain translucency to its texture, allowing her hands to almost glow with an amber red tone that is reminiscent of burning coal. This work is especially relevant in Myanmar's context, where blackouts have become daily occurrences. The torchlight is therefore a common household object that holds an intimate and familiar place in the hearts and minds of ordinary Myanmar citizens. *Me and Another Process* becomes the artist's way of overcoming existing obstacles. Light is seen here as a symbol of empowerment, which the artist holds in the palm of her hands.

     Nge Lay (b. 1979, Myanmar) received her Bachelor of Arts in painting at the University of Culture in Myanmar in 2003 and went on to do jewellery design in 2004. Her interest in photography emerged in 2007. She participated in 'Angsana: Southeast Asian Photographers Taking Flight' at 2902 Gallery in Singapore (2011) and 'Magnetic Power' at the Asian-Korea Contemporary Photography & Media Art Exhibition in Korea (2009).

(NW)

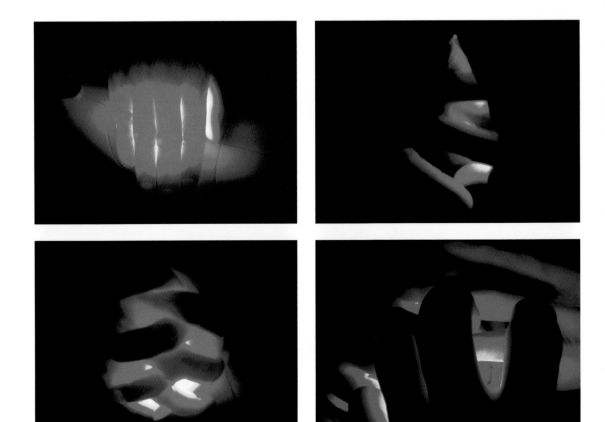

Nge Lay
(Hlaing Yupar Wint)

Imagination Sphere

2008–2009
Photo installation including
45 light boxes
Light boxes: 25.4 x 30.5 cm (each)
Installation dimensions variable

Singapore Art Museum
collection

MYANMAR

This photography light box installation involves two techniques of photography: digital photography and glass film negatives. In this work, Nge Lay uses a digital camera to capture the image of a glass film negative portrait of a deceased relative. Using a torchlight to represent luminosity amidst darkness, the artist plays with notions of light as a signifier for recollection, mediating between lost and found, known and unknown. In this way, Nge Lay questions the very essence of 'truthfulness' in photography through attempts to relate the familiar with the unfamiliar. Unidentifiable to the artist's family, the "mysterious relative" in the glass film negative explore ideas of lost memories and the limits of human recollection. The 'truthfulness' in photography perhaps lies in its ability to capture memories in a permanent form, adding more meaning and context to our understandings of a given past.

Nge Lay (b. 1979, Myanmar) received her Bachelor of Arts in painting at the University of Culture in Myanmar in 2003 and went on to do jewellery design in 2004. Her interest in photography emerged in 2007. She participated in 'Angsana: Southeast Asian Photographers Taking Flight' at 2902 Gallery in Singapore (2011) and 'Magnetic Power' at the Asian-Korea Contemporary Photography & Media Art Exhibition in Korea (2009).

(NW)

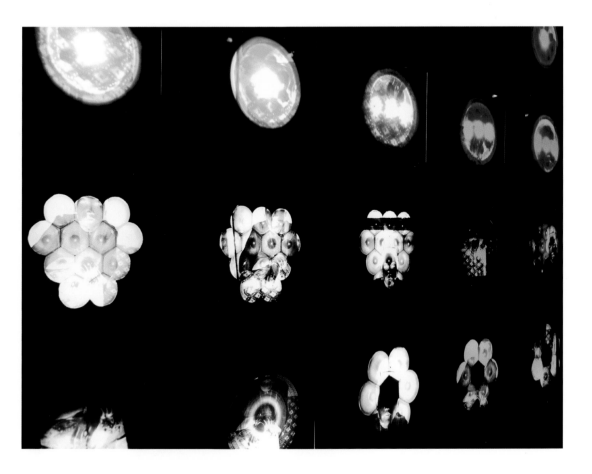

Nge Lay
(Hlaing Yupar Wint)

The Relevancy of Restricted Things

2010
Prints on archival paper
Set of 9 prints
90 x 120 cm (each)

Singapore Art Museum
collection

The Relevancy of Restricted Things is a tribute to the artist's father who passed away when she was a teenager. This body of work examines the role of a father – the male figurehead, central to the family unit. In Nge Lay's examination of Myanmar's paternalistic culture, she revisits the trauma of her younger years by attempting to understand the gender role of men and the significance of paternalism in Myanmar. The role of a father as a signifier of unity, authority and leadership is explored as Nge Lay dons her father's garb, and wears a mask that was moulded to resemble that of her father's face.

Nge Lay's sense of disorientation through the loss of her father mirrors what she noticed to be a similar sense of confusion and disarray in Myanmar society when General Aung San was assassinated in 1947. Widely acknowledged to be the voice of authority and de facto political leadership in post-independennce Myanmar, the turbulent period that followed after General Aung San's death continues to be plagued by a similar sense of loss and disruption, as was felt by Nge Lay when her father passed away.

Nge Lay (b. 1979, Myanmar) received her Bachelor of Arts in painting at the University of Culture in Myanmar in 2003 and went on to do jewellery design in 2004. Her interest in photography emerged in 2007. She participated in 'Angsana: Southeast Asian Photographers Taking Flight' at 2902 Gallery in Singapore (2011) and 'Magnetic Power' at the Asian-Korea Contemporary Photography & Media Art Exhibition in Korea (2009).

(NW)

Southeast Asia

THE PHILIPPINES

Poklong Anading
Alfredo & Isabel Aquilizan
Agnes Arellano
Felix Bacolor
Victor Balanon
Ringo Bunoan
Annie Cabigting
Frank Callaghan
Mariano Ching
Louie Cordero
Kiri Dalena
Leslie de Chavez
Patricia Eustaquio
Roberto Feleo

Nona Garcia
Geraldine Javier
Jose (Jojo) Legaspi
Renato Orara
Gary-Ross Pastrana
Alwin Reamillo
Norberto Roldan
Jose Tence Ruiz
Briccio Santos
Gerardo Tan
Rodel Tapaya
Steve Tirona
Wire Tuazon
Alvin Zafra

Poklong Anading

Anonymity

2005–2008
Photographic transparency,
light boxes, set of 9
155 x 122 cm (each)

Singapore Art Museum
collection

The subject of photographic street portraiture is often the unknown and anonymous individual – the 'man on the street' who is invariably nameless – and Poklong Anading's **Anonymity** continues in a similar vein, but here, the artist has also performed a sleight of hand and sight. Friends and strangers were asked to pose in front of the camera and by using a surprisingly simple device – a circular mirror held up to reflect the sun – their heads have 'exploded' in a halo of pure light. Anading's images capture the encounter with the Other, but with the subjects' faces 'hidden' by light, attention is directed to the background to try and get some sense of their identities and glean some information about the locale. In an elegant and ironic reversal of the camera's gaze, Anading has used light itself – the means by which vision and seeing are made possible – to 'blind' the viewer and conceal the identity of the subject.

Poklong Anading (b. 1975, Philippines) received his Bachelor of Fine Arts from the University of the Philippines, College of Fine Arts in 1999. He has held several solo shows in the Philippines, and has participated in group exhibitions in California, New York, Denmark, Hong Kong, as well as the 4th Gwangju Biennale, Korea (2002). Poklong Anading was conferred the Thirteen Artists Award in 2006 by the Cultural Center of the Philippines.

(JT)

Alfredo & Isabel Aquilizan

Wings

2009
Mixed media with used rubber
thongs, fibreglass and
stainless steel
Dimensions variable

Singapore Art Museum
collection

Comprising of hundreds of used rubber slippers, *Wings* is an extension and development from an earlier public artwork, *Flight*, which was commissioned and presented at the Singapore Biennale in 2008. Although the slippers are all of same make and type, closer examination reveals specific numerical markings and letters that differentiate each pair of thongs. This is a feature attributed to the fact that all these slippers were originally worn by inmates in a Singapore Correctional Facility, and then collected by the artists through the Yellow Ribbon project. Rather than being the traditional 'mark of the artist', each marking was made by an inmate as a means to identify which pair of slippers belonged to him while incarcerated in a place which allows precious few personal possessions.

In both manifestations of the work, the slippers – the very objects that kept the inmate literally and figuratively bound to the ground – undergo a transformation by taking flight (when perched on tall bamboo sticks, in *Flight*) and by becoming the means to fly (in *Wings*). When reconfigured into three massive sets of wings, the symbolism of hope and the metaphor of the redemptive journey are manifestly clear. However suggested here too are the notions of escape, and the cautionary tale found in the unhappy ending that befell the mythic figure of Daedalus, and his son, Icarus, who ignored advice and flew too close to the sun.

Alfredo Aquilizan (b. 1962, Philippines) and Isabel Aquilizan (b. 1965, Philippines) have participated in several biennales, including the Biennale of Sydney (2006), Singapore Biennale (2008) and the 50th Venice Biennale (2003). Themes of migration and re-location, community and family, home and belonging, identity and memory have featured prominently in the practice of the husband-and-wife team. They currently work and reside in Brisbane, Australia.

(JT)

(Detail)

Agnes Arellano

Haliya Bathing

1983
Coldcast marble and
crushed marble
Dimensions variable

Singapore Art Museum
collection

Haliya Bathing recounts the Philippine Bicol myth of the goddess Haliya who would descend to earth periodically to bathe in a sacred spring, but became ensnared in her mortal guise after a woodsman hid her clothes. Though the cause of her entrapment, the woodsman eventually won her love and the goddess is shown heavy with child. Half-immersed in the holy waters and with her face partially concealed, Haliya contemplates her fate and future at the very moment she is about to birth a demigod. The power of the goddess on the cusp of a momentous occasion is heightened by the concentric circles that radiate from her body like magnetic fields or energy waves; these lines raked into the crushed marble were inspired by Agnes Arellano's visit to the zen gardens in the Ryoan-ji Temple in Kyoto.

Haliya Bathing also contains an autobiographical reference, and the result is a work in which myth and reality, hope and fulfilment powerfully coincide. The sculpture marks the first time Arellano used live-casting and at the time when the work was 'conceived', the artist was hoping for a child. To mimic the condition, she built a mound of plasticine on top of her cast torso, superimposed her hand and livecast the piece once more. During the setup, Arellano placed Haliya on the ground to face the star Sirius and wished for a daughter; nine months later, Arellano gave birth to a girl.

Agnes Arellano (b. 1949, Philippines) is regarded as one of the Philippines' foremost sculptors, known for her surrealist and expressionist plaster, bronze and cold-cast marble sculptures. Charged with the sensuality of the human body, Arellano's works have also sought to assert the place and power of the feminine principle and female creative force, especially as a counter to the patriarchy of monotheistic religions. In an artistic career spanning three decades, Arellano has exhibited in Berlin, Fukuoka, Havana, Johannesburg, New York, Brisbane and Singapore.

(JT)

Felix Bacolor

Stormy Weather

2009
Installation with plastic wind
chimes and fans
Dimensions variable

Singapore Art Museum
collection

Comprising of some 1,000 multi-coloured wind chimes, ***Stormy Weather*** is at once a cacophony of colour and harmony of ethereal sounds. Made out of cheap, mass-produced plastic, the wind chimes are everyday objects that may ordinarily be regarded as kitsch decorations. However, hung slightly above eye level, the installation now invites the viewer to become immersed amongst the wind chimes, and the chimes soon reveal themselves as a dissimulation of translucent tiny birds, teeny horses and miniscule bells. A series of industrial fans sets the chimes in motion, and the rotating action of the fans causes the chimes' twinkling to crescendo and fall in synch with the movement of the air. ***Stormy Weather*** is a play upon the senses of sight, sound and physical sensation, and the work effects the transformation of the mundane into the magical, redirecting our attention to ordinary things that are oft ignored.

In less technologically advanced times, wind chimes were also used to ward off evil spirits and give forewarning about impending storms, and even a slight variation in melody and tone could signal the kind of weather to come. In ***Stormy Weather***, they have taken on a contemporary and ironic twist for the wind chimes are now sited in a gallery and the 'storm' is a comparatively tame affair – one manufactured by machines and powered by electricity. 'Real' storms however, continue to defy our expectations and despite the increasing use of sophisticated equipment to make weather forecasts today, the weather still manages to confound predictions and the installation touches upon humankind's troubled relationship with nature, especially in a time of climate change.

Felix Bacolor (b. 1967, Philippines) has worked across a wide range of media, including paintings, assemblages and installations, often working with readymade objects and revealing the poetic possibilities of found or factory-made materials. He graduated from the University of the Philippines College of Fine Arts with a Bachelor of Fine Art in Painting in 1989.

(JT)

Victor Balanon

Acid Test

2010
Pen, brush, correction fluid,
masking medium on canvas paper
66 x 51 cm

Desalination

2010
Pen, brush, correction fluid,
masking medium on canvas paper
66 x 51 cm

Our Lady of the Flowers

2010
Pen, brush, correction fluid,
masking medium on canvas paper
66 x 51 cm

Singapore Art Museum
collection

This suite of drawings begin with the photographic image but depart rapidly from the realistic and faithful representation of the subjects through Victor Balanon's distinctive technique in which abstraction, 'obstruction', elimination and extensive re-workings, coalesce on the picture surface. The works owe their source imagery to photography but assert their autonomy as drawings by calling upon old-fashioned draughtsmanship and an unusual mixture of drawing media (pen, brush, ink, correction fluid and masking medium), arriving at a sophisticated synthesis of mark-making and erasure.

Grotesque, disturbing and enigmatic, Balanon's worlds are inhabited by figures whose identities are under assault, for their faces are often masked or distorted, even 'melting' into utter disfigurement. A sense of confrontation is also evident in **Desalination** – a plate brimming with animal carcasses (or innards) is depicted front-down and close-up, proffering the viewer a meal that serves up unease in place of sustenance. In their oblique references to old-world Europe (the man in the café adorned in suit-and-tie in **Acid Test**), western art history (Marcel Duchamp in the persona of Rrose Selavy in **Our Lady of the Flowers**) and Catholicism (by referring to Duchamp as '**Our Lady of the Flowers**'), the images also reveal a certain cultural orientation towards the west that has been discernable in Philippine art and culture.

Victor Balanon (b. 1972, Ilocos Sur, Philippines) took up dental medicine at the University of the East, Philippines, in 1989, but left before completing his studies to pursue his interest in art and went on to become a self-taught artist. His drawing practice shows a resonance with the language of graphic novels and comics, combined with a distinctly 'dadaesque' humour and sensibility. Balanon also works as an illustrator and animator, and was part of the now-defunct Philippine artists collective, Surrounded By Water.

(JT)

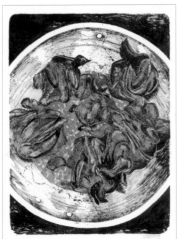

From left: *Acid Test*, *Desalination*, *Our Lady of the Flowers*

Ringo Bunoan

In The Same Breath

2003
C-prints, pillows and pillow cases
Dimensions variable

Singapore Art Museum
collection

Laying 12 photographs of tombstones upon soft pillows, Ringo Bunoan has created a poignant statement about the kind of final resting place we desire for loved ones. ***In the Same Breath*** is an intensely private memorial to the artist's late mother but also addresses universal concepts of remembrance, loss, sorrow and recovery. Marking the date of her mother's death, Bunoan found eight other people who passed away on the same day – 1 June 1986 – and the photographs of their gravestones are laid gently on the pillows. Arranged in the archetypal form of the circle, the pillows necessitate a kind of ritualised viewing for each of the images. Walking around the work, the viewer also encounters the headstone of Bunoan's mother four times, placed at the cardinal points of north, south, east and west. Strangers in life, nine individuals have been brought together on the day of their departure from the mortal world, leaving 'in the same breath'. The work is part of a series that Bunoan developed using pillows – personal objects associated with the bed and comfort – but placed in strange and awkward places, they have become tragic markers of loss and a constant search for belonging.

Ringo Bunoan (b. 1974, Philippines) is an artist, writer and curator. She graduated with Bachelor of Fine Arts in Art History from the University of the Philippines, College of Fine Arts in 1997. The founder and director of the independent art space, Big Sky Mind Artists' Projects Foundation (2001-2004), she continues to support young artists through exhibitions, exchanges and residencies. She received the Thirteen Artists Award by the Cultural Center of the Philippines in 2003.

(JT)

Annie Cabigting

On the Shelf, On the Shelf (After Michael Craig-Martin)

2010
Oil on canvas and painted bookshelf (wood and metal brackets)
20 x 30 cm (painting)

Singapore Art Museum collection

Contemporary artists have long and cannily referenced art history and the works of other art practitioners, and it is a mode adopted here by Annie Cabigting, in a work that based on the wall sculpture, *On the Shelf* (1971), by the British conceptualist artist Michael Craig-Martin. Here, Craig-Martin's original sculpture – comprising a tilted row of milk-bottles placed on a wooden shelf – has been depicted by Cabigting as a photo-realistic painting, and the painting is, in turn, then placed on a near-identical wooden shelf held up by metal brackets. Cabigting also riffs off Craig-Martin's penchant for literal and wry descriptive titles. However, by repeating the phrase "on the shelf", the work enacts and goes beyond simple verbatim repetition: it makes obvious the 'objecthood' of the painting (by underscoring its need for structural support), but also obviates the identification of the artwork (since there are two artworks contained in the one). It is thus repetition and deviation at once, and the result is a sophisticated mind-bending triple *mise-en-abyme*: of image, word/title, and of the artwork itself.

Annie Cabigting's (b. 1971, Philippines) conceptualist paintings may be seen as an attempt to grapple with some of the most fundamental questions in art: representation, originality, appropriation, art and reality, object and image. She majored in Painting at the University of the Philippines and was a recipient of the Ateneo Art Awards, Philippines, in 2005.

(JT)

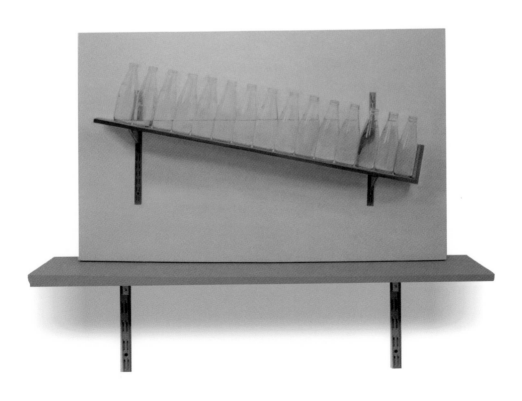

Frank Callaghan

101
2009
Archival inkjet print, edition 2/5
69 x 102 cm

308
2009
Archival inkjet print, edition 3/5
69 x 102 cm

501
2009
Archival inkjet print, edition 1/5
69 x 102 cm

Guarding the Woods
2008
Archival inkjet print, edition 3/5
41 x 61 cm

Clothes Lines
2008
Archival inkjet print, edition 2/5
41 x 61 cm

Singapore Art Museum
collection

Saturated with colour and awash in the unnatural glow of electrical lighting, these night-time images of shanty towns and low-cost housing suggest the effects of digital imaging or Photoshop manipulation. Yet they are 'natural' insofar that the works were shot using the existing and ambient light of the city, captured through a long exposure process and without additional lighting. Where the found object has become a staple in contemporary art, these photographs, in a conceptual shift, use 'found light' to illuminate and make visible the nocturnal world of Manila. In so doing, they also cast back to some of the foundational processes and concepts of photography, notably the role of light in seeing, vision and image capture.

The photographs are frank portrayals of Manila's prevalent poverty in the city, but they also sidestep overt social commentary on the problems associated with the Philippine urban environment, such as overcrowding or poor sanitation. Instead, concrete structures, metal grills and zinc hoarding take centre-stage – formally dominating the images with their sheer and unapologetic presence. These elements of make-shift construction and rapid urban development – so 'ugly' under the glare of the daytime sun – take on an uncanny beauty and otherworldly aesthetic through Callaghan's lens. Windows, interiors, doorways and even a 'forest clearing' in the urban jungle hum with night lighting; it is a world that pulses with electricity but is devoid of human presence. In a city (in)famous for its bustle, crowds and thronging noise, Callaghan has sought to, in his own words, capture its "unintentional beauty", a beauty revealed in such rare moments of stillness and quiet. Thus his poetic images render anew, images of Manila that are otherwise commonplace and unsightly in the bright light of the day.

Frank Callaghan (b. 1980, United Kingdom) was born in England and grew up in Baguio, Philippines. After studying finance and management at the Wharton School of Business, University of Pennsylvania, United States, he began pursuing photography full-time, and has held solo and group exhibitions in the Philippines and the region.

(JT)

Right: *101*

Facing page:
Top: *Guarding the Woods*
Bottom: *501*

Mariano Ching

Elephant Man

2011
Acrylic on canvas
150 x 150 cm

Four-Legged Woman

2011
Acrylic on canvas
183 x 152 cm

Singapore Art Museum
collection

In Mariano Ching's first foray into portraiture, the artist has chosen to focus on human oddities and 'freaks'. In **Elephant Man** and **Four-Legged Woman** – which are based on Charles Eisenmann's photographs of New York circus performers in the mid-1800s – the subjects' grotesque physical deformities compel a conflicted fascination. On the one hand, the figures appear imbued with a solemn dignity and the title of Ching's exhibition, 'Even Bad Days are Good' (2011), in which the paintings were shown, suggests a resilient hope and optimism in the face of despair, and the two figures also confront the viewer squarely in the eye. However Ching's sympathy towards the figures remains ambiguous for under his brush, two already physically distorted human beings have been metamorphosed into something even more bizarre: a fountain of exuberant colour gushes forth from the chest of the four-legged lady and a large cavity in the elephant man's head reveals strange rock formations. Where humans might otherwise inhabit a landscape or environment, Ching has performed a reversal, transforming the human body into a vessel or site for an interior world – and no less, an alien world with a life force of its own. In his world, the weird and wonderful collide and its only constant is mutation, but it is one that now arguably obscures, rather than reveals, the subjects' fraught humanity.

Mariano Ching's (b. 1971, Philippines) practice encompasses painting, photography and illustration. He received his Bachelor of Arts from the University of the Philippines and also studied printmaking at the Kyoto City University of Fine Arts. He is a recipient of the Monbusho Japanese Grant, and also received the Thirteen Artists Award from the Cultural Center of the Philippines in 2006.

(JT)

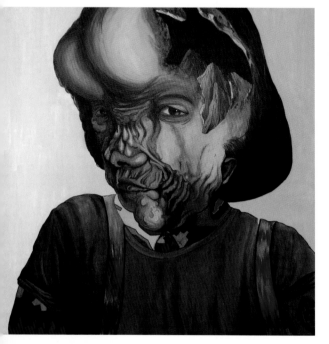

Elephant Man

Four-Legged Woman

Louie Cordero

MY WE

2011
Mixed media installation with a
videoke machine, video, paintings
and fibreglass sculptures
Dimensions variable

Singapore Art Museum
collection

Stepping into the lurid pink room filled with kitsch paintings and off-key singing from a 'videoke' machine, one is immediately reminded of a bad bar scene. In this Singapore Biennale 2011 commission work by Louie Cordero, the sensory overload is pushed even further by four life-size zombie sculptures that inhabit the ghastly scene, each 'suitably' replete with eyeballs dangling from sockets and wounds that ooze green and orange. Yet a macabre, if sly wit, also underpins the work: one zombie comes clad in a bright Hawaiian t-shirt, another bears a fried egg on his head. In Cordero's world, horror and humour go hand-in-(bloody)-hand.

Despite its otherworldly character, the installation takes as its starting point, a real-life social phenomenon in the Philippines: a spate of killings in the country associated with the singing of Frank Sinatra's classic song, "My Way". Karaoke is a popular and inexpensive pastime in the Philippines, and 5 pesos (15 Singapore cents) will buy enthusiasts a momentary respite from life's brutal grind. In a country which has felt the strong influence of American popular culture in music and film, Frank Sinatra has proved to be an enduring icon, and his bow-out song – with its mixture of bravado and machismo (its chorus refrain climaxes in the line, "I did it my way") – has garnered heated debates on how it should be sung. These disputes have occasionally resulted in violent fights and a number of deaths, as well as a growing urban legend surrounding the song.

Louie Cordero (b. 1978, Philippines) currently lives and works in Manila. He is a recipient of numerous awards including an Ateneo Art Award in 2004, and the Thirteen Artists Award from the Cultural Center of the Philippines in 2006, and his exhibitions include the Singapore Biennale in 2011.

(JT)

(Detail)

Louie Cordero

MY WE

2011
Mixed media installation with a
videoke machine, video, paintings
and fibreglass sculptures
Dimensions variable

Singapore Art Museum
collection

Louie Cordero

**Smash the Cool, No. 6
(Death by the Most Holistic
Influential Utopian Goals)**

2008
Mixed media with acrylic on
canvas, fibreglass sculpture, wood
162 x 101 x 155 cm

Singapore Art Museum
collection

Zombies, monsters and the living undead are the frequent inhabitants of Louie Cordero's paintings and sculptures. His works delight irrepressibly in blood and gore, and the shock value is more akin to that of a B-grade horror movie – more entertaining than genuinely terrifying – for Cordero's notion of horror is also shaped by an abiding fascination with pop and counter culture. Consequently, Cordero's visual imagery is an explosive fusion of tattoo motifs, rock music icons, underground comics and graphic art, as well as Catholic iconography, such as the sacred heart and crown of thorns. It is a distinctive graphic sensibility and syncretism also calls to mind the rich visual vernacular found on the colourful jeepneys that plough the streets of Manila.

Smash the Cool, No. 6 is an exception to the explicit depiction of guts and gore commonly found in Cordero's paintings and sculptures, but the work is a scene of 'violence' nonetheless. A heavy metal rock fan – tattooed and garbed in requisite black t-shirt with band logo – lies dead on the floor, his body cut in two by a painting. Bifurcation is a formal composition device frequently used by Cordero, as in this case when the painting is symmetrically divided like a Rorschach inkblot, and the painting itself (as physical object) is also the victim's cause of death, having severed the teenager squarely in half across the torso. In more ways than one, the work seems to say that Art that has killed the young man – or as Cordero suggests in the work's deliberately rambling title – ideals and aspirations are also to blame.

Louie Cordero (b. 1978, Philippines) currently lives and works in Manila. He is a recipient of numerous awards including the Ateneo Art Award in 2004, and the Thirteen Artists Award from the Cultural Center of the Philippines in 2006, and his exhibitions include the Singapore Biennale in 2011.

(JT)

Kiri Dalena

Erased Slogans
2008
Video projection on desk
62 x 92 x 78 cm (table),
41 x 41 x 61 cm (stool)

Red Book of Slogans
2008
Hardcover red book with
wood arm rest
9 x 6 x 8 cm (red book),
56 x 23 x 2 cm (wood arm rest)

Singapore Art Museum
collection

Protest art in the Philippines came to the fore during the period of Marcos rule and Kiri Dalena's works carry on the spirit of social realist art, while provoking questions about the oft-ambiguous place of the artist in such encounters with history. In these two companion pieces, Dalena has consciously assumed the twin roles of social activist and state censor. Too young to have been at the historic events herself, Dalena delved into the Lopez Museum library archives and collected over a hundred journalistic photographs of scenes of mass protest and public demonstration during the Martial Law years of 1972-1981. Now projected onto an old desk, the steady stream of images offer a documentary-style presentation of those tumultuous years and the trauma of state brutality is replayed, but it is staged upon the memories of others – on 'borrowed memories'. Moreover, in these photographs of activists brandishing placards, banners and streamers, there is something else amiss: all the signs are blank, oddly devoid of a single word of urgent protest and propaganda. Replicating the actions of government authorities, Dalena 'censored' all the slogans in the photographs and those words of dissent were then compiled into the adjoining artwork, the ***Red Book of Slogans***. With one slogan per page, the 700-page book is dense with 'protest', and its form is akin to a thick communist red book or the bible.

Kiri Dalena (b. 1975, Philippines) graduated with a degree in human ecology from the University of the Philippines, Los Banos, and then furthered her studies in documentary filmmaking and 16 mm cinematography at the Mowelfund Film Institute in Quezon City, Philippines. Her works often aim to highlight the social issues faced by the ordinary Filipinos and marginalised groups, such as the effects of militarisation on farming and indigenous communities.

(JT)

Right:
Red Book of Slogans

Facing page:
Top: Video still from
Erased Slogans
Bottom: Installation view of
Erased Slogans

Leslie de Chavez

Governators

2010
Mixed media with resin, wood,
steel, nylon rope
35 x 19 x 15 cm (figures each),
35 x 21 x 244 cm (swing)

Singapore Art Museum
collection

The intertwining of art and politics has a long history in the art of the Philippines. Social realist art, in particular, was instrumental during Martial Law years (1972-1981) in articulating the abuses of the political system and the hardships endured by the average person. Growing up in the post-Marcos period, Leslie de Chavez continues to employ the tools of symbolism and allegory to critique a system that does not seem to have changed despite a succession of leaders and elected officials.

Governators comprises of 23 corpulent, hooded figures on a swing. Its title, a conflation of the words 'governor' and the 'terminator', is phonetically evocative, suggesting that those who hold office are merciless, unfeeling beings with scant regard for ordinary people. Dressed in the Filipino men's national dress of Barong Tagalog, it points to politicians who regard themselves as respectable, but their hooded faces and blood on their hands give away their true selves as robbers and abusers of the system. Seated back-to-back and shoulder-to-shoulder, the *governators* form an impenetrable pack of brothers whose chief interest is to protect themselves and one another, gesturing to the cronyism that is often rife in world of politics. There is obvious reference to the 'seat of government', but in de Chavez's use of a swing – which associated with play and the trapeze – it suggests that the *governators* are perpetrators in a political system that is, essentially, a circus.

Leslie de Chavez (b. 1978, Philippines) graduated from the University of the Philippines Fine Arts program in 1999; since then, he has held several solo exhibitions in the Philippines, China, Korea and Switzerland. His finely executed works confront the prevalence of problems like the misuse of power in politics and religion, as well as issues in contemporary society, such as the degradation of the environment.

(JT)

Patricia Eustaquio

Horns
(Deer, Columbine, Paine)

2008
Oil on canvas and oil on linen
122 x 488 cm (triptych)

Singapore Art Museum
collection

Horns (Deer, Columbine, Paine) is a conceptually driven exploration about the formal and experimental processes of composition. It turns upon the play of visual and phonetic puns, and probes the relationship between word, sound and image. Riffs, echoes and resonances traverse aural and visual realms, and the work delights in the transformations and translations that occur between the sense of sight and sound.

The motif of horns – and death – runs through the three paintings, but each of the 'horned' subjects also carries its own specific connotations. The severed deer's head alludes to the triumphant deer hunt, a familiar subject in the western art canon. The central panel is dominated by a Columbine flower, which once signified melancholia but in more recent times, the word conjures up the horrific bloodshed of the American school massacre in 1999. The dead tree evokes Roxy Paine, the American artist known for making tree sculptures of stainless steel, but the homonym also connotes hurt and suffering. Juxtaposing different genres, the triptych performs like a postmodern musical composition, but the individual images also come together visually, composed like the stanzas of a poem.

Patricia Eustaquio (b. 1977, Cebu) is a magna cum laude graduate of the University of the Philippines, College of Fine Arts. With a background in fashion and design, Eustaquio is versatile across a range of media and injects her works with elements of design processes and materials. In 2009, she was the winner of the Ateneo Art Awards, Philippines, as well as the recipient of the Thirteen Artists Awards, conferred by the Cultural Center of the Philippines.

(JT)

Roberto Feleo

Ambaristo in Life

2008
Mixed media: acrylic on sawdust
on wood carving, vitrine
42 x 29 x 29 cm

Ang Pinteng ni Ambaristo
(Ambaristo in Death)

2007
Mixed media: acrylic on sawdust
on wood carving, vitrine
46 x 30 x 30 cm

Los Soldados de Espiritu
Santo (Soldiers of the
Holy Spirit)

2007
Mixed media: acrylic on sawdust
on wood carving, vitrine
35 x 27.5 x 27.5 cm

Kathang Isip na Larawan
ni Esteban Villanueva at
Ang Kanyang mga Tularan
(Fictional Portrait of
Esteban Villanueva and His
Models)

2008
Mixed media: acrylic on sawdust
on wood carving, vitrine
47 x 28.5 x 28.5 cm

Auto Retrato

2008
Mixed media: acrylic on sawdust
on wood carving, vitrine
57.5 x 36 x 36 cm

Singapore Art Museum
collection

In the Philippines, the *virinas* were traditionally glass bell jars that held holy figures and *santos* – often exquisitely carved from ivory – as well as scenes from the Biblical narrative for the purposes of religious devotion. In this series of contemporary *virinas* (vitrine) works, Feleo turns instead to an episode in Philippine history: the Basi Revolt of 1807, a rebellion sparked by the Spanish monopoly of *basi* (sugarcane) wine. While they originate from a singular historical episode, the works also speak of multiple stories: of history as it slides into myth and legend, of religious and indigenous beliefs, and a tale of Philippine art history itself.

One of the central figures is that of Pedro Ambaristo, a leader of the Basi Revolt. In life, he is portrayed heroically astride a water buffalo and with guns ablaze. However, he was killed by the Spanish, who believed that they were soldiers of the Holy Spirit, aided by their Christian God in a battle with consequences beyond the mortal world. In death, the Ambaristo returns as the terrifying *pinteng*, for in Ifugao myth, a valorous warrior who dies in battle is rewarded with a head of fire in the afterlife to strike fear into the hearts of his enemies. Importantly, the Basi uprising was first captured by the Filipino artist Esteban Villanueva in 1821. Commissioned by the Spanish as a triumphant record of their victory over the native fighters, the 14 oil panels by Villanueva also documented the brutality of the army. Today, the paintings by Villanueva are possibly the oldest surviving paintings of a secular subject in the Philippines, but of that early artist, almost nothing is known. Thus while the enigmatic Villanueva is portrayed towering over his models, it is a 'fictional portrait' for this portrait is not based on facial likeness but is conceived entirely from Feleo's imagination.

Of note as well is the final vitrine, **Auto Retrato** – Spanish for 'self portrait' – which depicts Feleo holding the tools of his craft and kneeling before a shaman figure. Against the context of the Basi Revolt and the imaging of Esteban Villanueva, the *virinas* proffer a complex portrait of the relations between the self, spiritual belief, the place of art, and strategies of resistance against political and religious dominion.

Roberto Feleo (b. 1954, Manila) studied history at the University of the Philippines and graduated from the Philippines Women's University with a degree in fine arts. The artist's sculptures speak of hybridity, by way of form and material, as a way of manifesting the diverse origins and manifold influences that comprise modern-day Philippine identity and culture. Feleo is known for his use of *pinalakpak*, a sculptural compound made of sawdust, water and glue. He has held several solo exhibitions in the Philippines and abroad, and his works are in the collections of the Fukuoka Asian Art Museum, Japan, and the National Museum of the Philippines.

(JT)

Clockwise from top left:

Auto Retrato

Ambaristo in Life

Ang Pinteng ni Ambaristo (Ambaristo in Death)

Los Soldados de Espiritu Santo (Soldiers of the Holy Spirit)
Kathang Isip na Larawan ni Esteban Villanueva at Ang Kanyang mga Tularan
(Fictional Portrait of Esteban Villanueva and His Models)

Roberto Feleo

Ang Retablo ng Bantaoay (The Retablo of Bantaoay)

2007
Planked marine plywood covered
with sawdust and eggshell dust
Installation size:
508 x 411 x 17 cm

Singapore Art Museum
collection

Starting from a specific historical episode in the Philippines, the **Retablo** swiftly extends into other narratives such as indigenous myth, religion and art history. It also speaks of feudal societal structures and the quandary of the common worker. Unlike the traditional Christian altarpiece that points upwards, Feleo's **Retablo** is always presented as an inverted triangle, indicative of the artist's interest to upturn colonial power structures and destabilise conventional hierarchies.

The central story relates to the Basi Revolt of 1807, a local uprising against the Spanish because of their heavy regulation of *basi* (sugarcane) wine, which was crucial for the natives' communion with the spirit world. Led with the battle cry "Kill all the lords and ladies", the insurrection may be regarded as one of many rebellions against Spanish colonial rule that culminated in a nationalist movement some 80 years later.

The Church's involvement in the affair is reflected in the figure of the sugarcane-faced friar, which is inverted. A number of other Christian references figure in the **Retablo**, such as the character of Longinus, the Roman centurion who supposedly pierced the side of Jesus Christ while he was on the cross. The Kristong Pango, the pug-nosed Christ, reflects the actions of Filipino revolutionaries who destroyed or defaced colonial images during the revolt. These acts of iconoclasm were potent symbolic gestures to assume domination over the coloniser, and in this instance, a radical move that would also 'switch' Jesus Christ to align on the side of the natives.

Other characters of interest include the *pinteng*. In Ifugao myth, the pinteng is the valorous warrior who falls in battle, but in death, he is rewarded with a head of fire to strike fear into his enemies' hearts. Both the fearsome warrior and a protector of women and children, the *pinteng* is, for the artist, a figure which stands as an alternative to western dichotomies of good/evil and angels/demons. Maguayen, the Manunggul boatman to the afterlife, is represented with coins on his eyes and lizards on his shoulder, which symbolise the horizon that separates this mortal life and the next one. At the base of the inverted triangle is the everyday worker who both holds up and labours beneath the feudal system of land ownership.

Roberto Feleo (b. 1954, Manila) studied history at the University of the Philippines and graduated from the Philippines Women's University with a degree in fine arts. The artist's sculptures speak of hybridity, by way of form and material, as a way of manifesting the diverse origins and manifold influences that comprise modern-day Philippine identity and culture. Feleo is known for his use of *pinalakpak*, a sculptural compound made of sawdust, water and glue. He has held several solo exhibitions in the Philippines and abroad, and his works are in the collections of the Fukuoka Asian Art Museum, Japan, and the National Museum of the Philippines.

(JT)

Nona Garcia

Fall Leaves After Leaves Fall

2010
Oil on canvas
274 x 547 cm

Singapore Art Museum
collection

In her most ambitious work to-date, Nona Garcia grapples with the seduction of scale, and amplifies a wrecked car to epic proportions. In this monumental painting, the horror of the subject is rendered remote, and the crash becomes the site of a formal and conceptual exercise for the moment of the collision is deliberately aestheticised in monochromatic greys and blacks, imbued with a strange, uncanny beauty that derives from Garcia's hyperrealist mode of painting. Visually and conceptually, the work turns upon the notion of mirroring – both in terms of its Rorschach-like symmetrical composition and its palindrome title – and as a result, the car simultaneously becomes the cause and consequence of its own collision.

Nona Garcia (b. 1978, the Philippines) graduated from the University of the Philippines with a Bachelor of Fine Arts in Painting. In 2000, she was both a recipient of the Thirteen Artists Award, Cultural Centre of the Philippines, and a Jurors' Choice winner of the Philip Morris ASEAN (Association of Southeast Asian Nations) Art Award.

(JT)

Geraldine Javier

*Ella Amo'
Apasionadamente y Fue
Correspondida (For She
Loved Fiercely, and She is
Well-loved)*

2010
Oil on canvas, with framed insets
of embroidery with
preserved butterflies
229 x 160 cm

Singapore Art Museum
collection

Initially trained as a nurse, Filipino artist Geraldine Javier brings a methodical approach to her paintings, which are often characterised by a sombre, melancholic air and mesmerising beauty. Echoing a leitmotif that recurs in her practice, ***Ella Amo' Apasionadamente y Fue Correspondida*** reveals a fascination with beauty and death, and life's transience is explored in this painting which contains ten framed cushions embroidered with flowers or caterpillars, each holding a preserved butterfly.

The central subject of ***Ella Amo' Apasionadamente y Fue Correspondida*** ostensibly portrays the Mexican artist Frida Kahlo, who produced over 50 self-portraits that captured and dramatised the severe physical and emotional pain she endured in life – personal traumas played out on canvas before a 'voyeuristic' audience. Intimately linked to the subject of the self-portrait, Kahlo has stood out in art history as the one female artist who was the most instrumental in creating her own iconic image, in physical likeness and as a symbol of 'female suffering'. It was passion and pain intertwined that characterised much of Kahlo's personal and artistic life, and arguably one that Javier herself identifies with, and romanticises. Many of Javier's paintings depict young girls or women (occasionally in poses of rigor mortis), which may be seen as Javier's projection of the self: self-portraits of sorts that explore the difficult relationship that she has with an aggressive art market. Now, centred amidst a profusion of flowers, Kahlo / Javier averts her gaze from the public and stands immortal as an icon of beauty and sorrow – a queen in a twilight paradise.

Geraldine Javier (b. 1970, Philippines) graduated from the University of the Philippines with a Bachelor of Fine Arts in 1997. Since the mid-1990s, Javier has been exhibiting widely in the region and has held several solo shows in the Philippines, as well as in group shows in the region. She participated in the Prague Biennale in 2009, and was awarded the Thirteen Artists Award, from the Cultural Center of the Philippines, in 2003.

(JT)

Jose (Jojo) Legaspi

Untitled

2009
Pastel on paper
100 x 70cm

Untitled

2009
Pastel on paper
100 x 70cm

Untitled

2009
Pastel on paper
100 x 70cm

Untitled

2009
Pastel on paper
100 x 70cm

Singapore Art Museum
collection

Jose Legaspi plumbs the depths of the human psyche with his drawings that explore the darker sides of human psychological and emotional states – psychosis, neurosis and obsession. His violent, scatological subjects may appear unabashedly graphic or even provocative, but for artist, they shock only because they visually articulate that which is unsaid or repressed. Locating the human body as the ultimate site of pain, the images unnerve and unsettle. However rather than intending to provoke simple outrage, these expressions of anguish are, in actuality, located within one of the oldest traditions in art – one in which pain and suffering have been the wellsprings from which art, and even beauty, come forth, such as images of Christ's agonies on the cross.

Executed at a painstakingly slow pace and with a meticulous attention to anatomical detail that reveals Legaspi's training in biology and zoology, the works' unexpected delicacy possess a disquieting beauty that seems at odds with their subject matter. They turn upon an exquisite tensive point between attraction and repulsion, an aesthetic tension further played out by Legaspi's use of colour in these four drawings, which are both minimalist (being mostly monochromatic) and rich (through the specific and precise points of colour, like the crimson red fingernails or midnight blue shorts).

Deeply autobiographical, Legaspi's works draw upon real-life events during a difficult childhood – such as the mistreatment of his mother by other family members – as well as the difficulties of living openly with his sexual orientation in a predominantly religious society. Although the works expose human cruelty, hypocrisy and its blatant indifference, Legaspi is no misanthrope for the drawings also reveal tenderness, sorrow and love. In so doing, Legaspi's portraits of family, friends and the self give moving expression to the extremes and breadth of the human condition.

Jose (Jojo) Legaspi (b. 1959, Philippines) received a Bachelor of Science in Zoology as well as a Master of Science in Biological Science, both from the University of Santo Tomas, Manila, and also studied at the College of Fine arts at the University of the Philippines. He has exhibited at several large-scale platforms like the 4th Asia Pacific Triennial of Contemporary Art, Brisbane, Australia (2002), and the 1st Singapore Biennale (2006), as well as in many solo exhibitions in Australia, Hong Kong, the Philippines and United States.

(JT)

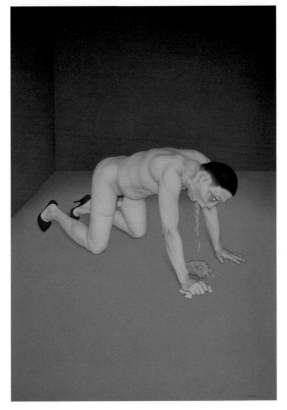

Renato Orara

Bookwork: NIV Compact Thinline Bible (page 403)

2008
Ballpoint ink drawing on paper
23 x 12 x 3 cm (opened size),
17 x 12 x 2 cm (closed size)

Singapore Art Museum
collection

In **Bookwork: NIV Compact Thinline Bible (page 403)**, Orara uses a ballpoint pen to portray a lamb chop in the holy book, an image which can be read as alluding to Jesus as the sacrificial lamb in the Biblical narrative. Rendered in slow and painstaking detail, the lamb chop draws the viewer in with its compelling, visceral beauty. The rawness of the subject appears to reiterate the blood sacrifice made by Jesus Christ and by encouraging a contemplative kind of viewing, the drawing also evokes the religious art of the past. Set in the Old Testament Book of Job, the first inclination is to interpret it as a herald of Christ's coming in the New Testament, but the artist did not deliberately choose the image for any specific connotations in relation to its textual base – the book page – which the drawing is rendered on. An outgrowth of Orara's monumental series, 'Ten Thousand Things That Breathe', the 'Bookworks' are his attempts to negotiate a space between the privacy of drawing and the need to exhibit as a visual artist. By situating the drawing in a book, the artwork can be intensely private and hidden (when the book is closed), or publicly accessible (when the book is open and displayed). It thus hovers between tensions of many kinds: the sacred and profane, secrecy and openness, the symbolic and literal.

Renato Orara (b. 1961, Philippines), an artist and an educator, lives and works in New York. He has been actively participating in solo and group exhibitions in the United States, Europe and the Philippines. In 2005, he was a recipient of the Pollock-Krasner Foundation Fellowship Grant.

(JT)

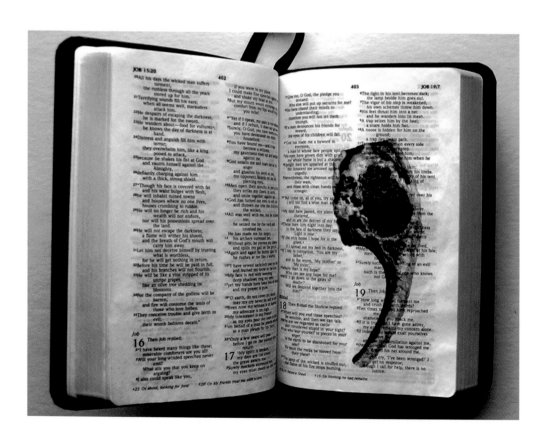

Gary-Ross Pastrana

1-36

2008
Collage on index cards
113 x 82.7 cm

89-124

2008
Collage on index cards
113 x 82.7 cm

Singapore Art Museum
collection

1-36 and *89-124* act as counter-points, different in character but belonging to the same series of collages. Meticulous and intimate the collages appear to be the products of deft skill and careful formal composition, exacting craft and workmanship. Indeed they are, but the notion of 'failure' also underpins the collages' conceptual foundations – but it is a 'failure' which has been rehabilitated and transformed to become the origination for new works.

In the Philippines, the medium of collage has been associated with the conceptualist artist and pioneering figure of Roberto Chabet. However, Gary-Ross Pastrana's collages emerged from an initial dissatisfaction with a Chabet assignment in school, and similarly, his use of index cards came about from a flipbook assignment in school, which he deemed as a failure then. Returning to the use of collage later on and outside the confines of a school assignment, Pastrana consciously used his freedom to set his own restrictions for the exercise. Using only 'rejects' – torn and cut paper from a 2003 exhibition – Gary-Ross Pastrana recycled and reworked discarded pieces into material for 'fresh' works five years on. The collages may be read as oscillations between repetition and variation, chance and control, accident and design, and deliberately eschew narrative or sequence, for the numberings do not reflect the chronological order in which the individual pieces were made.

Gary-Ross Pastrana (b. 1977, Manila, Philippines) is an artist and a curator. He graduated with a Bachelor of Fine Arts in Painting from the University of the Philippines. He exhibited in 'The Ungovernables', the New Museum Triennial, New York (2012), and also participated in the Busan Biennale, Korea (2008). Gary-Ross Pastrana was also a co-founder of the independent and now-defunct art space, Future Prospects.

(JT)

1-36

89-124

Gary-Ross Pastrana
in collaboration with Zoe Dulay

Echolalia

2009

19 mixed media objects: sawdust, glue, resin, ashfall, fake snow, lightening soap, text, Bulul figurine, musical box mechanism, wood, wood filler and others, and a collection of short stories by Zoe Dulay
Dimensions variable

Singapore Art Museum collection

Each of the objects in ***Echolalia*** is a 'relic' from a particular story but collectively, they also play with the idea of echoes and reverberations, repetition and variation, dubious beginnings and alternate endings, and in so doing, this assortment of curios proffers an unlikely tale about the life 'lived' by stories and objects.

Working in collaboration with writer Zoe Dulay, Gary-Ross Pastrana collected stories from myriad sources and re-imagined these narratives back into ordinary life. Taking after the title headings of a number of Dulay's stories, such as "Frame", "Keys", "Rung" and "Tongue", Gary-Ross Pastrana's list of 'mundane' objects includes a picture frame, keys, a rung, a tongue scraper, as well as other items like needle and thread, and a cassette tape. However, the cassette turns out to be made of sawdust and glue, the 'wooden rung' is sculpted out of wood filler, and the delicate thread in a needle is comprised of eraser 'dust' from a vigorously rubbed book page. Others are made from similarly unlikely materials, such as ashfall from Mt. Pinatubo, 'found' clay, and lightening soap. Deemed as discards, debris or just insignificant, these materials have been re-fashioned and sculpted into 19 not-so-common objects. Adding a twist to the 'original' story, Gary-Ross Pastrana's objects are ultimately more simulacrum than genuine: they replicate likeness to the 'real thing' but each is an ingenious counterfeit, a little fiction and a refracted copy of reality.

Gary-Ross Pastrana (b. 1977, Manila, Philippines) is an artist and a curator. He graduated with a Bachelor of Fine Arts in Painting from the University of the Philippines. He exhibited in 'The Ungovernables', the New Museum Triennial, New York (2012), and also participated in the Busan Biennale, Korea (2008). Gary-Ross Pastrana was also a co-founder of the independent and now-defunct art space, Future Prospects.

(JT)

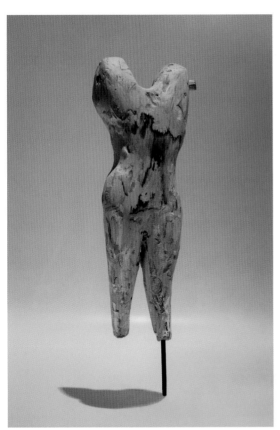

Alwin Reamillo

in collaboration with
Jaime Pastorfide,
Tranquilino Tosio Jr. &
Rabino Sabas Jr.

Mang Emo + Mag-himo
Grand Piano Project
(3ʳᵈ Movement: Manila-
Fremantle-Singapore)

2007–2009
Mixed media installation with
found Wittemberg grand piano
iron frame, structural wooden
backpost, Watanabe musical
instrument parts and video
Installation dimensions variable

Singapore Art Museum
collection

The ***Mang Emo + Mag-himo Grand Piano Project*** is a work of many stories and journeys. The artist descends from a well-known piano-making family in the Philippines, and following the closure of the family business, Reamillo went back in search of the lost techniques and now-forgotten methods that his late father had developed. Collaborating with the former factory craftsmen, he has produced a work which is both a 'social sculpture' and functioning musical instrument.

A parlour grand piano occupies the central space, and on the surrounding walls are 'wings' of varying sizes – wooden sculptures which take their symmetrical form from the shape of the piano lid and hinged in the middle so they resemble butterfly wings. Adorned on various points on the piano and 'wings' are images associated with travel and migration, such as the whale and cartographic markings, while others are more personal, like the face of Reamillo's father, half-concealed under the piano strings.

Of note is the work's title which is a combination and phonetic play of 'Mang Emo' ('Mang' suggesting uncle or an affectionate way of addressing a senior figure, 'Emo' being his father's nickname) and 'Mag-himo' is a waray word meaning 'to make, to create, to craft'. On one level, the work is a conceptual and moving portrait in commemoration of Reamillo's father, but the project also draws heavily upon the Filipino notion of *bayanihan* (community solidarity) because it was realised through the spirit of collaboration and support of many individuals.

Alwin Reamillo (b. 1964, Manila, Philippines) has been based in Western Australia since 1995. He studied painting at the University of the Philippines, College of Fine Arts, Philippines. A versatile artist, he has experimented with various art forms, from installation to sculpture and performing arts.

(JT)

MANG EMO + MA...   ...NO PROJECT
3RD MOVEMENT...   ...GAPORE (2007-2009)

Noberto Roldan

Invisibilitus Est 1

2010
Assemblage with old Roman
Chasuble, metal amulets,
assorted bottles
183 x 122 x 5 cm

Singapore Art Museum
collection

Although the Philippines is the only predominantly Catholic country in Southeast Asia today, a certain syncretism has also characterised the practice of Catholicism in the country. It is one which sees an intermingling of faith and magic, religion and animism, spiritual and superstitious belief, and Noberto Roldan has long examined this phenomenon in a distinctive body of works.

'Invisibilitus Est' is pidgin-Latin for "it is invisible" and the assemblage is dominated by an old Roman chasuble, the vestment worn by the priest during the celebration of the Holy Eucharist. Presented frontally, the chasuble takes on the appearance of invincible armour, and the artist has also studded the garment with 18 metal amulets, known colloquially as *anting-anting*. Although 'Christianised' through the incorporation of Christian imagery and sold near churches, these ubiquitous talismans still bear the traces of a more ancient, animist system of magic, ancestral worship and native spiritual beliefs that continue to pervade across much of the region today. Historically, the *anting-anting* were used by soldiers and rebels in the Filipino fight for liberty during the years of colonial rule, and are still widely worn as protective talismans against bad luck or accidents.

Here, the chasuble and *anting-anting* – as objects symbolic of specific beliefs that carry complex histories in the Philippines – may be regarded as the artist's attempt to visually signify the many facets of doctrine and faith. Placed in formal proximity with each other, and together with the miniature bottles, they come together in an improvised 'altar' that hints at the subversion of Christian dogma and its practice in the Philippines, and serves as an oblique comment on the country's troubled colonial past.

Norberto Roldan (b. 1953, Philippines) is a co-founder and artistic director of the alternative art space, Green Papaya Art Projects. He has held solo exhibitions in Malaysia, Singapore, Manila and Australia, as well as participated in several group exhibitions in cities such as New York, London and Tokyo.

(JT)

Jose Tence Ruiz
in collaboration with Danilo Ilag-Ilag

Paraisado Rampa Blanko (White)

2007–2008
Mixed media installation
168 x 91 x 137 cm (kariton),
823 x 274 x 290 cm (installation)

Paraisado Sorbetero (Orange)

2004
Mixed media
198 x 122 x 198 cm

Singapore Art Museum
collection

Bottom:
Paraisado Rampa Blanko (White)

Facing page:
Paraisado Sorbetero (Orange)

The Philippines is better known for the noisy and colourful jeepney, but here, Tence Ruiz has adopted another conveyance, the humble *kariton*, as a vehicle for social critique. The *kariton* is a pushcart commonly used by the urban poor to collect odds and ends, not merely rubbish, but discarded items that can be recycled and reused. Often holding personal effects, the *kariton* also doubles up as a temporary home for those who cannot afford a more permanent abode. Now as a base or foundation for the iconic architecture of a Gothic cathedral, the *kariton* also performs as a 'church on wheels'. In conjoining the poor person's *kariton* with the grandeur of the gothic cathedral, these two sculptures also point to the extreme disparity between the two worlds, suggesting a disjuncture between the Church and those that it claims to offer salvation to. The term 'paraisado' is itself an imaginary term that conflates two words: 'paradise' and 'paralysed', and suggests that some people are so fixated on going to Heaven, they are desensitised to the pain and suffering of others around them on earth.

With its bright orange colour and large wheels, **Paraisado Sorbetero** also calls to mind a third kind of conveyance: the ice cream cart. It thus collapses three disparate but iconic motifs into a single hybridised sculpture, resulting in a work that is critical, comical and compelling.

Although **Paraisado Rampa Blanko** is a stark austere white, it is far from 'pure' for its entire surface is tainted with the numerals 0 and 1; it is utterly infected by the binary code. When installed on a ramp, **Paraisado Rampa Blanko** also suggests the 'dangerous' possibility that this cart may well meet a fateful end by careening over the edge.

Jose Tence Ruiz (b. 1956, Manila, Philippines) graduated with a Bachelor of Fine Arts in Painting from the University of Santo Tomas, Philippines, in 1979. He has held several solo exhibitions in the Philippines and has also participated in major platforms like the 2nd Asia Pacific Triennial of Contemporary Art, Brisbane, Australia (1996), and the Havana Biennial, Cuba (2000). A key figure in several art collectives, Tence Ruiz has been involved for more than 30 years in fields ranging from art, set design, editorial illustration and education.

(JT)

Briccio Santos

Heritage Tunnel

2010
Books, mirrors, wood
244 x 99 x 99 cm

Singapore Art Museum
collection

Laden with tomes, it is apt that the **Heritage Tunnel** also finds its origin in the world's oldest book, the Chinese I-Ching, also known as the Book of Changes. In this ancient book of divination, the well is a powerful symbol of a permanence that stands outside the confines of time and space. The image of the well signifies endless depth, but the **Heritage Tunnel** both descends and ascends upwards to infinity. Conveying an impression of an endless tunnel of books, it suggests that heritage is a corpus of knowledge built up with infinite accretions of history, meaning and memory. With its seemingly infinite tunnel of books and mysterious, if immeasurable, worlds 'contained' between the pages, the work also calls to mind Jorge Luis Borges' Library of Babel which stood as an allegory of the Universe. However similar to the optical device employed by the sculpture, **Heritage Tunnel** also hints at the notion of limitless knowledge being more illusory than real.

Second-hand fiction and non-fiction Filipina books line the shelves and Santos' sculptural 'library' points to histories – the real and the imagined – of the Philippines, as well as its possible futures. Notably, the books of non-fiction are placed with their spines facing outwards, alluding to the conscious mind; conversely, the fiction books are placed with their pages out and titles hidden, suggesting that it is the imagination that lines the unconscious mind.

Briccio Santos (b. 1949, Philippines) is a photographer, filmmaker and also a painter. In 1977, Santos moved back to the Philippines after living abroad for many years, where he began to experiment as a painter and sculptor, while continuing to work with photographs and films.

(JT)

Gerardo Tan
in collaboration with David Griggs

Skateboard Drawing 1

2008
Acrylic on paper, and video
221 x 546 cm (drawing)

Singapore Art Museum
collection

With its back lines darting across the surface plane, this work by Gerardo Tan seems very much a drawing in its most traditional and fundamental form: the act of mark-making on a two-dimensional surface. Although the outcome very much appears that way, the process of creating it has been far less conventional: the drawing was made through the act, and action, of a skateboarder (Tan's friend David Griggs) zipping over the paper, with the skateboard wheels covered with paint.

Although seemingly abstract, the human body is vividly evoked here – even by its visual absence – for it is the body in motion and 'performance' that has directly resulted in this dramatic drawing. This action-based work calls to mind the abstract expressionist paintings of Jackson Pollock and indeed, both are works hung on walls but created on the floor. However, where Pollock has used the gesture of hand and sweep of arm, carefully controlled by the artist leaning over the canvas, Tan's drawing summons the whole body into spontaneous free play over the surface and the result is a drawing made not by the hand, but rather of leg and foot. Drawing practice is recast here as an expansive and dynamic field, its process performative as it is playful.

Gerardo Tan (b. 1960, Manila, Philippines) obtained his MFA in 1992 from the State University of New York at Buffalo, where he majored in Painting, on a Fulbright Hays Fellowship. He received his BFA from the College of Fine Arts, University of the Philippines, in 1982. Tan was awarded a Thirteen Artists Award from the Cultural Center of the Philippines in 1988, and represented Philippines at the first Melbourne International Biennial (1999). He has held several solo exhibitions in the Philippines, and has shown widely in the region and further abroad, including the Fukuoka Asian Art Museum, Japan, Burchfield Art Center, New York, and MOP Projects at Sydney, Australia.

(JT)

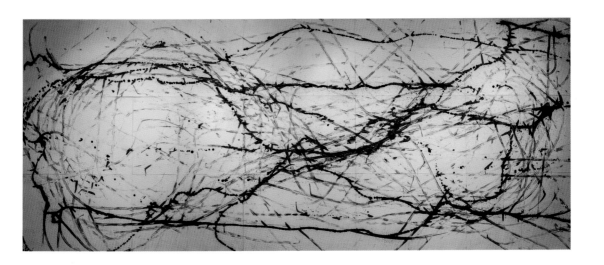

Rodel Tapaya

Pedro and the Witch
2009
Mixed media
60 x 38 x 28 cm

The Hunter of Pinamaloy
2009
Mixed media
60 x 38 x 28 cm

Origin of Grain
2009
Mixed media
60 x 38 x 28 cm

The Wise Monkey and the Foolish Giant
2009
Mixed media
60 x 38 x 26 cm

Singapore Art Museum
collection

Rodel Tapaya's practice has constantly drawn from the rich mythology of the Philippines, harnessing the stories, legends and folklore of the myriad indigenous groups that existed prior to the arrival of Western colonialism. Here, he has adopted dioramas as a mode of storytelling – three-dimensional objects that are reminiscent of museum tableaux. With the pointed roofs, the forms of the containers are akin to altarpieces (or *retablos*, as they are commonly referred to in the Philippines) or miniature houses on stilts, and may suggest an attempt to re-configure indigenous spirituality within a folk Christianity. For Tapaya, the dioramas also serve as a site to 're-stage' stories that have otherwise been forgotten; illustrative in style and technique, they continue his abiding interest in looking towards the country's indigenous history and oral cultures to construct rich visual narratives in post-colonial Philippines.

Pedro and the Witch shows the climax of the story in which the hero, Pedro, aided by an enchanted horse, flees from the winged witch Boroka. Tapaya has chosen to depict the scene in which the hero is surrounded by flames after he drops one of the three magical handkerchiefs in his possession.

The Hunter of Pinamaloy tells of the creation of Lake Pinamaloy. A great hunter was seriously injured after he had killed a wild boar. Using the pig's ears, he creates a garland that he puts around his faithful dog and sends him off to town to seek help. Yet there is a tragic end to the story, which is not shown here. The dog utters words of warning to the hunter's beloved, and in doing, breaches the language divide between Man and animals; the volcano erupts and the ruins of the town are eventually submerged in a lake.

The Wise Monkey and the Foolish Giant is a folktale about how a small animal was able to outsmart a creature that was many times bigger, one who had the advantage of size but not of wit. The scene depicts the monkey tying the giant to a tree, after the former had tricked the giant into believing that was the only way to survive an impending storm. The monkey then proceeds to whip the giant with the vines. Later on in the story, after a succession of tricks, the monkey convinces the giant that the open mouth of a crocodile is the entrance to a room, and the giant enters, only to be swallowed up whole.

Origin of Grain is a myth about how the barren Earth got her first grains. Labangan, a mortal, pleaded to the sky god Kabuniyan for food, who threw a line for him to climb to the other world for a meal of rice, under the condition that he was not to bring back any to Earth. But Labangan defied Kabuniyan and thus began the cultivation of rice on Earth.

Rodel Tapaya (b. 1980, Philippines) graduated from University of the Philippines, before travelling to University of Art and Design, Helsinki, Finland, and Parsons School of Design in New York City for further studies. He was the Grand Prize winner of the Asia Pacific Breweries Foundation Signature Art Prize in 2011. In 2001, Tapaya also won the Grand Prize of the Nokia Art Awards Asia Pacific. Since 1999, Tapaya has been actively participating in solo and group exhibitions in the Philippines and the region.

(JT)

Clockwise from top left:
Pedro and the Witch
The Hunter of Pinamaloy
Origin of Grain
The Wise Monkey and the Foolish Giant

Rodel Tapaya

The Creation Myths

2009
Painting and wall installation: acrylic on canvas, acrylic on wood, ceramic
330 x 440 cm (painting), wall installation dimensions variable

Singapore Art Museum collection

Rodel Tapaya takes on the role of the master storyteller, setting the scene within each canvas and condensing multi-narratives into a single narrative, constantly drawing from the ancient myths, folklore and legends of pre-colonial Philippines. Because many of these indigenous tales were passed down through the oral tradition, they exist in fragments and must be filled in by the (artist as) storyteller – each tale is re-shaped even as it is re-told and re-presented. In *The Creation Myths*, the artist incorporates several pre-colonial myths and intertwines them in this dreamscape, making it impossible to separate one from the other. The mythical bird Manaul, whose feathers are said to have transformed into different animals, including humans, dominates here. Other stories are depicted as well, such as the Creator and King of Time, Kan-Laon, shown sitting on a cloud, and the tales about the children of Bathala – Apolaqui and Mayari – who are the Sun and the Moon respectively. Echoing how stories can take new lives of their own in the re-telling, the painting spills out beyond the confines of the canvas, extending itself and its many stories to occupy the very wall itself.

Rodel Tapaya (b. 1980, Philippines) graduated from University of the Philippines, before travelling to University of Art and Design, Helsinki, Finland, and Parsons School of Design in New York City for further studies. He was the Grand Prize winner of the Asia Pacific Breweries Foundation Signature Art Prize in 2011. In 2001, Tapaya also won the Grand Prize of the Nokia Art Awards Asia Pacific. Since 1999, Tapaya has been actively participating in solo and group exhibitions in the Philippines and the region.

(JT)

Wire Tuazon

Resurrecting Resurreccion

2005
Oil on canvas
244 x 488 cm

Singapore Art Museum
collection

Philippine art history and the spectre of grand masters haunt this large-scale painting by Wire Tuazon. The work's title, ***Resurrecting Resurreccion***, and the words on the surface, "Christian Virgins Exposed to the Public", make a direct reference to one of the Philippines' most famous paintings, *Las Virgenes Cristianas Expuestas al Populacho (The Christian Virgins Being Exposed to the Populace)*, painted by Felix Resurrección Hidalgo in 1884. In Hidalgo's painting, two Christian maidens are shown overcome with shame as they are stripped before a mob of lascivious Roman slave traders, and the work is conventionally read as an allegory against Spanish colonial abuse, becoming a powerful symbol of the early Philippine nationalist cause.

In contrast, Tuazon's painting is based upon a 1960s photograph from Life magazine which shows a mass of people in skimpy swimwear. Men and women now form a voluntary parade of human flesh, a stark contrast to the Hidalgo painting in which the salacious display of female form before the male gaze was cloaked under a guise of moral censure at the behaviour of lecherous men. This monumental painting by Tuazon may thus be read as an oblique commentary on notions of morality and social mores in the primarily Catholic country. Moreover, by punning upon the name of the 'original' artist, Tuazon's painting questions the iconic work, and its creator's place and relevance, for a modern-day Philippine public.

Wire Tuazon's (b. 1973, Angono, Philippines) conceptualist paintings often combine a specific word juxtaposed in front of a sourced image, both seeming to have no direct relation with each other. Tuazon was a founder of the artists group "Surrounded by Water" and has held several solo shows and group exhibitions in the Philippines, Australia, Singapore, Japan and Korea.

(JT)

Steve Tirona

Imelda Collection #1 - #5

2006
Digital C-prints, set of 5
Edition 3/15
61 x 91 cm (each)

Singapore Art Museum
collection

This series by Steve Tirona centres on the infamous and iconic Imelda Marcos, while critically exploring the nature of modern myth-making. Calling upon his background as a commercial photographer, Tirona has created a series of images that deftly uses the techniques and approaches of advertising and fashion photography to 'frame' the subject – but a subject who is, herself, a consummate manipulator of the media and of her own image. Tirona portrays Imelda in a range of 'comic catastrophes' and absurd situations that appear to critique her and the indulgences of the Marcos years. The photographs appear unrelenting in their use of parody and kitsch to lampoon its subject. Yet the series was actually approved by Imelda Marcos herself and was commissioned by her grandson to launch her line of fashion accessories sold on the Internet. The photographs oscillate, rather ambivalently, between advertising, parody, criticism and marketing. Despite her many years of living in the public eye, Imelda Marcos remains an enigmatic, if controversial figure, and the photographs by Tirona both reveal and 'display' her as an object of unceasing fascination.

Steve Tirona (b. 1976, Manila, Philippines) has worked primarily in the field of fashion photography and received his Bachelor of Art in photography from the Art Center College of Design, Pasadena, California, United States.

(JT)

Alvin Zafra

Pepe

2008
Live bullet on sandpaper panel,
set of 3 panels
122 x 180 cm

Marcial Bonifacio

2006
Live bullet on sandpaper panel,
set of 3 panels
122 x 180 cm

Singapore Art Museum
collection

Pepe and *Marcial Bonifacio* come from Zafra's 'Headshot' series in which martyrs and executioners are rendered using an M16 round. Each image uses one entire live bullet round as a drawing implement, each image is thus drawn with – or more accurately, *ground into* – the sandpaper panel.

Pepe depicts the haunting image of Jose Rizal, the Philippine patriot and polymath whose writings seeded a growing Philippine national consciousness during the late 19th century. Tried and convicted by the Spanish colonial government on charges of treason, Rizal was executed by firing squad and his politically-motivated death transformed him into a martyr for the Philippine Revolution. Pepe was Rizal's nickname when he was a boy.

In a similar vein, the spectral portrait *Marcial Bonifacio* captures Benigno Aquino, the Philippine opposition senator who was assassinated at Manila International Airport after returning home from exile in 1983 to challenge Ferdinand Marcos. Marcial Bonifacio was the alias Aquino used on his passport because the Philippine authorities would not issue him a passport. 'Marcial' stood for martial law, and 'Bonifacio' referred to Fort Bonifacio, the prison in Manila where he was incarcerated for seven years. Aquino's assassination provided the catalyst for the People's Power Revolution which brought down the dictatorial Marcos rule.

In each of these portraits, an entire bullet shell is literally and metaphorically 'spent' in making the work – an implement of death is now the instrument of creation. In the process, the minimalist sculptural form of the bullet appears to 'dissolve' but does not disappear, for it undergoes a transformation and re-emerges as 'image', translated into a recognisable portrait. Poignant and poetic, *Pepe* and *Marcial Bonifacio* also implicate the artist as he takes on the binary positions of executioner/victim, creator/destroyer, good/evil. Representation, abstraction and medium converge onto a single surface, and the sandpaper's subtly shimmering grains hold fast the haunting images of two men who died in their prime.

Multi-disciplinary artist Alvin Zafra (b. 1978, Philippines) is a painter, production designer, film director and a musician. A graduate of the University of the Philippines with a Bachelor of Fine Arts degree in Painting, Zafra experiments widely with his choice of medium for his works, incorporating unusual materials and employing innovative processes, such as using his fingernails and bullets as drawing tools.

(JT)

Facing page:
Top:
Pepe
Bottom:
Marcial Bonifacio

Southeast Asia

THAILAND

Francesc Xavier Comas de la Paz	Sudsiri Pui-Ock
Yuree Kensaku	Araya Rasdjarmrearnsook
Sakarin Krue-On	Navin Rawanchaikul
Sutee Kunavichayanont	Pinaree Sanpitak
Torlarp Larpjaroensook	Michael Shaowanasai
Kamin Lertchaiprasert	Vasan Sitthiket
Kedsuda Loogthong	Manit Sriwanichpoom
Nipan Oranniwesna	Natee Utarit
Wit Pimkanchanapong	Promthum Woravut

Francesc Xavier Comas de la Paz

Jiuta-mai

2009
Inkjet colour prints on
archival paper, set of 14 prints
Edition 1/7
100 x 66 cm (each)

Singapore Art Museum
collection

This series of work resulted from Xavier Comas' chance encounter with Noe Tawara, a Japanese *jiuta-mai* dancer, on the streets of Tokyo's red-light district. *Jiuta-mai* is an ancient and secretive style of Japanese classical dance and its obscure origins can be traced back to the 13th century. Characterised as being intensely intimate, *jiuta-mai* is a dance form usually performed for the solitary viewing pleasure of a male witness. Traditionally performed only for those of high nobility, *jiuta-mai* is revealing of the multi-layered Japanese social class system. Subtle and delicate yet purposeful, much of a woman's physical and emotional expressions of strength and tenacity is captured in this art form. Noe invited Xavier Comas to witness her performance at the Daijo-ji temple in 2007 and 2008, where she performs once every year to mark the beginning of Autumn. This personal friendship enabled Xavier Comas to witness a rare art form, which would otherwise have been traditionally inaccessible to foreigners.

Francesc Xavier Comas de la Paz (b. 1970, Spain) is a graduate of the University of Barcelona's Faculty of Fine Arts. He has worked as a freelance designer and illustrator and his works have been published worldwide. He is currently based in Bangkok, Thailand where in 2011 he organised a solo exhibition, 'The House of the Raja' at H Gallery in Bangkok.

(NW)

Yuree Kensaku

Last Room – The Buddha

2009
Mixed media in acrylic, with
ribbons, painted wood snakes,
metal butterflies, door curtain
and wood panel
203 x 86.5 cm

The Killer From Electricity Authority

2009
Mixed media in acrylic, with
carved window, painted toy skull
and plastic blinds
112 x 80 cm

Singapore Art Museum
collection

Yuree Kensaku is known for her pop-surrealist aesthetics, in which she combines paintings with discarded objects and everyday utensils. Weaving them into a stylised form of narrative illustration, the artist highlights her environmental concerns in depictions of an ecological Armageddon, a theme that frequently appears in her works.

A graduate of visual arts from Bangkok University, Yuree Kensaku (b. 1979, Thailand) has exhibited in both group and solo exhibitions in Thailand such as 'Brand New' at the Art Gallery, Bangkok University (2003), '108 Paths to Vanity' at 100 Tonson Gallery (2004), 'One On Other at About Café' (2005), 'Love In Platinum Frame' at the Art Center, Chulalongkorn University (2007), and 'Same Place While the Clock's Hands Pace' at Gallery VER (2008). Internationally, she has presented her work 'The Adventure of Momotaro Girl' at the Yokohama Museum of Art (2007), and also the Kuandu Biennale in Taipei, Taiwan (2010).

(MH)

The Killer From
Electricity Authority

Last Room –
The Buddha

Sakarin Krue-On

Cloud Nine

2005
Mixed media installation:
ceramic dogs, table, plates
and plastic fruits
Dimensions variable

Singapore Art Museum
collection

Stray dogs are a common sight in the streets of Thailand, and artist Sakarin Krue-on employs them as a potent visual metaphor in this installation. By modelling these unwanted dogs into exquisite-looking porcelain figurines, poised in a kitschy *nouveau-riche* home setting, the artist alludes to the social inequalities embedded in Thai society, as well as its class divides.

Cloud Nine illustrates the notion of "empty hope" (or "lom lom, lang lang" in Thai), and Sakarin's street dogs can only dream of an alternative life of a more elevated status. By portraying the common stray as winged, angel-like entities, yet bound by their instinctive nature, the artist presents a tragic and yet farcical parody of Thai social realities. The work also reflects Sakarin's Buddhist beliefs of the limitations and inherent emptiness of dreams and self-delusion.

Sakarin Krue-On (b. 1965, Maehongsorn, Thailand) graduated from Silapakorn University, Bangkok, in Thailand. His past solo exhibitions include 'Cloud Nine' at 100 Tonson Gallery in Bangkok (2004) and 'Yellow Simple' at Open Arts Space in Bangkok (2001), and other notable exhibitions in the international arena includes his participation in the Venice Biennale (2002 and 2009), as well as Documenta 12, Kassel, Germany (2007).

(MH)

Sakarin Krue-On

Manorah and Best Friends of the Snake

2010
Single-channel black & white
video, edition 1/5
Duration 28:00 mins

Singapore Art Museum
collection

Using allegory to draw references to Thai realities, ***Manorah and Best Friends of the Snake*** is Sakarin Krue-On's remake of the famous folk story from the Jataka tales. This tale follows the journey of a heavenly being, who takes the form of a half-maiden and half-swan, as she faces trials that ensue from being kidnapped by a hunter, and finally, falling in love with the prince of the fable's ancient city Panjalanakhon. Her celestial wings become the subject of the myth. After she shares her secret gift of flying with the prince, many others in the kingdom covet the ability, and soon, the kingdom dissolves into pandemonium.

The artist's film can be read in the light of Thailand's social and political climate of public protests, particularly in the past five years, where the pursuit of freedom or democracy can result in unwanted violence. Imbued with several layers of references that combine Thai folklore with contemporary culture and society, the work presents varied readings into the state of contemporary Thai society, and its complex relationship with the Thai monarchy.

Sakarin Krue-On (b. 1965, Maehongsorn, Thailand) graduated from Silapakorn University, Bangkok, in Thailand. His past solo exhibitions include 'Cloud Nine' at 100 Tonson Gallery in Bangkok (2004) and 'Yellow Simple' at Open Arts Space in Bangkok (2001), and other notable exhibitions in the international arena includes his participation in the Venice Biennale (2002 and 2009), as well as Documenta 12, Kassel, Germany (2007).

(MH)

Sakarin Krue-On

No Fly Zone

2005
Single-channel black & white
video, edition 1/10
Duration 6:38 mins

Singapore Art Museum
collection

The title of this satirical work *No Fly Zone* also refers to its Thai translation, "No flies allowed". It can be seen as the artist's playful response to the issue of international border disputes, as reported in the international news media. Using a pile of fermented fish to represent the frontier of a landscape, the artist presents a parody of territorial infringement. A woman enacts different scenarios of her attempts to chase away a fly, from swatting the fly with her hand, to the employment of optical tricks, and finally, to the using light-reflecting compact discs to repel the fly. Her progressive tactics can be seen akin to the strategies that countries use to safeguard their borders ranging from the display of patrolling guards to military power. To the artist, the race in the development of arms technology to protect one's borders, and the creation of national boundaries and restricted zones, have resulted in human beings being alienated from each other.

Sakarin Krue-On (b. 1965, Maehongsorn, Thailand) graduated from Silapakorn University, Bangkok, in Thailand. His past solo exhibitions include 'Cloud Nine' at 100 Tonson Gallery in Bangkok (2004) and 'Yellow Simple' at Open Arts Space in Bangkok (2001), and other notable exhibitions in the international arena includes his participation in the Venice Biennale (2002 and 2009), as well as Documenta 12, Kassel, Germany (2007).

(MH)

Sutee
Kunavichayanont

History Class

2000
Installation with wooden
classroom tables and wooden
chairs (sets of 14)
Dimensions variable

Singapore Art Museum
collection

History Class was conceived in 2000 to commemorate the centenary of the birth of ex-Thai Prime Minister, Pridi Banomyong, a renowned if somewhat controversial figure in 20th century Thai politics. *History Class* is an interactive installation work, comprising 14 ordinary wooden classroom desks. On the desktops are engraved images and texts drawn from various episodes in modern Thai history, especially marked by the people's uprisings, student protests, assassinations, military crackdowns and torture.

Kunavichayanont draws attention to the notion of history as a succession of milestones and crises leading to change. Ordinary citizens with conviction and determination have the ability to effect positive change in society. The work engages its audience, as it is invited to make image rubbings (by placing a paper over, and pencil shading, the etched surfaces) of these episodes. In this way, they also symbolically play out the process of history making. As *History Class* demonstrates, Kunavichayanont's installations reflect eloquently the changing social, economic and political landscapes in Thailand. Audience participation is often sought to complete the meaning of works, making artistic transmission and audience reception of ideas a two-way process.

Sutee Kunavichayanont (b. 1965, Thailand) graduated with a Bachelor's in Fine Arts from Silpakorn University, Bangkok, in 1989 and a Master's degree in Visual Arts from the University of Sydney, Australia. He has exhibited internationally including the 5th Asia Pacific Triennial of Contemporary Art, Brisbane, Australia (2006).

(KH)

(Detail)

Torlarp Larpjaroensook

Bookshelf

2011
Mixed media installation:
acrylic on canvas, wood
Dimensions variable

Singapore Art Museum
collection

With all books, the full value of their content is transacted when the book is read. However, in the case of art books, where heavy visual elements complement the written word, a person may skim through its pages, focusing only on the pictures and assume that s/he has satisfactorily understood its content. For an artist such as Larpjaroensook, who primary language is Thai, this case is not only habitual but also personal and circumstantial. As an artist, he often feels frustrated and unfulfilled when 'reading' such books, which are mostly written in English. His access to knowledge to a wider, more international and current practice of art is limited to the number of pictures illustrated in them. Through ***Bookshelf***, Larpjaroensook reverses the function of these books, where they are now consumed directly through their visual and tactile quality.

These 'books' are actually appropriated thick, impasto-styled acrylic paintings based on popular and coffee-table styled art books that are widely and internationally available. Traversing definitions, between the genres of painting and installation art, ***Bookshelf*** also reminds us of the indoctrination and popularisation of certain artworks, artists and art practices today by authors who are typically made of established international art critics, curators and taste-makers of the day.

Torlarp Larpjaroensook a.k.a Hern (b. 1977, Thailand) is an emerging Thai artist based in Chiang Mai. At the age of 16, he embarked on formal art education at the College of Fine Arts in Bangkok and later graduated from the Fine Arts Faculty at Chiang Mai University with a BA (Visual Art) in Painting and Printmaking. Larpjaroensook's practice shuffles between art and design, and dwells between function and aesthetics.

(KH)

Kamin Lertchaiprasert

Lord Buddha said, "If you see Dhamma, you see me"

2003–2004
Shredded Thai bank notes
244 x 73 x 73 cm

Singapore Art Museum
collection

The Buddha statue is regarded as an important part of Thailand's cultural landscape where a majority of its population is Buddhist. As a symbol of Buddhism, it acts as a reminder in encouraging equality, harmony and peace for the individual and the society, as well as equilibrium and righteousness in daily life. In the sculpture, ***Lord Buddha said, "If you see Dhamma, you see me"***, Thai artist Kamin Lertchaiprasert references the Asian financial crisis of 1997-1998 that began in Thailand when its government released the Thai Baht from its peg against the American dollar. This invited heavy speculation of the Thai Baht, causing it to collapse and the country to become bankrupt due to foreign debts. In the midst of this crisis, many Thai businessmen seemed disinterested in helping to stabilise and recover the economy; instead, many took advantage of the weak Thai Baht to reap quick and large profits. This act is seen by the artist as revealing an "appalling inner-condition" of the Thai society, specifically, in their love for personal and material wealth over faith and society, hence, the representation of the Buddha here as one that is broken and created out of destroyed currency.

Kamin Lertchaiprasert (b. 1964, Lopburi, Thailand) graduated from Silpakorn University in Bangkok, majoring in printmaking in 1987. Between 1987 and 1992, he was based in New York, working while attending art school. He has exhibited prolifically in numerous exhibitions in Thailand, and is also the co-founder of the The Land Project, an artist commune in Chiang Mai, in Northern Thailand. His exhibitions in the international arena include the Sydney Biennale (1993), Venice Biennale (2003) and Busan Biennale, Korea (2008), among others.

(KH)

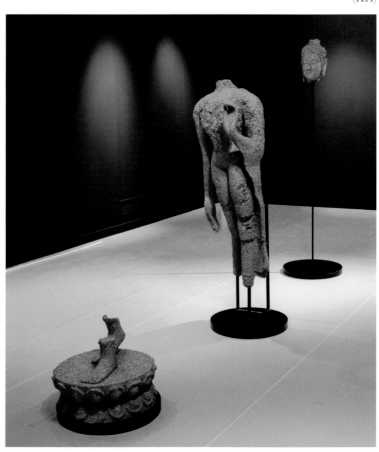

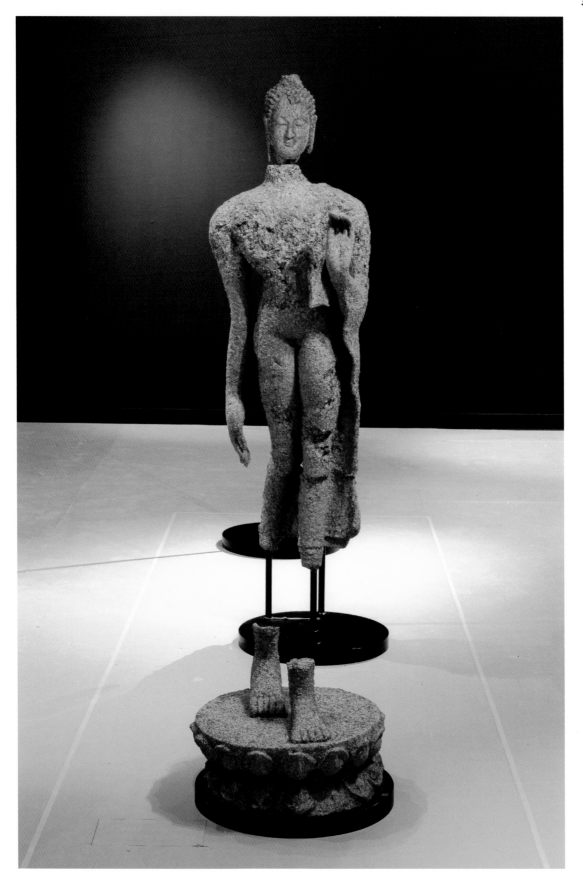

Kamin Lertchaiprasert

Sitting

2004
Installation with sculptures
(wood, wire; set of 366) and
drawings (charcoal on handmade
paper; set of 366)
Dimensions variable

Singapore Art Museum
collection

Sitting comprises of a series of drawings and sculptures that the artist had executed each day for over a year. As a collective installation, it reflects the accumulation of life's experiences. These 366 drawings and sculptures are testament to the process of everyday living, as the artist incorporates his personal daily reflections and meditations into his artmaking. Portraying time as an expressive dimension, the sculptures and the drawings, when viewed together, reveal the interplay and overlap of meaning and significance in the daily rituals of the artist.

Kamin Lertchaiprasert (b. 1964, Lopburi, Thailand) graduated from Silpakorn University in Bangkok, majoring in printmaking in 1987. Between 1987 and 1992, he was based in New York, working while attending art school. He has exhibited prolifically in numerous exhibitions in Thailand, and is also the co-founder of the The Land Project, an artist commune in Chiang Mai, in Northern Thailand. His exhibitions include the Biennale of Sydney, Australia (1993), Venice Biennale, Italy (2003) and Busan Biennale, Korea (2008).

(MH)

Kedsuda Loogthong

Letters from Songkla

2006
Installation with watercolour
works (set of 27), embroidered
canvases (set of 6), 1 bronze
envelope, 1 bronze box and
school table and chair (1 set)
Dimensions variable

Singapore Art Museum
collection

Hailing originally from southern provincial Thailand, Kedsuda Loogthong moved from a village childhood in Songkhla to study in the city of Bangkok. She left behind parents and brothers, who called and wrote to her often. In 2006, Loogthong began her *Letters from Songkhla* series, illustrating aspects of her correspondence with her family, by using a variety of materials to convey simple and yet poignant messages that have been exchanged. In the installation, mailed envelopes have been recreated as watercolour miniatures. The memory of a cardboard package from home has been preserved in the form of a bronze sculpture. Kind words, extracted from letters that had touched her deeply, have been stitched onto canvas, as the artist's way of expressing her gratitude and yearning for kinship.

Collectively, the installation reminds one of the intrinsic values that form the basis of human relationships, which modern means of communication, such as email, despite its speed of delivery, cannot convey. In *Letters from Songkhla*, the artist shows us how some of life's most precious and intangible experiences may well be the ones that transcend the trappings of an advanced and technologically driven society.

Kedsuda Loogthong (b. 1983, Thailand) graduated from the Faculty of Fine and Applied Arts in Bangkok University in 2006. She has exhibited in Singapore, Malaysia, Thailand, Finland and Korea. She lives and works in Bangkok.

(MH)

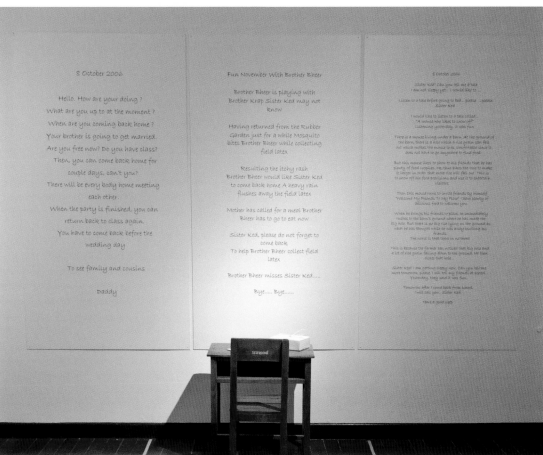

8 October 2006

Hello. How are your doing ?
What are you up to at the moment ?
When are you coming back home ?
Your brother is going to get married.
Are you free now? Do you have class?
Then, you can come back home for
couple days, can't you?
There will be every body home meeting
each other.
When the party is finished, you can
return back to class again.
You have to come back before the
wedding day

To see family and cousins

Daddy

Fun November With Brother Bheer

Brother Bheer is playing with
Brother Krap Sister Ked may not
know

Having returned from the Rubber
Garden just for a while Mosquito
bites Brother Bheer while collecting
field latex

Resulting the itchy rash
Brother Bheer would like Sister Ked
to come back home A heavy rain
flushes away the field latex

Mother has called for a meal Brother
Bheer has to go to eat now

Sister Ked, please do not forget to
come back
To help Brother Bheer collect field
latex

Brother Bheer misses Sister Ked.....

Bye..... Bye......

Nipan Oranniwesna

Let Us Progress Towards...

2009
Hand-pierced paper, set of 4
78 x 108 cm (each)

Singapore Art Museum
collection

In this series of paper works, Thai artist Nipan Oranniwesna explores the concept of nationalism, and the roles that language and meaning play in the fostering of national identity. Taking national anthems as a subject of scrutiny, Oranniwesna believes that they can be instrumental in creating a nation's collective memory, as generations of citizens, through repeated choruses of the anthem, produce a collective sentiment about nationhood. Made of delicate paper, and pierced holes that form the lyrics of selected national anthems, the work can be seen as the artist's query on idea of national identity as both a form of cultural conditioning as well as a constructed entity. *Let Us Progress Towards...* features the lyrics of the Singapore national anthem.

Nipan Oranniwesna (b. 1962, Bangkok, Thailand) has participated in international exhibitions such as the Busan Biennale, Korea (2008) and the Thai Pavilion at the 52nd Venice Biennale (2007). He lectures at the Visual Arts Department in Bangkok University.

(MH)

(Detail)

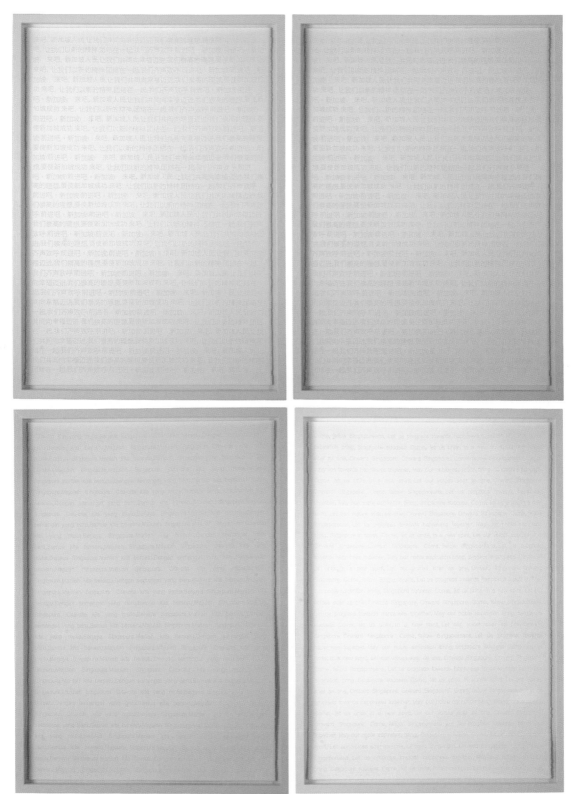

Wit Pimkanchanapong

Not Quite A Total Eclipse

2009
Mixed media installation with
motorised parts of wood, metal,
electronic circuit board and
electric cable
Dimensions variable

Singapore Art Museum
collection

Trained in architecture, Wit Pimkanchanapong's interest in space and design can be seen in his diverse artistic practice which includes installation and animation. His practice is also known for its use of everyday materials to create interactive environments that draw audiences into the creative process of artmaking. *Not Quite A Total Eclipse* is a motorised installation that is made of basic materials and cabling processes to achieve astounding effects. His version of the phenomena of a planetary eclipse exploits the play between light and shadow, which is controlled by electronic programming.

Wit Pimkanchanapong (b. 1976, Thailand) has taken part in many international art festivals including the Asia Pacific Triennial of Contemporary Art, Brisbane, Australia (2009), the Singapore Biennale (2008), the Sharjah Biennale, United Arab Emirates (2007) and Yokohama International Triennial of Contemporary Art, Japan (2005). His work has been shown in many museums including the MOT Museum of Contemporary Art, Tokyo (2007), San Diego Art Museum (2007), as well as the Singapore Art Museum (2010 and 2011). The artist resides in Bangkok and is also involved in collaborative projects such as the Fat Music Festival and the Soi Project, an ongoing "laboratory" project that fosters exchanges amongst artists and practitioners from a variety of disciplines.

(MH)

Sudsiri Pui-Ock

Draw My Life With Blue On White

2005
Installation with ceramic dinner plates, set of 34
Dimensions variable

Singapore Art Museum collection

Sudsiri Pui-Ock is part of an emerging generation of young female Southeast Asian artists whose works examine the notions of identity, culture and history from her cultural perspective. ***Draw My Life With Blue On White*** was created during her stay in the Netherlands, where the artist began to reflect on how one's new living environments necessarily influences one's being, just as the histories of the encounters between foreign cultures may in turn, impact their respective individual cultures. By creating her work in the style of Dutch delftware in this work, the artist attempts to show its influence by 17th century Chinese ceramics that were imported into Europe. The installation features 34 pieces of dining ware, each piece painted with an anecdotal illustration of her journey and musings in the Netherlands.

Sudsiri Pui-Ock (b.1976, Chiang Mai, Thailand) obtained her Bachelor Degree of Fine Arts from Chiang Mai University in 1999, and Master Degree from Silpakorn University, Bangkok in 2003. She has participated in group exhibitions such as 'Short Film Festival Oberhausen', Germany (2009), '7th World Film Festival of Bangkok' (2009), 'Incheon Women Artists Biennial', Korea, (2009), 'Traces of Siamese Smile: Art+Faith+Politics+Love', Bangkok Art and Culture Centre, Bangkok, (2008), 'The Ethics of Encounter', Bangkok (2008), and 'Happy Hours', ZAIM, Yokohama, Japan (2007). She also represented Thailand at the 53rd Venice Biennale (2009) and the Yokohama Triennale (2011).

(MH)

Araya Rasdjarmrearnsook

Thai Medley I, II and III

2002
3-channel video, edition 1/4
Duration 4:35 mins, 5:23 mins
and 6:19 mins

Singapore Art Museum
collection

Araya Rasdjarmrearnsook is known for her work that explore death and the rituals of mourning. The process of working with a hospital morgue began in 1998 when the artist first sought permission to use unclaimed dead bodies, and developed this body of work, based on the idea of caring for those who had not received cremation rituals. In the videos, the artist walks through rows of female corpses, reading *Inaow*, an ancient Thai text. *Inaow* is a love story through which the artist reads as a way of connecting with each of the deceased, whom she believed must have had a love in their lives. Her recitation of excerpts about being in love, and the nature of love amongst different genders, can be seen as an act of consolation for the deceased, as well as a compellingly poetic eulogy for those who had passed on anonymously without their last rites being performed for them.

Araya Rasdjarmrearnsook (b. 1957, Trad, Thailand) is known for her works that reflect on identity, gender roles, death and cultural contexts. She lives and works in Chiang Mai, northern Thailand, and has exhibited widely, including in international exhibitions such as the 1st Asia Pacific Triennial of Contemporary Art, Brisbane, Australia (1993), 1st Johannesburg Biennale (1995), Biennale of Sydney (1996 and 2010) as well as the 51st Venice Biennial (2006).

(MH)

Araya Rasdjarmrearnsook

Three Female Scapes

2002
3-channel video, edition 1/4
Duration 9:00 mins, 8:50 mins
and 6:25 mins

Singapore Art Museum
collection

Three Female Scapes is part of Araya Rasdjarmrearnsook's practices that deals with communication with the dead. In this series, the artist chooses to highlight details and close-up images of a female dead body as a way of confronting death in its immediate form. But far from being terrifying, the textures of flesh and fabric in water present an intimate vision of death as a part of nature, with this indelible impression of body as landscape, to which her representation draws a parallel.

Araya Rasdjarmrearnsook (b. 1957, Trad, Thailand) is known for her works that reflect on identity, gender roles, death and cultural contexts. She lives and works in Chiang Mai, northern Thailand, and has exhibited widely, including in international exhibitions such as the 1st Asia Pacific Triennial of Contemporary Art, Brisbane, Australia (1993), 1st Johannesburg Biennale (1995), Biennale of Sydney (1996 and 2010) as well as the 51st Venice Biennial (2006).

(MH)

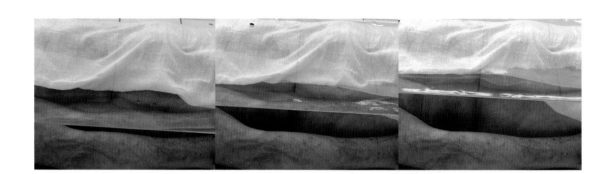

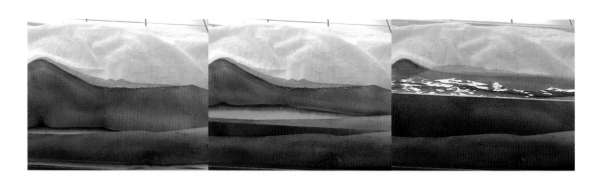

Araya Rasdjarmrearnsook

Two Planets

2008
4-channel video, edition 1/5
Duration 20:00 mins

Singapore Art Museum
collection

A work which explores the construction of art history narratives as well as the context in which art is being viewed, *Two Planets* emerges from the artist's experiences as a university professor and her observations of her students' responses to renowned works of Western art. If a work of art is being introduced as one of great significance, how is one to assess its merits within one's own different cultural context or artistic practice?

Two Planets combines the two worlds of art history and the rural life in Thailand, as the artist arranges for images of well-known Western masterpieces to be displayed, and discussed, by an unlikely audience – Thai farmers. Featuring works such as French artists Édouard Manet's 'Luncheon on the Grass' (1863), Jean-François Millet's 'The Gleaners' (1857), Pierre-Auguste Renoir's 'Ball at the Moulin de la Galette' (1876) and Vincent van Gogh's 'The Midday Sleep' (1889-90), Araya records the spontaneous conversations between the farmers, who do not possess any art history knowledge. The piece provokes questions of whether we can appreciate the value of art works without knowing anything of their importance in art history, and whether such knowledge may influence our responses.

Araya Rasdjarmrearnsook (b. 1957, Trad, Thailand) is known for her works that reflect on identity, gender roles, death and cultural contexts. She lives and works in Chiang Mai, northern Thailand, and has exhibited widely, including in international exhibitions such as the 1st Asia Pacific Triennial of Contemporary Art, Brisbane, Australia (1993), 1st Johannesburg Biennale (1995), Biennale of Sydney (1996 and 2010) as well as the 51st Venice Biennial (2006).

(MH)

Navin Rawanchaikul

Navins of Bollywood

2006
High Definition Video (HDV)
Edition 5/9
Duration 10:34 mins

Where is Navin?

2007
Painted fibreglass, cloth and
wood, edition 3/3
67 x 45 x 176 cm

Singapore Art Museum
collection

In the sculptural work, **Where is Navin?**, the artist has sculptured his own figure, holding a sign that reads his name: "Navin". Through both the sculpture and video, Navin Rawanchaikul seeks to find his inner self, yet at the same time too, find other people in the world who share the same name and similarities of destiny.

The **Navins of Bollywood** video follows the same line of enquiry and exploration, with the insertion of more theatrical elements. Inspired by a journey he made from Thailand to India, he wrote, directed and starred in a musical that combines comedy with the absurdity of society, parodying the over-the-top style of Bollywood movies. The film is a performance by the artist who completes the circle of searching for one's identity, origin, companionship and fame.

Navin Rawanchaikul (b. 1971, Chiang Mai, Thailand) is of Indian descent. His works focus on the conflicts and interactions between globalisation and localisation. Over the past years, Rawanchaikul has been experimenting with a very lively and practical artistic approach, which allows him to do the following: get involved in the community and interact directly with the audience; develop a platform for social criticism; and incorporate his experiences and those of the community into a science fiction novel. He has exhibited in the 54th Venice Biennale (2011).

(KH)

Pinaree Sanpitak

Noon-Nom

2011
Organza and synthetic fibre
Dimensions variable

Singapore Art Museum
collection

Pinaree Sanpitak expanded ideas from a body of work in a series collectively titled 'Vessels and Mounds' to produce **Noon-Nom**. Sanpitak created this work to challenge and expand our perception, altering our attitudes through the senses aroused by this strong female bodily symbol: the breast. Since the series of work 'vessels and mounds' began, her artworks have become more and more interactive and continues to incorporate a wide range of materials such as silk, mulberry fibre, wax, cast metal, terracotta, rattan, live fish and food. They cross gender lines and attempt to explore the humour, the fragility and the vigour of the senses through sight, touch, sound, scent and taste. **Noon-Nom** is Sanpitak's first sculpture installation, one in which the artist intentionally seeks audience engagement with the artwork through physical interaction. The audience is asked to take off their shoes and immerse in the work as they please. They become part of the artwork itself, transforming into both the examiner and the examined.

Pinaree Sanpitak (b. 1961, Bangkok, Thailand) has participated in various residencies and biennales including the 3rd Asia Pacific Triennial of Contemporary Art, Brisbane, Australia (1999), and the 2nd Fukuoka Asian Art Triennale, Japan (2002).

(KH)

Michael Shaowanasai

Four Faces of Faith:
A Girl in Rose Blouse

2005
C-prints, edition 2/4
76 x 76 cm (each)

Singapore Art Museum
collection

Michael Shaowanasai's *Four Faces of Faith: A Girl in Rose Blouse* looks at women in religion, represented by the four major faiths; Judaism, Buddhism, Islam and Christianity. These heavily made-up women, with false eyelashes and long hair played by Shaowanasai himself, hints at female subjugation in religion and how they are controlled by patriarchal systems. Although engaging the audience in the context of religiosity, this depiction also suggests women as both victims and temptresses as commonly found throughout various religious narratives.

Shaowanasai uses photography as a theatrical device in his performative projects that explore female identities in society. The artist role-plays in his attempts to understand the various social roles of women through their negotiations between fashion and appropriated environments. Shaowanasai's manufactured interpretations reveal the imposition of ideals and pressures that women have to navigate on a daily basis as individuals, mothers, wives and daughters.

Michael Shaowanasai (b. 1964, Philadephia, United States) received a Bachelor of Fine Art from the San Francisco Art Institute and a Masters of Fine Art from The School of the Art Institute of Chicago. Based in Bangkok, he is multidisciplinary artist whose work encompasses film, performance, photography and installation.

(KH)

THAILAND

Michael Shaowanasai

**Portrait of
a Man in Habits 1**

2000
C-prints, edition 8/9
142 x 91.5 cm

**Portrait of
a Man in Habits 2**

2000
C-prints, edition 8/9
35.5 x 28 cm

Singapore Art Museum
collection

Portrait of a Man in Habits 1 and *2* generated much controversy and discussion when it was first exhibited. Much has been written on the concept and intention of this work, ranging from social commentaries to gender analyses. For Michael Shaowanasai, the need for 'freedom of speech' resonates the strongest as an underlying impetus for the work.

Created and exhibited for 'Alien-(gener)-ation' (curated by Bangkok-based curator, Grigthiya Gaweewon) in 2000 in Thailand, the artwork originally consisted of only one photograph – *Portrait of a Man in Habits 1* – the larger piece, depicting a Buddhist monk in his yellow robe. This depiction of a monk with cosmetic make-up, angered the Thai Buddhist association so much that they staged a protest days after the exhibition opened and demanded the work be removed. The association threatened to shut down the exhibition should the work remain on exhibit.

In response, Shaowanasai created a smaller, companion piece – *Portrait of a Man in Habits 2* – which had a much smaller photo of the same monk, now dressed in a white shirt, holding a blue handkerchief and wearing a despondent look on his face. This character is commonly known as 'Tid', or a man who had just left the Buddhist monkhood. This picture was placed underneath the image of the larger monk portrait, which remained on exhibit albeit rolled up so that the image was no longer visible.

Michael Shaowanasai (b. 1964, Philadephia, United States) received a Bachelor of Fine Art from the San Francisco Art Institute and a Masters of Fine Art from The School of the Art Institute of Chicago. Based in Bangkok, he is multidisciplinary artist whose work encompasses film, performance, photography and installation.

(KH)

Vasan Sitthiket

American Dream

2004
Woodcut on paper and board
Woodcut 180 x 90 cm,
print 200 x 98 cm

Singapore Art Museum
collection

Criticising the unabashed advertising of the 'American dream' – an almost utopian vision that stands on the ethos of liberty and democracy – Vasan Sitthiket laments how many have been lulled by these lofty ideals and got burnt in its pursuit.

American Dream predominantly features a white dog dressed in a blue suit, black boots and top hat, embellished with stars and stripes from the American flag. This 'dog' is illustrated defecating and wielding a rocket, while standing between two black clouds: one inscribed with the word "democrazy" and the other, "liberty". A speech bubble from the dog says: "Follow me and you'll be save, ha, ha..." On the lower segment of the artwork, there are depictions of five blue, naked human figures spinning round a glowing orb, as if they are drifting in a dream, towards a flaming sun.

Vasan Sitthiket (b. 1957, Nakhorn Sawan, Thailand) graduated from the College of Fine Art in Bangkok. Sitthiket's works confront the exploitation of the poor by the wealthy as well as the corruption present in politics. Sitthiket explores multiple mediums to articulate his ideas. The use of paintings, drawings, woodcut prints, installations and performances are some of the media he has used for his works. Sitthiket has participated in various exhibitions abroad and represented Thailand at the Venice Biennale in 2003.

(KH)

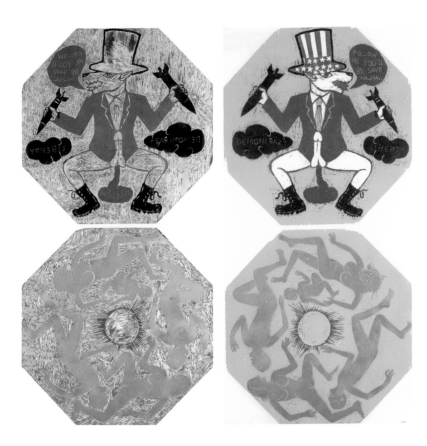

Vasan Sitthiket

Committing Suicide Culture: The Only Way Thai Farmers Escape Debt

1995
Plywood, metal, rope, rice and paint
450 x 250 x 150 cm

Singapore Art Museum collection

Committing Suicide Culture: The Only Way Thai Farmers Escape Debt is bold as it presents a social problem in an unapologetic and confrontational stance, and is a reminder of the price a society has to pay for the degeneration and disregard of traditional values and knowledge. Here, the cause of suicides is blamed on bad credit, a phenomenon not unusual amongst farmers in developing countries such as Thailand who, in today's capitalist climate, have to pay a high price for unpredictable returns. The plight of farmers is understandably a subject that is very close and personal to Vasan Sitthiket as he comes from a lineage of farmers. According to Sitthiket, his farming family is "inspiring yet still poor".

Farming and its traditions are fast rendered obsolete by urban migration and technological advancements. As described in the title of the work, suicides amongst farmers in Thailand are real, unjust and unnecessary. Rice, the crop/commodity featured in this installation through the use of mounds of husks, is the staple diet of Thailand (and the rest of Southeast Asia) and, to the artist, also represents the masses, the common people. This work is a striking example of Sitthiket's oeuvre as a long-time social crusader and national critic.

Vasan Sitthiket (b. 1957, Nakhorn Sawan, Thailand) graduated from the College of Fine Art in Bangkok. Sitthiket's works confront the exploitation of the poor by the wealthy as well as the corruption present in politics. Sitthiket explores multiple mediums to articulate his ideas. The use of paintings, drawings, woodcut prints, installations and performances are some of the media he has used for his works. Sitthiket has participated in various exhibitions abroad and represented Thailand at the Venice Biennale in 2003.

(KH)

(Detail)

Manit Sriwanichpoom

Coup d'etat Photo Op

2006
Gelatin silver print, set of 12
Edition 1/9
49 x 49 cm (each)

Singapore Art Museum
collection

Manit Sriwanichpoom's photographs deal with themes of consumerism and other Thai social and political issues, through critical documentation, as well as his staged satirical depictions of Thai society today. This series of photographs show Sriwanichpoom's documentation of the extensive protest of Thai people, resulting in Thailand's *coup d'etat* on the 19th September, 2006. The transition was motivated by four beliefs: firstly, the social segregation caused by the former Prime Minister Thaksin Shinawatra; secondly, the country being corruptly managed to benefit groups of associates; thirdly, the intervention of independent organisations; and lastly, the commitment of *lèse majesté*. The *coup d'etat* was carried out while the former Prime Minister attended a United Nations conference in New York. The incident did not result in any bloodshed, nor were there any reports of injuries. While many countries voiced their disapproval of the *coup d'etat*, a large number of Thai citizens and foreign tourists flocked to the Royal Plaza to give each other flowers and encouragement, as well as take photographs as souvenirs of the gathering.

Manit Sriwanichpoom (b. 1961, Bangkok, Thailand) has exhibited extensively around the world, including at the 6th Asia Pacific Triennial of Contemporary Art, Brisbane, Australia (2010), the 6th Gwangju Biennale, South Korea (2006), the 1st Pocheon Asian Art Festival, Korea (2005), and the 50th Venice Biennale, Italy (2003).

(MH)

Manit Sriwanichpoom

Horror in Pink (#1, #3 and #5)

2001
C-prints, edition 4/7
189 x 120 cm, 120 x 165 cm,
120 x 160 cm

Singapore Art Museum
collection

Known for his 'Pink Man' series of works that critiques the consumerism and political apathy of present-day Thai society, *Horror in Pink* is a further development of this body of works that began in 1997. Sriwanichpoom features *Pink Man* in a historically significant event, the 6 October Massacre, in which many left-wing students were killed as the army and paramilitary forces stormed the Thammasat University campus in Bangkok in 1976. By inserting *Pink Man* in these photos, the artist evokes the memory of this painful episode in Thai history in the present, raising the complex issues of democracy that Thai society has historically had to grapple. *Pink Man* is performed by Thai artist-poet, Sompong Thawee.

Manit Sriwanichpoom (b. 1961, Bangkok, Thailand) has exhibited extensively around the world, including at the 6th Asia Pacific Triennial of Contemporary Art, Brisbane, Australia (2010), the 6th Gwangju Biennale, South Korea (2006), the 1st Pocheon Asian Art Festival, Korea (2005), and the 50th Venice Biennale, Italy (2003).

(MH)

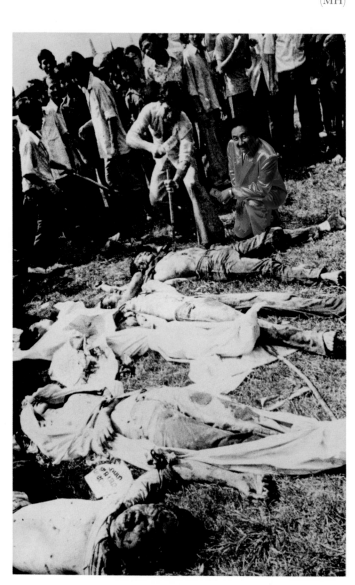

Right:
Horror in Pink #5

Facing page:
Top:
Horror in Pink #1

Bottom:
Horror in Pink #3

Manit Sriwanichpoom

Waiting For the King (Sitting)

2006
Gelatin print, set of 13
Edition 1/9
60.5 x 50.5 cm (each)

Singapore Art Museum collection

In *Waiting for the King (Sitting)*, Manit captures the psyche of Thai society and its relationship with its revered king, Bhumibol Adulyadej (Rama IX). In Thailand, where the monarchy is preserved alongside an elected government, King Adulyadej remains a key symbolic figure for Thai people. The images were taken on 5th December 2006, the King's birthday as well as Thailand's National Father's Day, and the year was particularly significant as it was the 60th anniversary of the King's coronation. At that time, tens of thousands of people from the different provinces of Thailand gathered on the Royal Ground for a glimpse of the king as his motorcade travelled past to the Grand Palace. Manit's frames a scenario in this series of 13 photographs, in which the crowd waits with stoic patience, behind grilled fences. They look out from behind the bars, toward the camera, which is you, their audience. The works convey a sense of irrevocable distance between the king and his subjects. The king remains absent, and the humdrum of anticipation is amplified in this series of repeated snapshots.

Manit Sriwanichpoom (b. 1961, Bangkok, Thailand) has exhibited extensively around the world, including at the 6th Asia Pacific Triennial of Contemporary Art, Brisbane, Australia (2010), the 6th Gwangju Biennale, South Korea (2006), the 1st Pocheon Asian Art Festival, Korea (2005), and the 50th Venice Biennale, Italy (2003).

(MH)

Manit Sriwanichpoom

Masters

2009
Epson archival ink on archival
paper, set of 18, edition 1/3
129 x 100 cm (each)

Singapore Art Museum
collection

Faith and devotion figure largely in the psyche of Buddhist Thailand, but according to Manit Sriwanichpoom, even this domain of worship is not spared from the mechanisms of consumerism. Revered Thai masters are being idolised in their mass-produced form of life-like resin replicas, and the veneration of these masters often stem from the popular belief in their reputed magical powers, rather than the faith in Buddhist teachings. Manit intentionally photographs the idols in this manner to make a statement about blind faith, revealing how commercialisation of Thai Buddhism can obscure true faith.

Manit Sriwanichpoom (b. 1961, Bangkok, Thailand) has exhibited extensively around the world, including at the 6th Asia Pacific Triennial of Contemporary Art, Brisbane, Australia (2010), the 6th Gwangju Biennale, South Korea (2006), the 1st Pocheon Asian Art Festival, Korea (2005), and the 50th Venice Biennale, Italy (2003).

(MH)

Natee Utarit

Tales of Yesterday, Today and Tomorrow

2009
Oil on linen
240 x 200 cm

Singapore Art Museum
collection

Tales of Yesterday, Today and Tomorrow is loosely based on the composition of renowned artist Diego Velázquez's 1656 painting, *Las Meninas*. *Las Meninas* is a depiction of a portrait-painting session set in one of King Philip IV of Spain's palace salons. It features a complex arrangement of 12 characters in a painting session: Princess Infanta Margarita, born of Philip IV's second wife Mariana of Austria, her two ladies-in-waiting, a chaperone, bodyguard, two dwarves, a dog and the Queen's chamberlain, the artist himself, and the King and Queen within the pictorial frame. It is unique in its composition and unusual arrangement of characters within the spatial scheme, with the King and Queen present only in their reflection in a strategically placed mirror, while their subjects are placed in the foreground. In terms of the spatial dynamics of painting, it is described as a masterpiece of 17th century portraiture.

 Tales of Yesterday, Today and Tomorrow employs a similar compositional strategy to Velázquez's work, but this time the 12 characters are replaced by a set of toys: a group of dwarves (from Disney's Snow White), a rabbit and a toy soldier in pink – a colour that bears obvious meaning in the context in Thailand. A cheeky artistic pun on the original work, ***Tales*** is also a complex work that alludes to both the history of the 17th century Spanish court and the Thai kingdom of today.

 Natee Utarit (b. 1970, Thailand) graduated from Silpakorn University, Bangkok, in 1992, majoring in painting, sculpture and graphic art. He has exhibited at the 3rd Asia Pacific Triennial of Contemporary Art in Brisbane, Australia (1999), and held his solo exhibition 'Natee Utarit: After Painting' at the Singapore Art Museum in 2010.

(MH)

Natee Utarit

The Ballad for Khrua In Khong / Greyscale

2005
Oil on canvas, set of 50
40 x 50 cm (each)

Singapore Art Museum
collection

A monk and celebrated court painter during the reign of King Rama IV, Khrua In Khong was known for his striking murals in the temples of Bangkok as well as those in Thai provinces. While his subject matter remained local, his painterly style was reminiscent of European traditions in painting, such as chiaroscuro techniques as well as perspectival influences of the Renaissance. Interestingly, Khrua In Khong developed these styles not under the tutelage of a Western master, but through the practice and mimicking of styles from European and American postcards sent to the palace at a time when photographic postcards were popular as an international trend.

In an attempt to examine copying as a legitimate means of representation, Utarit retraces the steps of Khrua In Khong in his creation of *The Ballad for Khrua In Khong*. By painting some 50 black-and-white postcards that he had procured from eBay, without having actually been to the featured destinations the cards portray, the artist creates a dialogue between the world of information and the world of imagination.

Natee Utarit (b. 1970, Thailand) graduated from Silpakorn University, Bangkok, in 1992, majoring in painting, sculpture and graphic art. He has exhibited at the 3rd Asia Pacific Triennial of Contemporary Art in Brisbane, Australia (1999), and held his solo exhibition 'Natee Utarit: After Painting' at the Singapore Art Museum in 2010.

(MH)

Natee Utarit

The Birth of Tragedy
2010
Oil on canvas
240 x 600 cm (triptych)

Singapore Art Museum
collection

Natee Utarit's paintings from 2005 to 2009 feature a variety of everyday life objects as his way of telling stories. Of significance during this period, is his shift in focus to commenting on the social situation in Thailand. The artist, who is known previously for paintings that applied Western stylistic conventions, also revisits the still life, a genre that is traditionally considered secondary to established categories like Mythology, History, Portrait and Landscape paintings.

Seen in this work is the tendency in this period to transpose fairy tales and fiction into national narratives; his employment of art historical styles and the depictions of toys, serves to signify a host of powerful meanings. *The Birth of Tragedy* is Natee's largest masterpiece to-date, painted during a critical juncture in the climate of politics in the Thai kingdom, and alluding to an uncertain future to come.

Natee Utarit (b. 1970, Thailand) graduated from Silpakorn University, Bangkok, in 1992, majoring in painting, sculpture and graphic art. He has exhibited at the 3rd Asia Pacific Triennial of Contemporary Art in Brisbane, Australia (1999), and held his solo exhibition 'Natee Utarit: After Painting' at the Singapore Art Museum in 2010.

(MH)

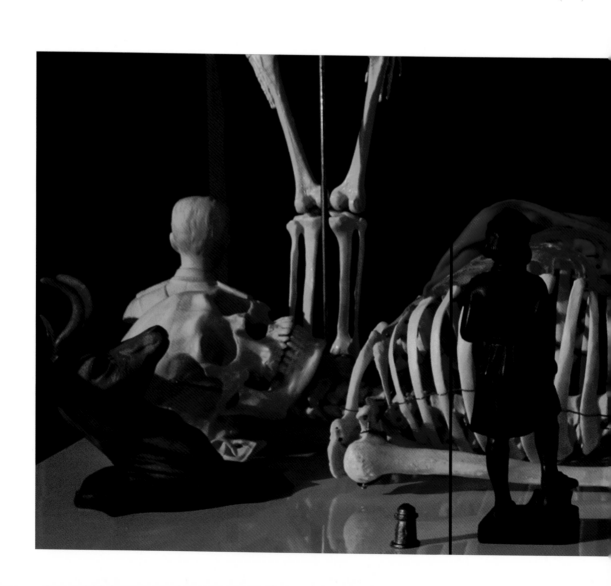

Natee Utarit

The Crown

2010
Bronze and gold leaf, edition 5/6
18 x 19 x 14 cm

Gift of Richard Koh Fine Arts

Singapore Art Museum
collection

The Crown can be seen as the artist's response to an important juncture in contemporary Thai society, when the future of the Thai monarchy is being deliberated. It is part of Utarit's 'Illustration of the Crisis' series of works, of which his masterpiece, *The Birth of Tragedy*, is part of, and follows from his artistic strategy of using still-life arrangements embedded with metaphorical meanings.

Natee Utarit (b. 1970, Thailand) graduated from Silpakorn University, Bangkok, in 1992, majoring in painting, sculpture and graphic art. He has exhibited at the 3rd Asia Pacific Triennial of Contemporary Art in Brisbane, Australia (1999), and held his solo exhibition 'Natee Utarit: After Painting' at the Singapore Art Museum in 2010.

(MH)

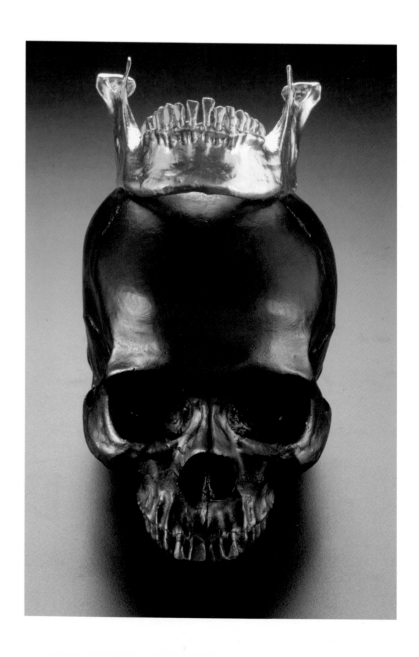

Natee Utarit

The Western Light No. 1

2006
Oil on canvas
200 x 180 cm

Singapore Art Museum
collection

The Western Light No. 1 features Rama V (King Chulalongkorn), Thailand's revered king and most successful reformer, who was also the first Thai monarch to travel to the West. During his reign, Thailand maintained her independence from European colonial rule. This work recalls the bronze equestrian statue of Rama V that was commissioned in 1908 at Bangkok city's Royal Plaza symbolising Thailand's promising future. In the Natee Utarit's rendition, the statue is rendered with a foreboding, dark palette in contrast to the actual monument, suggesting a tarnished present-day reality instead of the blazing destiny it is meant to represent.

Known for the adherence to established Western painting traditions, Natee's ultimate aim was to develop new possibilities for painting. Of late, the artist's recent work since the mid-2000s, however, have increasingly been commentaries on Thai society and identity, as he uses painting as a powerful means of commenting on the changing socio-political situations in his country.

Natee Utarit (b. 1970, Thailand) graduated from Silpakorn University, Bangkok, in 1992, majoring in painting, sculpture and graphic art. He has exhibited at the 3rd Asia Pacific Triennial of Contemporary Art in Brisbane, Australia (1999), and held his solo exhibition 'Natee Utarit: After Painting' at the Singapore Art Museum in 2010.

(MH)

Promthum Woravut

My First Day

2010
Graphite on paper
175 x 184 cm

Singapore Art Museum
collection

In this work, Promthum Woravut chooses the subject-matter of childhood memories, particularly defined by early school days to explore the concerns and psyche of the generation of Thai youths today. At first glance, **My First Day** appears as a nostalgic depiction of a child's first day at school, guided by her parents on her side, as she embarks on her journey of learning, and passage into adulthood. Upon closer look however, the work which is made up of individual pieces of Multiple Choice Question (MCQ) answer sheets often used in examinations, seems to suggest that childhood is not as carefree as it is commonly thought to be.

Imitating the same practice used in school examinations, the artist coloured various areas of the MCQ options to render the image. By doing so, he highlights how children have been imposed with modes of standardised learning and systematic thinking in the school environment where they are constantly being graded. To the artist, children are not exempted from the pressures of contemporary society to excel, having to face the rat race that begins at school, at a tender age.

Promthum Woravut (b. 1985, Thailand) is an emerging Thai contemporary artist who graduated from the School of Fine and Applied Arts in Bangkok University in 2010.

(MH)

Southeast Asia

VIETNAM

Tiffany Chung
Dinh Q. Le
Jun Nguyen-Hatsushiba
Nguyen Van Cuong
Tung Mai
The Propeller Group
Richard Streitmatter-Tran
Tran Luong
Vu Dan Tan
Vuong Van Thao

Tiffany Chung

Enokiberry Tree in Wonderland

2008–2010
Mixed media installation with 8
C-prints and 2 MDF sculptures
Dimensions variable

Singapore Art Museum
collection

Tiffany Chung represents a new wave of young Vietnamese artists who have returned to Vietnam, after prolonged periods of residence abroad. Works by many of these artists often deal with notions of diaspora and frequently highlight the rapid socio-political changes of a country driven by drastic redevelopment plans. Chung also references other forms of popular culture in many of her works, thereby making astute statements about the porosity of globalisation. Through the lens of spatial and cultural transformations in Vietnam, Chung's works attempt to re-imagine the urban landscape by referencing the rapid pace of economic development in Vietnam. She imagines an increasingly urban Vietnam, where the vibrant city life is part sci-fi, part cosplay, and part fantasy. The Enokiberry tree installation alludes to Japanese Enoki mushrooms and references the parasitic nature of mushrooms. Urban development parallels this parasitic sprouting of mushrooms, in that they overtake host sites and destabilize existing eco-systems.

Tiffany Chung (b. 1969, Vietnam) is a freelance film editor, script supervisor and graphic designer. She graduated with a Bachelor of Fine Art in Photography at the California State University, Long Beach, United States in 1998, and completed her Masters of Fine Art in Studio Art at the University of California, Santa Barbara in 2000. Notable solo exhibitions include 'Play' at Tyler Rollins Fine Art, New York, and 'Wonderland' at Galerie Quynh in Ho Chi Minh City, Vietnam. Chung currently lives and works in Ho Chi Minh City, Vietnam.

(NW)

Dinh Q. Le

The Farmers and
the Helicopters

2006
3-channel video installation with
3 digital files with colour and
stereo sound, PAL, edition 3/5
Duration 15:00 mins (loop)

Singapore Art Museum
collection

The Farmers and the Helicopters is a video installation consisting of present-day interview footages of Vietnamese farmers, clips from Hollywood war movies, and archival clips of helicopters during the war. Set in the context of the Vietnam-American war, this work is significant as this was the first war where helicopters were extensively used (over 12,000 American helicopters). The visual impact on the population in Vietnam is thus profound and ever-present. In this video, a spectrum of memories evoked by the sight and sound of a helicopter is explored. While some associate helicopters with war and violence, others perceive it a machine of peace, referencing its more recent function of transporting food and aid to disaster-areas. The latter opinion, championed by Le Van Danh (a farmer) and Tran Quoc Hai (a self-taught mechanic), is also expressed through their combined efforts in building a helicopter from scrap materials and machine remnants over a six-year period. This self-built machine of peace is utilised to assist in agricultural needs and to evacuate people in emergency situations.

This work is a collaboration by Dinh Q. Le with Tran Quoc Hai, Le Van Danh, Phu-Nam Thuc Ha, and Tuan Andrew Nguyen.

Dinh Q. Le, (b. 1968, Vietnam) received his Bachelor of Arts in art studio at UC Santa Barbara, United States, and his Master of Fine Art in Photography and Related Media at The School of Visual Arts in New York City. Notable solo exhibitions include 'Project 93: Dinh Q. Le at Museum of Modern Art' in New York (2010), the 4th Fukuoka Asian Art Triennale (2009), and the Venice Biennale (2003).

(NW)

Jun Nguyen-Hatsushiba

Breathing is Free: 12,756.3

2009
Video installation, 6 digital files
with colour and sound, NTSC
Dimensions variable
Durations 13:30 mins,
17:30 mins, 25 mins, 9:30 mins,
15 mins, 19:30 mins

Singapore Art Museum
collection

Breathing is Free: 12,756.3 is the culmination of the artist's memorial projects to date. In this video, the artist has selected running videos from Ho Chi Minh City, Tokyo, Taipei, Luang Prabang and Singapore. The artist runs the distance of 12,356.3 km, the diameter of the earth. A Global Positioning System (GPS) is used to track the data of the run, which is then transferred onto aerial photographs of cities, drawing paths over the infrastructure of the land. The recorded data references the hardship of refugees and the struggles of their physical displacement. The marathon is a literal reference to refugees who are constantly on the run. The frame-by-frame sequence employed by the artist allows viewers to visually experience space through motion, thus tracking the artist's physical migration across time and place.

In Nguyen-Hatsushiba's words, "Running is a part of human existence. We run to hunt, to fight, to compete, to conquer, to condition, to escape, to survive, to move and to migrate. Inevitably, the act of running is invested with the power of humanity, a force invisible like the potential energy of coal – we possess the vitality to initiate these footsteps." This work stands as a testimony to a variety of themes that speak to the artist on a personal level: his experiences with migration, place and belonging, and overall identity.

Jun Nguyen-Hatsushiba (b. 1968, Japan) resides and works in Vietnam. He received his Masters of Fine Arts from the Maryland Institute College of Art, United States, after receiving his Bachelor of Fine Arts from the School of the Art Institute of Chicago, United States. Notable solo exhibitions include the Museo d'arte Contemporanea in Rome (2003 to 2004), and New Museum of Contemporary Art in New York (2003). He also participated in the Venice Biennale (2005) and Tel Aviv Biennale (2002).

(NW)

Jun Nguyen-Hatsushiba

Memorial Project Nha Trang, Vietnam: Towards the Complex – For the Courageous, the Curious and the Cowards

2001
Video projection
Duration 13:00 mins
Edition AP 6/6

Singapore Art Museum collection

Filmed in Nha Trang, the southeast coast of Vietnam, ***Memorial Project Nha Trang, Vietnam: Towards the Complex – For the Courageous, the Curious, and the Cowards*** examines the impact of historical events on present-day Vietnam. This series started in 1994 and is a dedication to the thousands of boat people who attempted to escape Vietnam for fear of political retribution during the Vietnam war. Shot entirely underwater, the artist engaged the participation of six fishermen he met on site. These men struggle to pull rickshaws along the ocean bed and constantly swim back to the surface for air. The divers eventually encounter several mosquito nets affixed to the bottom of the ocean bed. According to the artist, the mosquito nets symbolise a grave for the souls of people who died in their attempt to flee Vietnam after the fall of Saigon in 1975. This procession thus pays homage to the lost lives, and highlights the tedious and challenging circumstances of dislocation. In addition, rickshaws – a common site in many Southeast Asian countries – also reference the aftermath of war as many soldiers became rickshawmen following the war, though recently these vehicles are being phased out from the streets. This work takes a critical look at the consequences of war, nearly 40 years on.

Jun Nguyen-Hatsushiba (b. 1968, Japan) resides and works in Vietnam. He received his Masters of Fine Arts from the Maryland Institute College of Art, United States, after receiving his Bachelor of Fine Arts from the School of the Art Institute of Chicago, United States. Notable solo exhibitions include the Museo d'arte Contemporanea in Rome (2003 to 2004), and New Museum of Contemporary Art in New York (2003). He also participated in the Venice Biennale (2005) and Tel Aviv Biennale (2002).

(NW)

VIETNAM

Nguyen Van Cuong

Cultural Pollution (Porcelain Diary)

1999–2001
Ceramics, set of 5
28 x 10 x 12 cm (each)

Singapore Art Museum
collection

In the late-1990s, Nguyen Van Cuong produced a series of porcelain vases, each hand-painted with narratives examining contemporary Vietnam and the struggles of the Vietnamese people in their search for democracy and a peaceful life. Each vase is unique and portrays a vivid portrait in polychrome, of the country and its contradictions as it embarks on a new course at the end of the 20th century. Crafted in the traditional Vietnamese way and hinting at the tremendous Chinese influence within Southeast Asia, the vases are particularly appealing because of their juxtaposition of contemporary ideas with traditional medium. In particular, they are an acute reminder of the fact that painting in Southeast Asia pre-dates paintings on canvas imported from the West.

Nguyen Van Cuong (b. 1972, Thai Binh, Vietnam) attended the Hanoi Fine Arts College and relatively few of his major works have survived as many were wall murals or works on paper that have subsequently been destroyed. His works were featured in the seminal 1999 exhibition 'Gap Viet Nam' at the House of World Cultures in Berlin, Germany.

(KH)

Tung Mai

Racing Forward

2008–2009
Interactive photo installation
Dimensions variable

Singapore Art Museum
collection

Racing Forward features a rotating screen attached to the front of a bicycle – one of the most common vehicles used in daily transportation. Attached to the screens are digitally manipulated images of Vietnam and Singapore. Visitors are encouraged to ride the bicycle, and the pedalling motion will cause the hexagonal box to spin. By referencing the motion and speed of riding a bicycle, the artist makes a literal reference to the pace of one's life, thus cautioning audiences of the need to moderate their lives. Engineered in this interactive display is also the need for participants to pedal backwards in order to spin the box. The ability to view all the images therefore depends on a reversal of conventional behaviour. Beyond a contemplative look into the pace of individual lives, *Racing Forward* also makes a poignant statement about the discord between the preservation of history and that of rapid economic progress in Southeast Asian countries such as Vietnam and Singapore.

Tung Mai (b. 1985, Vietnam) graduated from Royal Melbourne Institute of Technology (RMIT) University in Vietnam with a major in Multimedia Design. He participated in the Singapore Biennale in 2008.

(NW)

The Propeller Group
(Tuan Andrew Nguyen, Phunam Thuc Ha & Matthew Charles Lucero)

Uh...

2007
Single-channel video projection
with 1 digital file, PAL, colour and
stereo sound, edition 2/7
Duration 7:00 mins (loop)

Singapore Art Museum
collection

The video features the work of a fictitious graffiti artist who goes by the alias, 'Uh'. In leaving his mark on numerous walls of Ho Chi Minh City's urban landscape, the artist makes a statement about one's state of presence and ownership in the city. This video work is particularly interesting because of the treatment of the graffiti work. Unlike most video works, where spaces are conventionally flattened, the 'floating' graffiti image gives a sense of an expansion of space, as seen by how pedestrians and motorists pass through behind the 'floating' graffiti image. This unexpected element plays on notions of the imagined and resonates strongly with the rapid urbanisation occurring in Vietnam and its impact on one's sense of physical displacement. Coupled with the influx of Western culture on the country's youth, the work speaks about a certain sense of cultural displacement in a home that is becoming physically alienating to a "local" sensibility.

The Propeller Group (formed 2006, Ho Chi Minh City, Vietnam) consists of Phunam Thuc Ha (b. 1974, Vietnam), Matt Lucero (b. 1976, United States) and Tuan Andrew Nguyen (b. 1976, Vietnam). Selected exhibitions include 'Open House', the 3rd Singapore Biennale (2011), 'Against Easy Listening' at 1A Space, Hong Kong (2010) and the 8th Shanghai Biennale's 'Rehearsal' (with superflex), Shanghai (2010).

(NW)

Richard Streitmatter-Tran

Missed Connections

2004–2010
Video installation, edition 1/5
Dimensions variable,
duration 8:00 mins

Singapore Art Museum
collection

Streitmatter-Tran was amongst the thousands of children who were part of 'Operation Babylift' – an American initiative in the 1970's, which enabled the adoption of Vietnamese children across the Western world. One of the biggest controversies to plague 'Operation Babylift' was the extent of accurate documentation which surrounds the circumstances of these adoptions. This video encapsulates the 'Operation Babylift' controversy through the personal story of Streitmatter-Tran.

Themes of memory, loss and nostalgia are explored in this video which makes direct reference to Streitmatter-Tran's personal experience of growing up not knowing his birth family. At the start of the video, individuals mirror each other's actions; this act of duplicity establishes a chord of camaraderie between them. Connection is however lost over time as each individual pursues his own activity. Literally referencing the title "Missed Connections", this video touches upon the ephemeral quality of chance and encounters.

Richard Streitmatter-Tran (b. 1972, Vietnam) participated in the Singapore Biennale (2008), Venice Biennale (2007) and Gwangju Biennale (2004). He also co-curated Mapping the Mekong in the 6th Asia Pacific Triennial of Contemporary Art, Brisbane, Australia (2009). Tran returned to Vietnam in 2003 and has since continued to live and work in Ho Chi Minh City, Vietnam.

(NW)

VIETNAM

Richard Streitmatter-Tran

The Jungle Book

2008–2009
Photo installation
Dimensions variable

Singapore Art Museum
collection

Borrowing its name from Rudyard Kipling's famous collection of stories, ***The Jungle Book*** is part of a larger project undertaken by the artist, where he attempts to examine the discord between fact and fiction in the Mekong sub-region. The two photographs were taken using a super wide-angle lens, after which the artist composited the models of the giant catfish and satellites into the images and then further altered the images to a tilt-shift in order to make it more difficult to distinguish between the real and the fictional.

In the first photograph, a giant catfish lies on the bank of the Mekong river. Its sheer size alludes to that of a whale and the phenomenon of 'whale worship' in Vietnam. In the second photograph, there is the same play on fiction and spectacle in the depiction of a satellite crashing into one of Ho Chi Minh City's many canals. Here, the artist references Vietnam's 2008 launch of its first national satellite into space, marking Vietnam's accelerated modernisation scheme. In blurring the boundaries between fact and fiction, ***The Jungle Book*** brings into question notions of belief systems and change, as well as the nature of perception and reality. In the artist's words, "While the series speaks of fluidity between fact and fiction, the photographs are fictional, being composed using 3-dimensional models. Making no attempt to be convincing, the artifices are to be celebrated."

Richard Streitmatter-Tran (b. 1972, Vietnam) participated in the Singapore Biennale (2008), Venice Biennale (2007) and Gwangju Biennale (2004). He also co-curated Mapping the Mekong in the 6th Asia Pacific Triennial of Contemporary Art, Brisbane, Australia (2009). Tran returned to Vietnam in 2003 and has since continued to live and work in Ho Chi Minh City, Vietnam.

(NW)

Tran Luong

Red Scarf / Welts

2010
Video, edition 1/1
Duration 2:51 mins

Singapore Art Museum
collection

Usually performed in front of a 'live' audience, *Red Scarf / Welts* was inspired by the artist's observation of a prank by his son and friends. It involves the use of a regular handkerchief, rolled quickly between two hands, then lashed repeatedly onto the body of the other. This action causes welts to form on the skin of the person whose body it had been inflicted. Although innocent and playful, this action can lead to bleeding and the tearing of one's skin. For the artist, this resembles how soft or invisible violence can be, which may be as hurtful and aggravating as one that is obvious. This video was specially commissioned by Singapore Art Museum for the 'Negotiating Home, History and Nation' exhibition in 2011.

Tran Luong (b. 1960, Vietnam) graduated from the Hanoi Fine Arts Institute in 1983 and began as a painter. He works with video, new media, performance installation and conceptual art.

(KH)

VIETNAM

Vu Dan Tan

Amazon Series No. 8

2001–2004
Metal bottle caps, screws, cut-out,
hammered and embellished
sheet metal
160 x 75 x 20 cm

Amazon Series No. 9

2001–2004
Screws, cut-out, hammered and
embellished sheet metal
160 x 75 x 20 cm

Singapore Art Museum
collection

Personally hand-made by the artist, only 13 of these metal-suits that form the *Amazon Series* were ever realised. Its production was physically demanding for the artist as he began making them when he was already in his late-fifties, several years before he passed away in 2009.

Amazon Series 8 and *9* expand Vu Dan Tan's dialogue on perceptions of shell and skin (exterior) in relation to content (interior). His exclusive use and depiction of the female figure and gender in both the earlier 'Fashion' and the 'Amazon' series was deliberate. He employs them as a point to negate issues of control and boundaries and to confront the views of women as objects of desire and contempt.

For the artist, these definitions are interchangeable and are susceptible to the perception/s of its beholder. As an example, in recent times, women in Vietnam enjoy respect and equal public status to men whereas before, during the French colonial rule till the late-1900s, they had been abused and exploited (through the use of repressive Nguyen code adopted from Qing Dynasty China), and as a result, often shut themselves in. These metal 'suits' can also be viewed as the very bodies of the women themselves. They appear sharp, hard and dangerous but at the same time sensuous. They suggest simultaneously an amour, a protection for the flesh, and a reinforced body or a weapon ready for confrontation.

Prior to this, Vu Dan Tan was already cutting, painting and manipulating materials such as Coke cans, cigarette boxes, plastic bottles, cardboard cartons and other similar 'wastes of consumerist culture' as part of his art practice. To the artist, this waste material is a modern signifier and result of the Doi Moi policy (socialist oriented market economy) in Vietnam introduced by its government in 1986. This is in opposition to the practice of most other Vietnamese artists who produced skilfully executed 'exotic', nostalgic and decorative artworks that, although popular with tourists, were almost purely commercial in nature.

One of the first experimental artists in Hanoi, Tan worked with found objects and other commonplace materials, allowing him to unleash his creativity without being limited by cost. At the same time, his use of the discards of consumer culture offers a stark social commentary, in contrast to his sometimes light-hearted creations.

Vu Dan Tan (1946–2009, Vietnam) was born into a literary family in Hanoi and had exhibited internationally. He was represented in the 8th Sculpture Triennial, Fellbach, Germany (2001), 10th Osaka Triennale (2001), Documenta X, Kassel, Germany (1997) and the 2nd Asia Pacific Triennial of Contemporary Art, Brisbane, Australia (1996). In addition to his artistic practice, Tan co-founded Salon Natasha with his wife, Natalia Kraevskaia. The first private and independent gallery in Hanoi, it has fostered the growth of experimental and contemporary art in Vietnam.

(KH)

Vu Dan Tan

Beauty Will Save The World

2003
Recycled cardboard and chinese
ink, suite of 12 sculptures
168 x 36 cm (each)

Singapore Art Museum
collection

Vu Dan Tan's approach to art-making is that of a craftsman. Tan often recycles discarded materials, symbolic of consumer societies and turns them into works of art, often infused with humour and playfulness. A quote from Dostoevsky's novel, "Beauty Will Save The World", provides the name for this suite of 12 cardboard figures, each representative of a female form. Ignoring the rules of conventional aesthetics, these female forms invite the viewer to re-define notions of beauty, beyond the world of physical appearances.

One of the first experimental artists in Hanoi, Tan worked with found objects and other commonplace materials, allowing him to unleash his creativity without being limited by cost. At the same time, his use of discarded materials such as the cardboard in the work, is a pointed critique of the wastages of our consumer society, in contrast to his sometimes light-hearted creations.

Vu Dan Tan (1946–2009, Vietnam) was born into a literary family in Hanoi and had exhibited internationally. He was represented in the 8th Sculpture Triennial, Fellbach, Germany (2001), 10th Osaka Triennale (2001), Documenta X, Kassel, Germany (1997) and the 2nd Asia Pacific Triennial of Contemporary Art, Brisbane, Australia (1996). In addition to his artistic practice, Tan co-founded Salon Natasha with his wife, Natalia Kraevskaia. The first private and independent gallery in Hanoi, it has fostered the growth of experimental and contemporary art in Vietnam.

(NW)

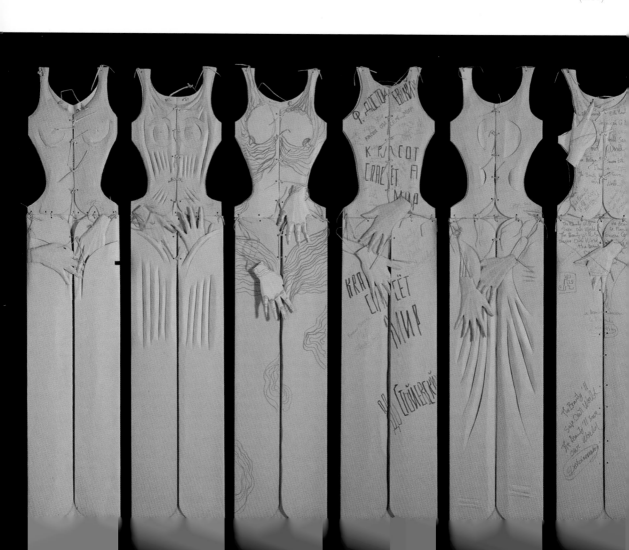

Vuong Van Thao

Living Fossils

2007
Acrylic, stoneware, glaze
Set of 72 pieces
Dimensions variable

Singapore Art Museum
collection

Vuong Van Thao's mixed-media work comprises replicas of 36 buildings located in Hanoi's historic Old Quarter. Each building was specially chosen by the artist for its traditional and historic architectural features and Thao encased his replicas in cracked resin blocks to imitate the look of an aged fossil. The installation maps the actual location of the buildings in the Old Quarter. With rapid modernisation and mass culture threatening the historic and cultural authenticity of Hanoi's Old Quarter, Thao's work touches upon the co-existence of the old and new, historical discontinuity, and displacement. It is also a reaction against uniformity of the city's development.

Vuong Van Thao (1969, Vietnam) graduated from the Hanoi Fine Art University in 1995. Vuong has participated in numerous solo and group exhibitions internationally. In 2008, he was nominated for the Asia Pacific Breweries Foundation Signature Art Prize.

(NW)

(Detail)

Asia

CHINA

Chi Peng
Gao Lei
He Jian
Jia Aili
Miao Xiaochun
Shen Shaomin
Su Xinping
Sun Yuan & Peng Yu
Xing Danwen
Zhang Peng
Zheng Bo
Zhou Xiaohu

Chi Peng

Apollo in Transit

2006
C-print, edition 8/8
66 x 800 cm

Singapore Art Museum
collection

Using the Greek mythological figure of Apollo as a symbol of truth and prophecy, art and culture, Chi Peng's ***Apollo In Transit*** is about contemporary China's youth, and their anxious search for truth in their world. The reference to a western myth is counterbalanced with the distinct format of the work. Its extensive length harks to the traditional Chinese handscroll which is meant to be unrolled from right to left, two to three feet at a time, a viewing process that also requires a certain progression of time.

The figure of the naked man running in front of the walls of The Forbidden City suggests a frantic and endless search for an unknown, higher order goal for his existence and being. Fantastical elements also dot the photograph: giant raindrops (or teardrops) encase the naked adult figures within, all of them in a foetal position, and suggest a new generation being symbolically 'birthed' against the backdrop of China's Forbidden City walls.

Chi Peng (b. 1981, Yantai, China) represents the new generation of Chinese artists born during the period of the One Child policy. He uses digital media and photography to express his thoughts and ideas in the midst of radical social change and transformation in China. His works have been presented in museums such as the Centre Pompidou, France, and at the 3rd Fukuoka Asian Art Triennale, Japan (2005).

(DC)

(Detail)

Gao Lei

Cabinet

2008
Installation with metal cabinet
and 3 rows of lightboxes
Edition 1/2
270 x 45 x 190 cm (each)

Singapore Art Museum
collection

Gao Lei's installation comprises of a custom-made metal cabinet that holds 24 prints of photographs from two series of works, *Building No.35* and *Scene*. *Building No.35* depicts rooms in nearly deserted buildings occupied by fictional inhabitants, and *Scene* – which was made to complement the first series – features the exteriors of buildings in China, and also similarly inserts a fictitious character into each street scene.

The use of peephole boxes to view the photographs recreates the experience of cultural surveillance as experienced in China today, in which the expressions and sentiments of contemporary China need to be kept hidden and can only be 'peeped at'. The 24 prints viewed through the peephole also feature computer-generated characters, from young female toy characters to plastic dinosaurs and aliens that come from the imaginary world created by the artist. Placed in scenarios reflecting the current economic reality of China, where construction and building are occurring at a rapid pace, these fictional characters convey the loss of childhood and innocence in contemporary China today, and also the increasing sense of displacement of today's young generation.

Gao Lei (b. 1980, Changsha, China) studied at the Digital Media Department of Central Academy of Fine Arts. In 2011, he participated in several group exhibitions. including the Mercator Foundation, Essen, Germany; Arario Beijing Gallery, China, and Arario Cheonan Gallery, Cheonan, Korea. In the same year, he also had a solo exhibition in White Space, Beijing, China.

(DC)

He Jian

Rostrum No. 1

2008
Chinese ink on paper
76 x 169 cm

Singapore Art Museum
collection

Chinese artist He Jian is best known for his contemporary paintings that are intentionally made to look old, using rice paper and dry pigments. Inspired by the Yuan Dynasty frescoes at the Yong Le Temple in Shanxi, he adopts the antiquated look and traditional aesthetics of an art form first used in temples to commemorate deities and gods in Chinese culture.

Capturing a seemingly mundane moment in which there is no human subject, *Rostrum No.1* references the politically tumultuous past of China through the innocuous depiction of a rostrum set up with flowers and a placard, in preparation of a meeting. The scene, however, examines the nation-building event of the Long March in China that took place between 1934 and 1936. This historical journey marks the ascent to power of Mao Zedong, whose leadership during the retreat gained him the support of the members of his party, securing their places as future leaders of China. This is referenced by the name plaque in front of the rostrum, which has the Chinese characters of the name of the missing person whose name reads 'nation building'. The work also recalls the importance of the Long March in determining the current power base of China, where the individuals who joined Mao on the March became the generation of leaders that went on to govern China. The absent official who has most power and influence holds the position of 'rostrum speaker' as suggested in this painting. This is one of the rare works by He Jian that centres on a historical event as its subject.

He Jian (b. 1978, Sichuan, China) graduated in 2000 from the Chinese Painting Department of Sichuan Fine Arts Institute, China. In 2007, he participated in exhibitions in Robischon Gallery, United States, as well as the 'Sichuan School of Painting 30 Years' exhibition in Beijing, China, and the third Guiyang Art Triennium Exhibition in Guizhou, China.

(DC)

Jia Aili

Old Painter I

2008–2009
Oil on canvas
229 x 400 cm

Singapore Art Museum
collection

The title of Jia Aili's work, which can be translated as "old painter" or "old artist", tries to sound an alarm to what the artist feels is the decline or marginalisation of painting in contemporary art. The painting is reminiscent of the monumental 'apocalyptic wasteland' paintings that Jia has done over the years, but in this case there are also semblances of a used car junkyard, in which an old figure now stands. The artist seems to be suggesting that this elderly man could stand for the ancient tradition of painting, which manages to survive and stay alive, despite being cast aside into the junkyard of history for newer artistic trends.

Jia Aili (b. 1979, Liaoning Dandong, China) resides and works in Beijing. He has been part of a group of Chinese artists who have wanted to explore the ultimate meaning of painting. Jia Aili has had recent solo exhibitions in London, Hong Kong, America and Beijing in 2010.

(DC)

Miao Xiaochun

Microcosm

2008
Fine art archival print, set of 9
panels, edition 3/5
300 x 1246 cm (total)

Microcosm: Garden of Heavenly Delights

2000
Video, edition 6/9
Duration 15:56 mins

The Last Judgement in Cyberspace

2006
C-prints, set of 17 panels
Edition 5/5
360 x 2080 cm (total)

Singapore Art Museum
collection

This series of works by multi-disciplinary artist Miao Xiaochun take as their starting point, two renowned works in Western art history, but the Chinese artist has used computer technology and digital imaging to recast these Western paintings as virtual cyberworlds, which offer multiple viewpoints of a single scene.

Microcosm's digital prints are based on Hieronymus Bosch's 15th century masterpiece, *The Garden of Earthly Delights*, which portrays the Christian narrative of mankind, starting with the union of Adam and Eve in the Garden of Eden, and ending in the horrors of hell for sinners during the Last Judgement. In Miao's version, the formal left-to-right composition that depict the Garden of Eden, earth and hell are similar as that of the original painting, but he offers multiple perspectives and new vantage points of these different scenes through the different panels of the work.

The video *Microcosm* conveys some of the ills and catastrophes that face the world today. The artist recreates a world in which different metaphors and allegories are constructed to "reflect modern people's views on life and death, their desires, and their view on humans' weaknesses", as he puts it. The work represents the deconstruction of history, and also the transition and crossing of traditional Chinese art into the virtual world.

In *The Last Judgement in Cyberspace*, Michelangelo's Sistine Chapel fresco is similarly re-imagined as a virtual computer world of the Apocalypse, where the Christian afterlife is tiered with heaven on top and hell below – only this time the same scene can be seen from various angles in the 17 panels of the work. The artist has individually replaced the 400 figures in Michelangelo's iconic work with a computer generated figure modelled after himself that represents the Everyman, again offering different vantage points of Christ's return, from both within and outside of the scene.

Miao Xiaochun (b.1964, Wuxi, Jiangsu, China) has been expanding the boundaries of new media art, creating installations of multiple dimensions that include photographs and 3D animation videos. Inspired by canonical art historical works, Miao's digitally manipulated worlds paint an alien view of contemporary China, conveying the alienated and disconnected sense of Chinese life today, while envisioning a new dynastic era.

(DC)

Below: *Microcosm*

Above: Detail of *Microcosm: Garden of Heavenly Delights*

Miao Xiaochun

The Last Judgement in Cyberspace
2006
C-prints, set of 17 panels
Edition 5/5
360 x 2080 cm (total)

Singapore Art Museum collection

Shen Shaomin

Summit

2010
Installation with silica gel
simulation, acrylic and fabric
Dimensions variable

Singapore Art Museum
collection

Summit simulates a congregation of world leaders whose agenda is to discuss political events of the world. The meeting consists of prominent communist leaders in history, such as Vladimir Lenin, Mao Zedong, Kim Il Sung, Ho Chi Minh and Fidel Castro. Significantly, however, the leaders have been placed in coffins that are open and serve as constant reminders to the living, and each coffin shaped like the actual coffin that exists in the hallowed mausoleums they each occupy. The exception is Castro, who is depicted as being on his last dying breath on a hospital bed, and is fitted out with a mechanism that makes him look like he is actually breathing.

The work is a reaction to the global financial crisis, attributed to the failure of capitalism. This piece mirrors the dreams these communist leaders possessed, but despite their idealist goals, have become lost visions due to the corruption of power, and the work hails this as the last summit among world leaders who have stood as towering ideological figures in modern world history.

Shen Shaomin (b. 1956, Heilongjiang Province, China) has taken part in group exhibitions such as the 17th Biennale of Sydney, in 2010, where *Summit* was shown, and in MAD Museum in New York, also in 2010. His recent solo exhibitions were held at ART CHANNEL, Beijing, China, and Eli Klein Fine Art, New York, USA, in 2010. He has since had 12 solo exhibitions in Hong Kong, Switzerland, Australia and the United States.

(DC)

Su Xinping

Comrade and Toast Series No. 4

2006
Lithograph on STPI handmade
white paper
Edition AP 3
102 x 127 cm

Comrade and Toast Series No. 5

2006
Lithograph on STPI handmade
white paper
Edition 7/15
102 x 127 cm

Singapore Art Museum
collection

Su Xinping's use of satirical stylistic imagery from government propaganda addresses his social concerns stemming from the fallout of the Cultural Revolution. Su had served as a soldier with the Red Guards but was later sentenced to hard labour in Inner Mongolia.

In *Comrade and Toast Series No. 4*, images of men wearing Mao and western business suits stand in perfect ease with each other. They are captured in the act of 'toasting', which is traditionally reserved for the celebration of a joyous occasion, and they seem to pose as if ready for an official's camera to document the occasion. Their superficial smiles and vacuous detached expressions however, imply otherwise. The men's hands are heavily blackened, in contrast to the resplendent red of the background. Black, which symbolically conveys a sense of tragedy and ominous gloom, is set against the red colour associated with communism. Su has used each of these two colours extensively in his artworks for the purposes of social commentary on China.

Su Xinping (b. 1960, China) graduated from the Tianjin Institute of Fine Arts, Painting Department, Inner Mongolia Teachers' College, Department of Fine Arts in 1983. A prominent arts educator, Su now heads the printmaking department at Beijing's prestigious Central Academy of Fine Arts. He has held solo exhibitions in the Shanghai Art Museum, National Art Gallery of China, Beijing, Seton Hall University, USA, and LASALLE College of the Arts, Singapore.

(SC)

Sun Yuan & Peng Yu

Hong Kong Intervention

2009
C-prints, set of 20
Edition 1/5
Dimensions variable

Singapore Art Museum
collection

Hong Kong Intervention explores a contemporary social phenomenon in Hong Kong where Filipino domestic workers are a key part of the social fabric of the city, and are also a growing phenomenon in other parts of Asia. This project invited 100 Filipino domestic workers in Hong Kong to photograph the households they worked in, with the inclusion of a toy grenade which the artists provided. These photographs capture the homes where the domestic workers work and live in, alongside their own portraits, as seen from the back.

A form of tension and anxiety arises from the insertion of the grenade prop in the otherwise assumed safe setting of the domestic household. The subjects photographed exude an uneasy calm as they allow viewers into their employers' homes, and into their most private and inner sanctums. The artists intended for this project to highlight the issue of domestic workers, whom many households are highly dependent on.

Sun Yuan (b. 1972, Beijing, China) and Peng Yu (b. 1974, Heilongjiang, China) are a collaborative artist duo from China whose controversial works test and push social conventions and ethical norms, often conveying an incisive social critique at the same time. Their parodies of everyday contemporary life are intended to shock viewers against mind-numbing acceptance, and to bring a return to more active deliberation on such issues.

(DC)

Xing Danwen

disCONNEXION

2002–2003
C-prints, set of 15
Edition of 8/15
76 x 62 cm (each)

Singapore Art Museum
collection

The tangled wires, circuit boards and broken cellphone casings in Xing Danwen's images in the *disCONNEXION* series reflect the raw economics at work in China's Guangdong province, regarded as a thriving dumping ground for the world's obsolete electronics.

The dark reality of 21st century technological development – of rampant junking of discarded electronic parts – portrayed by the artist through these abstract, almost beautiful images. The extensive reliance on newer technology and the disposable culture of the quickly obsolete in America result in a nightmare landscape of a technological graveyard in which decomposing e-trash ends up in Guangdong to be sorted manually and processed by the villagers there. Complete villages are devoted to sorting and processing specific materials, and the primitive processes used result in harm to the villages. Many of them that have the lingering smell of burnt plastic as the villagers melt wires to obtain the copper inside.

A self-taught photographer, Xing Danwen (b. 1967, Xi'an, China) has used the medium to make observations about Chinese society in the late-1980s and early 1990s. She pushed the boundaries of photography in China then by using it to challenge notions of humanity, female identity, charting a generation that was born in the 1960s and had experienced huge cultural transformation in China.

Xing Danwen graduated with a Master in Fine Arts from School of Visual Arts in New York, United States. She had originally trained in painting at the Central Academy of Fine Arts in Beijing. In 2011 and 2010, she was the part of the Jury for the SOCIETE GENRALE Chinese Art Awards. In 2008, she was an Award Finalist, ING REAL Photography Award in the Netherlands. In 2012, she had two solo shows in N-ce, Bogota, Columbia, and in the Institute of Contemporary Arts at the LASALLE College of the Arts, Singapore.

(DC)

Zhang Peng

Little Red

2008
C-prints
Edition of 2/5
180 x 228 cm

Acquired with support
from Pontiac Investment Pte Ltd

Singapore Art Museum
collection

Zhang Peng's photographs often show an elaborate theatrical set in which a little girl is featured. These images are digitally manipulated, with the eyes and the slenderness of the girls' bodies being enhanced and emphasised. The haunting expressions of these little girls, sitting timidly on the richly coloured settees, evoke an unsettling response as well as a heightened sense of drama. They convey a disarming vulnerability that leaves a sense of discomfort. The overly elaborate and luxurious sets seem to overwhelm and oppress these tiny figures, complicit as they are in them. The loss of innocence of the girls, as well as their relative sizes to the sets, point to the artist's intended message about the relentless expansion and development of China, and its impact on the individual.

Zhang Peng (b. 1981, Shan Dong, China) graduated from Central Academy of Fine Art, Beijing, China. His works were exhibited in ART Singapore in 2005 and in the same year, he exhibited in the Beijing International Triennium Exhibition. In 2007, he exhibited in Tang Contemporary Art in Bangkok, Thailand, and had a solo show with Art Seasons in Beijing, China.

(DC)

CHINA

Zheng Bo

The Karibu Islands

2007
Digital video and text
Dimensions variable
Video duration 8:38 mins

Gift of the Artist as part of the
Asia Pacific Breweries Foundation
Signature Art Prize 2008

Singapore Art Museum
collection

Responding to the vast transformations affecting China and the rapid pace of urban life, Zheng Bo produced this video work which takes place on the fictional land of the Karibu Islands. Taking its name from the poem by Tang Dynasty poet Li Po, the Karibu Islands also operate on a radically different temporal reality for time travels backwards on the fictional isle. On one level, it results in absurd scenes in which people walk backwards, but a more serious philosophical query also underpins the work. Using the device of a temporal reversal, the work considers what happens to historical developments that unfold against their natural chronology and society's 'progress' when it now occurs in the reverse: latest advancements become primitive and 'backward', and hierarchical structures are reduced to their raw beginnings. Far from alienating, the islands can be a refuge from the frenzy of the contemporary city. In "A Letter Home", one of the three video segments of the work, a young lady who has time-travelled from this world informs her family about her decision to stay on in the Karibu Islands. The work is part of an ongoing major project by the artist which has been presented at various exhibition platforms.

Zheng Bo (b. 1974, China) received his Masters of Fine Art from the Chinese University of Hong Kong in 2005, and participated in the 4th Auckland Triennial (2010) as well as the 3rd Guangzhou Triennial (2008).

(JT)

Zhou Xiaohu

Crowd of Bystanders

2003–2005
Clay statues and 10 video
animations (installed in a
circular ring)
Edition 3/3
800 x 800 cm

Singapore Art Museum
collection

Zhou Xiaohu's ***Crowd of Bystanders*** is an interrogation of the interaction between mass media and political developments. Although ostensibly about China, it finds relevance throughout the world, given that we often view violent and social change through the television and mass media images.

The work comprises of 10 videos – which portray events such as the trial of Saddam Hussein and the September 11 attacks – and the videos are paired with 10 ceramic dioramas. The claymation style of the videos evoke an absurdly infantile view of obscenity and violence, a strategy that ultimately renders the violence more real and shocking. Yet, as the artist himself notes, "because of the overflow of information today in the media, the shocking actualities that we see nightly on our TVs have become entertainment". In his paintings, videos and sets of sculptures, Zhou continually registers the media reality prevalent in China and the role of government policies within Chinese society.

Zhou Xiaohu (b. 1960, Changzhou, Jiangsu Province, China) graduated with a Bachelor in Fine Art from the Sichuan Academy, China. His group exhibitions include the 40th International Film Festival Rotterdam in the Netherlands, and 'Selections from Projects 35: International Video', at New Orleans Museum of Art (NOMA), United States. His also held a solo show at ART BASEL 42 in Switzerland, 2011.

(DC)

Asia

INDIA

Vibha Galhotra
G.R. Iranna
Ranbir Kaleka
Jitish Kallat
Nalini Malani

Vibha Galhotra

Neo-Camouflage

2006
Digital print on archival paper
(Hannemul photo rag)
Set of 6, edition 3/4
55.88 x 83.82 cm
(Prints nos. 1,2,3,4 & 5);
55.88 x 147.32 cm (Print no. 6)

Singapore Art Museum
collection

Neo-Camouflage confronts its viewer with pertinent urban issues such as destructiveness, overcrowding, pollution and psychological distress. It depicts how the artificial environment has become an almost uncontrollable phenomenon, overflowing from and intruding into public and personal spaces. Urbanisation and its effects is a subject often adopted by artists from Asia and Southeast Asia, particularly those living in environments undergoing rapid change. Galhotra imagines a need to reinvent the idea of the military fatigue (camouflage uniform) as if it is needed to blend into the concrete jungle rather than the natural foliage. The work has also been described by the artist as "coming from a satirical urge, following strands of thought about the urban takeover of environment".

Vibha Galhotra (b. 1978, New Delhi, India) graduated with a Bachelor from the Government College of Arts in Chandigarh, and later her Masters from Kala Bhavana, Visva Bharti, Santiniketan, India. Her works frequently address the complex and at times convoluted relationships between the city and its inhabitants. Her works can be found in the collections of Gate Foundation, United States; Devi Art Foundation, India, and Essel Museum, Austria.

(KH)

G.R. Iranna

Wounded Tools

2007
Mixed media: fibreglass, artificial
fur, iron, wood, acrylic
colouring, cloth
127 x 183 x 61 cm

Gift of the Artist as part of the
Asia Pacific Breweries Foundation
Signature Art Prize 2008

Singapore Art Museum
collection

Wounded Tools touches on the high human and ecological cost of humankind's never-ending quest for advancement and progress. The donkey has long been a beast of burden, labouring in farms and fields, but it is also a creature associated with the traits of stubbornness and stupidity. Those human follies are suggested here, as well as exploitation and subjection, and the naturalistic sculpture offers a commentary on the darker side of civilisation. The saddle on the donkey's back holds a variety of agrarian tools, such as the hammer, but interestingly, they have been wrapped with blood-stained bandages. The artist has effected an ironic reversal because the tools – which, when misused, can inflict violence – have become wounded themselves, a critique on the oft-fluctuating nature of power, and relationships between victor and victim.

G.R. Iranna (b. 1970, Karnataka, India) has held several solo exhibitions in United States and India. A multi-disciplinary artist, he obtained his Bachelor of Fine Art from the college of Visual Arts in Gulbarga in 1992, and Masters of Fine Art from Delhi College of Art in 1994. Iranna was also the recipient of National Academy Award (India) in 1997 and his works are in the collection of the National Gallery of Modern Art, Delhi.

(JT)

Ranbir Kaleka

He Was A Good Man

2007–2008
Oil on canvas on easel and
single-channel video projection
with sound
Edition 3/3
130 x 172.7 x 20 cm
Video duration 5:03 mins (loop)

Singapore Art Museum
collection

He Was A Good Man combines painting with video to create a lyrical narrative of one man and his life passing by, and his single-minded absorption in the seemingly mundane or trivial task of threading a needle. The protagonist's attempts to thread the needle parallel the practice of painting, another solitary pursuit which requires intense concentration and hand/eye co-ordination. All the while, the play of light and movement on the surface of the canvas dissembles and dissolves its subject matter, extending the artwork's self-reflective commentary on art, vision and visuality. This work is probably one of Kaleka's best-known works, having been exhibited extensively worldwide, including presentations at the Sydney Biennale in 2008, as well as at MOCA Taipei in 2010.

Ranbir Kaleka (b. 1953, India) studied Art at the Punjab University, and received a MFA in Painting from the Royal College of Art, London. His unique artworks combine easel painting with video projection. This layering explores the interaction between two markedly different media: one traditional and static, one contemporary and dynamic. The results are often lyrical and startling, as viewers watch paintings literally 'come to life', animated by the light and motion of the flickering projection; at other times, the layering of the video on top of the painting calls attention to the very illusion of 'life-likeness' that both media have tried to create, by drawing attention to the fact that what we are viewing is in fact a flat surface, manipulated by light, shadow and movement. Kaleka's work extends the traditional limits of either medium, and by combining them, conjures up poetic and phantasmagorical narratives, while calling attention to our modes of seeing.

(TSL)

Jitish Kallat

Annexation

2009
Black lead, paint, resin and steel
Edition 2/3
183 x 150 x 130 cm

Singapore Art Museum
collection

Annexation was made one year after a terrorist attack in 2008 in Mumbai, India, at the Victoria Terminus train station built by the British in 1887 to commemorate the Golden Jubilee of Queen Victoria. The large sculpture of a larger-than-life kerosene stove is filled with more than 100 images of animals depicted in the friezes at the station. As in the original friezes, animals are depicted devouring the weaker ones while clinging on to various things such as pots of food and plants, enacting scenes that the artist describes as "not unlike the daily grind of survival that this (terminal) porch witnesses everyday". The use of the kerosene stove serves to further localise the context. In India, many still use kerosene as a source of energy, be it to cook or to provide light in areas and villages that do not have ready access to electricity. The work is a depiction of allegorical scenes of a constant and daily human struggle in a country such as India. The sculpture has been dusted with graphite powder, a carbon that gives the sculpture sheen but also suggests a dark, burnt, expended and rather redundant resource.

Jitish Kallat (b. 1974, Mumbai, India) graduated from the Sir Jamsetjee Jeejebhoy School of Art in 1996. He is known to construct his art around local issues and geography and *Annexation* is a classic example of his practice. He has exhibited widely in international solo and group shows in venues including the Art Institute of Chicago, United States (2010), Lille 3000, Lille, France (2006) and House of World Cultures, Berlin, Germany (2005).

(KH)

(Detail)

Nalini Malani

Unity in Diversity

2003
Single-channel video installation with sound, living room setting with flat screen/projection in golden frame on a crimson wall, two lamps and a framed black/white photographs
Edition 1/10
Dimensions variable
Video duration 7:00 mins

Singapore Art Museum collection

Unity in Diversity was prompted by an incident in 2002, when a train transporting Hindu pilgrims returning from Ayodhya was attacked by a large Muslim mob and burned while it passed the city of Godhra in the Indian state of Gujarat. The part of the train that was badly burned contained mostly women and children, 58 of whom were killed. Retaliatory riots by the Hindus ensued, beginning from the city of Ahmedabad in Gujarat. In a period of communal violence, more than 700 Muslims and 250 Hindus were killed, with more than 200 others missing. Places of worship were attacked and either destroyed or damaged and over 70,000 people fled their homes.

As suggested by India's own political commentators then, the violence in Gujarat and the massacre of the Muslims could have been the ploy of its very government; it was a cynicism arising from the government's failure to prevent and contain the riots as they unfolded, despite their supposed belief in and invocation of 'unity in diversity', an age-old motto of India often cited and activated by national leaders such as Mahatma Ghandi, Chandra Bose and Jawaharlal Nehru.

This work appropriates a 19th century painting of the same title by Indian master painter Raja Ravi Varma. The latter work depicts 11 female musicians dressed in various traditional costumes, again unified through the expression 'unity in diversity'.

Nalini Malani (b. 1946, Karachi, Pakistan) and graduated from the Sir Jamsetjee Jeejebhoy School of Art in 1969. A veteran in the Indian contemporary art landscape, Malani has been featured in museums and galleries in New Zealand, New York, Ireland and Denmark. She was a resident artist at LASALLE College of the Arts, Singapore in 1999 and Fukuoka Asian Art Museum from 1999–2000, where she created *Hamletmachine*.

(KH)

Nalini Malani

Hamletmachine

2000
4-channel video, three wall
projections and one floor
projection on a bed of salt
surrounded with mirrors
Edition 2/5
Dimensions variable
Video duration 20:00 mins

Singapore Art Museum
collection

Hamletmachine is an appropriation of the play by Heiner Müller of the same name and from Shakespeare's eponymous Hamlet. Written in 1977, Müller's 'Hamletmachine' explores the 'consequence of inactivity', or the inability to respond to a crisis causing it to perpetuate in a vicious cycle; violence similarly, Malini suggests, seems to be deliberately perpetuated throughout history in such a cycle. Even some 30 years on, Müller's play that looks at issues of victimisation and redemption, how disenfranchised groups of people can turn upon one another; it is as chilling today as it was then, even if only excerpted in Malini's work.

The installation appropriates fragments of Müller's play and transforms them into a parable of the Hindu-Muslim conflict in South Asia, rising above religious and nationalist sentiments to offer a universal standpoint. This universal quality is represented in the video in which Harada Nobuo, a Japanese Butoh dancer, uses his body as a screen onto which images of history and icons of capitalist culture are etched. The use of a bed of salt in the installation also references the Salt March in 1930 by Mahatma Ghandi who embarked on a 240-mile walk as a protest and act of civil disobedience against British rule and monopoly on salt.

Nalini Malani (b. 1946, Karachi, Pakistan) and graduated from the Sir Jamsetjee Jeejebhoy School of Art in 1969. A veteran in the Indian contemporary art landscape, Malani has been featured in museums and galleries in New Zealand, New York, Ireland and Denmark. She was a resident artist at LASALLE College of the Arts, Singapore in 1999 and Fukuoka Asian Art Museum from 1999–2000, where she created *Hamletmachine*.

(KH)

Asia

JAPAN

Tetsuya Nagato

Tetsuya Nagato

I Against I

2002
Digital print
27 x 250 cm

Gift of the Artist

Singapore Art Museum
collection

I Against I is created using images taken of Nagato's hometown, Tokyo. These are generally gritty images of an urban city – "neon lights covered with auto exhaust dust, or jammed trains", and "the feel that people don't think much about the future", as the artist recounts. Based on hand-made drawings that were then fed into the computer, the resulting duotone work is the emblem of a city that is a 'mismatch' with what one would imagine a 'hometown' to be: beautiful, with a river running through it and mountains as its backdrop. It was also with an ironic insight that Nagato rediscovered after years abroad, that Tokyo remains his hometown.

This work, which won the Excellence Prize at the Japan Media Arts Festival in 2002, embodies the theme of polarity and integration. It blends realistic and surrealistic images, organic and inorganic forms in an elaborate composition. Eschewing cutting-edge technology for a more orthodox collage technique, this work suggests that technology is only a means to an end.

Nagato's body of digital photo collage works, is the result of his pursuing his early interest in new technology – first in scanned images that later consequently progressed to digital imaging processes. Such investigations concluded with his cultivating a collage technique, using various images, culled from old books, papers and prints and also his photo prints, to illustrations, and at times, his preferring to paint directly on the surface.

Tetsuya Nagato (b. 1970, Japan) graduated from Senshu University High School, after which he left for the United States where he studied art. He returned to Japan in 1996, whereupon his work ranged from designing CD album covers for top musicians, to illustrations for fashion publications and documentary filmmaking. Among the many awards he won were the 18th The Choice award in 2001, the "Digital Art (Non interactive) Division Excellence Prize" at the Japan Media Arts Festival in 2002, and Tokyo Wonder Wall prize in 2003. His work ranges from photography, to mixed media collages and digital photo collages.

(SW)

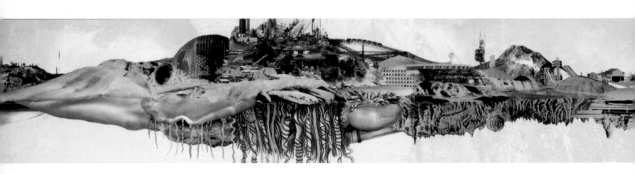

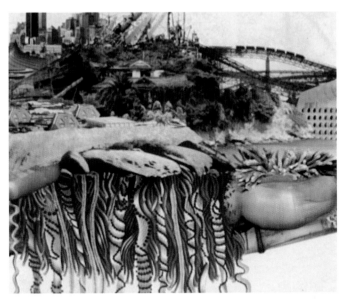

(Detail)

Asia

KOREA

Osang Gwon
Park Dae Cho

Osang Gwon

BluRay_B

2009
C-prints and mixed media
275 x 88 x 60 cm

Singapore Art Museum
collection

Works by Korean artist, Osang Gwon, defy simple categorisation. Categories such as sculpture, mixed media or photography no longer suffice as a means to accurately identify and classify his work. **BluRay_B** is one of a series of similarly sculpted figures in 'Deodorant Type', begun in 2001, which launched him to fame. Inspired by pop culture and media (advertisements), his 'Deodorant Type series are photo-sculptures made by collaging hundreds of photographs taken of a subject (a person), onto a 3-dimensional sculpture carved out of pink foam. A layer of resin is then applied over the completed piece to strengthen the work.

For Gwon, the term 'Deodorant Type' means "covering something up and changing its odour". It was inspired by a Nivea advertising campaign on deodorants in Korea. Produced using a Middle-Eastern model, it reveals a certain ignorance of their target consumers – Koreans, in this case – that Asians generally do not 'perspire'. As a result, his figures are "off a bit" to reflect these disjunctions of beliefs and attitudes, a comment on the effects of globalisation.

Compared to Gwon's earlier works from the series, the more recent figures gradually lose exact replication, as the photographs become more haphazardly layered. The viewer, however, may chance upon a deliberately manoeuvred angle of vision, of seeing a clear and distinct visage. Otherwise the illusory form of the figure is characterised by a disruptive quality. **BluRay_B** is inspired by pop culture of celebrity athletes and Korean street-fashion.

Osang Gwon's (b. 1974, Seoul, Korea) first debut took place in Korea in 1999, a year before he graduated from his Bachelor of Fine Art studies in Sculpture. Since 2002, he has held solo shows and participated in international group exhibitions like Japan, France, Italy, Netherlands, the United States, Germany, Chile, Argentina, Switzerland, the United Kingdom and China. His works are collected by The National Museum of Contemporary Art, Korea; Busan Museum of Art, Busan, Korea; Youngeun Museum of Contemporary Art, Gwangju, Korea; Embassy of Switzerland; Burger Collection; Universal Music Group; and many others.

(SW)

Park Dae Cho

Rainbow

2010
Transparency print mounted
on light-box
60 x 79 cm

Singapore Art Museum
collection

In creating ***Rainbow***, Park has used a combination of traditional and laborious photographic processing methods together with digital image manipulation. Although the image morphs through a range of 'rainbow' colours, the work's haunting focus is always on the young girl's eyes, which reflect the mushroom cloud of a nuclear bomb explosion. The effect is that the viewer is both a voyeur looking at the subject, and also a witness to the devastating catastrophe that the child is facing. Like many of Park's other works, ***Rainbow*** examines the trials and difficulties faced by children as they negotiate their way through the world of adults.

Park Dae Cho (b. 1970, South Korea) received his MFA in Korean Art from the Sang Myung University, where he is also pursuing his PhD. Since 2010, has had several solo shows, including 'Innocence Lost' at the Chelsea Art Museum, United States, and has also participated in numerous group exhibitions.

(TJ)

Asia

MONGOLIA

Davaa Dorjderem

Davaa Dorjderem

The Voice in the Space

2006
Mixed media: bone, leather,
wood, paper, artificial stone
Set of 3 pieces
40 x 60 x 60 cm (each)

Gift of the Artist as part of the
Asia Pacific Breweries Foundation
Signature Art Prize 2008

Singapore Art Museum
collection

The moment of childbirth is usually associated as the time of beginnings, signalling a human being's entry into the world. Here however, Davaa Dorjderem has reached back to an even earlier stage in human life – the period when a foetus is in the mother's womb – to explore ideas of existence, consciousness and pre-beginnings. Two babies, sculpted from artificial stone, are each depicted emerging from a pair of gnarled, sheep horns; they flank a box which contains a menacing mask and another sheep horn. The placement of the two babies inside the sheep horns seems an unlikely combination at first, but juxtaposed, the horns evoke the maturity of life to come, while also offering the vulnerable foetuses a sense of protection. For the artist, the embryonic state is regarded as a time of potential and promise, and in that regard, the foetus' existence is god-like and it possesses a powerful consciousness all of its own, hearing voices that those in the outside world are deaf to. This work was the winner of the People's Choice Award at the Asia Pacific Breweries Foundation Signature Art Prize 2008.

Davaa Dorjderem (b. 1981, Mongolia) has exhibited at the 4th Fukuoka Asian Art Triennale, Japan (2009), the Asia Pacific Breweries Foundation Signature Art Prize, Singapore (2008), as well as several other group exhibitions in Mongolia.

(JT)

Asia-Pacific

AUSTRALIA

Tracey Moffatt

Tracey Moffatt
in collaboration with
Gary Hillberg

Artist

2000
DVD
Duration 10:00 mins (loop)

DOOMED

2007
DVD, edition 218/499
Duration 10:00 mins (loop)

Love

2003
DVD
Duration 21:00 mins (loop)

Lip

2000
DVD
Duration 10:00 mins (loop)

Mother

2009
DVD, edition 48/200
Duration 20:00 mins (loop)

Other

2009
DVD, edition 55/200
Duration 07:00 mins (loop)

Revolution

2008
DVD, edition 113/250
Duration 14:00 mins (loop)

Acquired with support from
Lee Foundation and ANZ Bank

Singapore Art Museum
collection

In the late-1980s, Tracey Moffatt came to prominence after a commission by Albury Regional Art Gallery, Australia, for a photographic series titled 'Something More'. These pictures, designed to look as if they were shot on a movie set, reference topics ranging from sexuality, history, race and cultural diaspora. From here, Moffatt expanded her practice to later include experimental video making.

These videos are part of a series of what the artist calls "montage films". Together with editor Gary Hillberg, Moffatt produced these films by re-editing, juxtaposing, re-mixing and carefully re-constructing readymade video clips from various genres to create commentaries and critiques of modern life as played in cinema. For example in the film **Mother**, Moffatt claims, "Loving mothers, slapping mothers, suffering mothers, protective mothers – I think I got them all." This description by the artist suggests the extent of influence Hollywood has had on all aspects of our lives – and vice-versa.

Tracey Moffatt (b. 1960, Brisbane, Australia) graduated with a Bachelor of Arts in Visual Communications from the Queensland College of Art in 1982. Now based in New York, Mofatt has shown in Kunsthalle Vienna (1998), Institute of Contemporary Art, Boston (1999), Venice Biennale (1997) and Sao Paulo Biennial (1996 & 1998).

(KH)

Clockwise:
Artist, **Mother**, **Lip**

Clockwise:
Revolution, ***Other***, ***DOOMED***, ***Love***

Asia-Pacific

MEXICO

Rafael Lozano-Hemmer

Rafael Lozano-Hemmer

Frequency and Volume: Relational Architecture 9

2003
Installation with projectors, cameras, computers, radio-electric scanners, antennae, radios and 48-channel sound system
Dimensions variable

Singapore Art Museum collection

Frequency and Volume is an interactive new media work that enables participants to tune into and listen to different radio frequencies by using their own bodies. Shadows of participants are projected onto the wall of the exhibition space, from which a computerised tracking system follows these shadows, using the movement and size of the shadows to scan the radio waves as well as controlling the volume of the signal. Up to 48 frequencies can be tuned simultaneously and the resulting sound environment forms a composition controlled by people's movements. This piece visualises the normally invisible radio-electric spectrum and turns the human body into an antenna.

The project was developed at a time when the Mexican Government was very active in shutting down rogue radio stations in indigenous communities in the states of Chiapas and Guerrero. Lozano-Hemmer wanted to, in his words, question "who has access to the public space that is the radio-electric spectrum", as he believes there is an inequality in the assignment of such frequencies by the government.

A Mexican-Canadian artist, Rafael Lozano-Hemmer (b. 1967), Mexico) develops large-scale interactive installations that cross between the fields of architecture and performance art, where he creates platforms for public participation by perverting existing technologies. This work was exhibited at the Singapore Biennale 2011, after which it entered the Museum's collection.

(DC)

Artist Index

Southeast Asia

Asia

Asia-Pacific

Writers Biographies

(SC) Silvia Chan is a Curatorial Projects Manager at the Singapore Art Museum. She holds a B.A. in Creative Arts from the University of Melbourne, Australia. From 2004 to 2012, she managed SAM's Artbank collection, providing art consultancy for various Singapore government ministries, such as the Parliament House, the Prime Minister's office and APEC (2009). Exhibitions which she has project managed include *Thai Transience, Seeker of Hope: Works by Jia Aili, Russel Wong: Photography 1980-2005* and *Ming Wong: Life of Imitation*, the latter which travelled to the United States, Australia and Japan.

(DC) David Chew is a Curator at the Singapore Art Museum and oversees its Singapore and China collections, and works on the Collections portfolio. He has a Masters in Contemporary Art Theory from Goldsmiths College, University of London, a BA in English Literature and Sociology from the National University of Singapore, and a Business degree from Monash University, Australia. His past exhibitions include *The Singapore Show: Future Proof, Trans-cool TOKYO: Contemporary Japanese Art from the Museum of Contemporary Art Tokyo Collection* and *Tags and Treats: Works by Vincent Leow.*

(KH) Khairuddin Hori is a Senior Curator at the Singapore Art Museum, and oversees its Malaysia collection and the Collections portfolio. He holds a Masters of Art from the Open University, UK. His past exhibitions include *Lee Wen: Lucid Dreams in the Reverie of the Real, The Singapore Show: Future Proof*, and *Negotiating Home, History and Nation: Two Decades of Contemporary Art in Southeast Asia 1991–2011.*

(MH) Michelle Ho is a Curator at the Singapore Art Museum and oversees its Thailand collection. She holds a Masters in Curatorship and a BA in Comparative Religion from the University of Sydney, Australia. Her past exhibitions include *Amanda Heng: Speak to Me, Walk with Me, Natee Utarit: After Painting* and *The Artists Village: 20 Years On.*

(TSL) Tan Siuli is Assistant Director of Programmes and Curator at the Singapore Art Museum, and oversees its Indonesia collection and Education portfolio. She holds a Masters in Art History from University College London, UK, a BA in Literature and Art History from the University of Nottingham, UK, and a Postgraduate Diploma in Education from the National Institute of Education, Singapore. Her past exhibitions include *Chimera (The Collectors Show: Asian Contemporary Art from Private Collections), Classic Contemporary: Contemporary Southeast Asian Art from the Singapore Art Museum Collection, The President's Young Talents 2009*, and *FX Harsono: Testimonies.*

(TJ) Jason Toh is a Senior Curator at the Singapore Art Museum. He holds a BA in Art History and French from Middlebury College, Vermont, USA. His past exhibitions at SAM include *It's Now or Never 1: New Acquisitions from Singapore*, *It's Now or Never 2: New Acquisitions from Southeast Asia* and he helmed the inaugural issue of *Visual Culture*, SAM's exhibition in-print that features the museum's permanent collection in publication form.

(JT) Joyce Toh is a Senior Curator at Singapore Art Museum and oversees its Philippines collection and Publications portfolio. She holds a Masters in Aesthetics (Philosophy of Art) from University of York, UK and a BA in Art History from Syracuse University, USA. Her past exhibitions include the *Asia Pacific Breweries Foundation Singapore Art Prize 2011* and *2008* exhibitions, *Thrice Upon A Time: A Century of Story in the Art of the Philippines*, and *is it tomorrow yet? Highlights from the Daimler Art Collection*.

(NW) Naomi Wang Zhenghui is an Assistant Curator at the Singapore Art Museum, and oversees its Cambodia, Laos and Myanmar collection. She holds a BA in Art History from the University of Toronto, Canada. She is currently working on an upcoming exhibition featuring recently acquired works by the museum, as well as the second edition of *Visual Culture*.

(SW) Susie Wong is an artist, writer and curator in Singapore. She has contributed to several publications and monographs since the late 1980s, including being a regular contributor to Life!The Straits Times, Singapore, in the 1990s. Her art works had been exhibited in Singapore and Malaysia.

Image Credits

Unless indicated otherwise, artwork images are courtesy of Singapore Art Museum.

Pg 13: **Song-Ming Ang**, *Be True To Your School*: Image courtesy of the artist

Pg 18: **Cheo Chai Hiang**, *Li Bo Xue*: Images courtesy of the artist

Pg 19: **Choy Ka Fai**, *Rectangular Dreams*: Image courtesy of the artist

Pg 20 – 21: **Genevieve Chua**, *After The Flood*: Images courtesy of the artist

Pg 22 – 23: **Chua Chye Teck**, *Wonderland*: Image courtesy of the artist

Pg 26: **Chun Kai Feng**, *¥ € $*: Images courtesy of the artist

Pg 27: **John Clang**, *The White Book*: Image courtesy of the artist

Pg 28: **Safaruddin Dyn**, *Maxwell Road, Ang Siang Hill* & *Tiffin Carrier*: Images courtesy of the artist

Pg 29: **Eng Joo Heng**, *Lotus #9, #14* & *#24*: Images courtesy of the artist

Pg 30 – 31: **Amanda Heng**, *Another Woman*: Images courtesy of the artist

Front inside cover, Pg 32 – 33: **Ho Tzu Nyen**, *The Cloud of Unknown*: Photographs by Russell Adam Morton and images courtesy of artist.

Pg 40 – 41: **Jane Lee**, *Status*: Image courtesy of the artist

Pg 42: **Jane Lee**, *The Object I* & *II*: Images courtesy of the artist

Pg 46 – 47: **Sean Lee**, *Everybody Knows You Cried Last Night* & *HOMEWORK*: Images courtesy of the artist

Pg 48 – 49: **Lee Wen**, *Strange Fruit*: Images courtesy of the artist

Pg 51: **Lee Wen**, *World Class Society*: Images courtesy of the artist

Pg 53: **Vincent Leow**, *Yellow Field*: Image courtesy of the artist

Pg 8– 9, 54 – 55: **Charles Lim**, *All Lines Flow Out*: Image courtesy of the artist

Pg 56: **Jessie Lim**, *Orbs*: Images courtesy of Gajah Gallery

Pg 58: **Gilles Massot**, *Retro Specks Future Pixs*: Image courtesy of the artist

Pg 59: **Kumari Nahappan**, *Om (Aum) Series-Vibration E*: Image courtesy of the artist

Pg 61: **Kumari Nahappan**, *Shakti Dimension Two A-B-C*: Images courtesy of the artist

Pg 62: **Kumari Nahappan**, *Surya Series 99 Number Two*: Images courtesy of Art Forum

Pg 63: **Kumari Nahappan**, *Nine-O-One B*: Image courtesy of the artist

Pg 65: **Francis Ng**, *Displaced*: Images courtesy of the artist

Pg 67: **Om Mee Ai**, *Triptych-W*: Image courtesy of the artist

Pg 68: **Donna Ong**, *Crystal City*: Image courtesy of Khairuddin Hori

Pg 74 – 75: **Sherman Ong**, *Life of Imitation, Ticket Seller; Life Imitation, Mr. Neo Chon Teck; Life of Imitation, Mr Wong Han Min*: Images courtesy of the artist

Pg 77: **PHUNK & Keiichi Tanaami**, *Eccentric City: Rise and Fall*: Images courtesy of the artist

Pg 78: **PHUNK**, *Electricity (Neon)*: Image courtesy of TAKAMURADAISUKE

Pg 84: **Sai Hua Kuan**, *Space Drawing 5*: Image courtesy of the artist

Pg 85: **Sima Salehi Rahni**, *Circle*: Image courtesy of the artist

Pg 95: **Tang Ling Nah**, *An Outer Space Within the House II Scene I & II*: Images courtesy of the artist

Pg 96: **Vertical Submarine**, *A View With A Room*: Image courtesy of the artist

Pg 97: **Vertical Submarine**, *DeComposition I: Dead Books*: Image courtesy of the artist

Pg 98: **Vertical Submarine**, *Fool's Gold*: Image courtesy of the artist

Pg 99: **Vertical Submarine**, *Flirting Point*: Image courtesy of the artist

Pg 102 – 103: **Suzann Victor**, *Bloodline: Third World Extra Virgin Dreams*: Photographs by Arwi Reamillo and images courtesy of the artist

Pg 104 – 105, Back inside cover: **Suzann Victor**, *Expense of Spirit in a Waste of Shame*: Images courtesy of the artist

Pg 108: **Ming Wong**, *Four Malay Stories*: Video stills images courtesy of the artist

Pg 111: **Ming Wong**, *In Love for the Mood*: Video still image courtesy of the artist

Pg 113: **Ming Wong**, *Life of Imitation*: Video still image courtesy of the artist

Pg 115: **Ian Woo**, *Lot Sees Salt*: Images courtesy of the artist

Pg 117: **Joel Yuen**, *The Human Condition*: Images courtesy of the artist

Pg 120: **Robert Zhao Renhui**, *If A Tree Falls in a Forest*: Image courtesy of Khairuddin Hori

Pg 130 – 131: **Meas Sokhorn, Srey Bandol, Keith Deverell & Sue McCauley**, *The Hawker Song*: Image courtesy of Java Arts

Pg 137: **Vandy Rattana**, *Bomb Ponds*: Image courtesy of the artist

Pg 142 – 143: **Apotik Komik**, *Under Estimate*: Image courtesy of Valentine Willie Fine Art

Pg 150 – 151: **Dadang Christanto**, *Kekerasan I (Violence I)*: Image courtesy of the artist

Pg 152 – 153: **FX Harsono**, *Burned Victims*: Image courtesy of the artist

Pg 154: **FX Harsono**, *Power And The Oppressed*: Image courtesy of the artist

Pg 155: **FX Harsono**, *Rewriting The Erased*: Image courtesy of the artist

Pg 162: **Mella Jaarsama**, *Shaggy*: Photograph by Mie Cornoedus and image courtesy of the artist

Pg 163: **Mella Jaarsama**, *The Last Animist*: Image courtesy of the artist

Pg 167: **Nasirun**, *Bajaj Pasti Berlalu (The Bajaj Will Surely Pass)*: Image courtesy of GARIS ART

Pg 168: **Nasirun**, *Tanah Airku Indonesia (Indonesia My Motherland)*: Image courtesy of GARIS ART

Pg 180: **Yudi Sulistyo**, *Mewujudkan Angan (Realising Dreams)*: Image courtesy of Agung Sukindra

Pg 189: **Agus Suwage & Davy Linggar**, *Pinkswing Park*: Image courtesy of the artist

Pg 189: **Titarubi**, *Bayang Bayang Maha Kecil #9 (Shadows of the Smallest Kind)*: Image courtesy of the artist

Pg 194: **Tromarama**, *Zsa Zsa Zsu*: Image courtesy of the artist

Pg 195: **Entang Wiharso**, *Temple of Hope: Forest Of Eyes*: Image courtesy of Primo Marella Gallery and Studio NoMaden

Pg 200: **Tintin Wulia**, *Nous ne notons pas les fleurs (We Do Not Notice The Flowers)*: Image courtesy of the artist

Pg 201: **Albert Yonathan**, *Cosmic Labyrinth*: Image courtesy of the artist

Pg 203: **Albert Yonathan**, *Silent Union*: Image courtesy of the artist

Pg 216: **Chong Kim Chiew**, *The Stamp of Misreading, The Picture of Misreading 2, 3 & 4*: Images courtesy of the artist

Pg 218: **Chong Siew Ying**, *Pulse*: Image courtesy of the artist

Pg 226: **Phuan Thai Meng**, *The WE Project*: Images courtesy of the artist

Pg 247: **Alfredo & Isabel Aquilizan**, *Wings*: Photograph by OCS Alvarez and image courtesy of The Drawing Room

Pg 249: **Agnes Arellano**, *Haliya Bathing*: Image courtesy of the artist

Pg 250: **Felix Bacolor**, *Stormy Weather*: Image courtesy of the artist

Pg 253: **Anni Cabigting**, *On the Shelf, On the Shelf (After Michael Craig Martin)*: Image courtesy of the Artesan Gallery

Pg 256: **Mariano Ching**, *Elephant Man & Four-Legged Woman*: Image courtesy of Silverlens Gallery

Pg 262 – 263: **Kiri Dalena**, *Erased Slogans & Red Book of Slogans*: Images courtesy of Silverlens Gallery

Pg 268: **Roberto Feleo**, *Ang Retablo ng Bantaoay (The Retablo of Bantaoay)*: Image courtesy of Silverlens Gallery

Pg 270 – 271: **Nona Garcia**, *Fall Leaves After Leaves Fall*: Image courtesy of Finale Art File

Pg 276: **Renato Orara**, *Bookwork: NIV Compact Thinking Bible (page 403)*: Image courtesy of the artist

Pg 279: **Gary-Ross Pastrana**, *Echolalia*: Image courtesy of the artist

Pg 298: **Francesc Xavier Comas de la Paz**, *Jiuta-Mai*: Images courtesy of the artist.

Pg 302 – 303: **Sakarin Krue-On**, *Cloud Nine*: Images courtesy of the artist and 100 Tonson Gallery

Pg 304: **Sakarin Krue-On**, *Manorah and Best Friends of the Snake*: Images courtesy of the artist and 100 Tonson Gallery

Pg 305: **Sakarin Krue-On**, *No Fly Zone*: Image courtesy of the artist and 100 Tonson Gallery

Pg 304: **Sutee Kunavichayanont**, *History Class*: Images courtesy of the artist

Pg 308 – 309: **Torlarp Larpjaroensook**, *Bookshelf*: Images courtesy of Khairuddin Hori

Pg 312 – 313: **Kamin Lertchaiprasert**, *Sitting*: Images courtesy of Raif Tooten Photography

Pg 314 – 315: **Kedsuda Loogthong**, *Letters from Songkla*: Image courtesy of Richard Koh Fine Arts

Pg 319: **Sudsiri Pui-Ock**, *Draw My Life With Blue On White*: Image courtesy of the artist

Pg 340: **Natee Utarit**, *Tales of Yesterday, Today and Tomorrow*: Image courtesy of the artist

Pg 341: **Natee Utarit**, *The Ballad for Khrua In Khong/Greyscale*: Image courtesy of the artist

Pg 342 – 343: **Natee Utarit**, *The Birth of Tragedy*: Image courtesy of the artist

Pg 344: **Natee Utarit**, *The Crown*: Image courtesy of the artist

Pg 345: **Natee Utarit**, *The Western Light No.1*: Image courtesy of the artist

Pg 351: **Tiffany Chung**, *Enokiberry Tree in Wonderland*: Image courtesy of the artist and Galerie Quynh

Pg 351: **Tiffany Chung**, *Enokiberry Tree in Wonderland*: Image courtesy of the artist and Galerie Quynh

Pg 354: **Jun Nguyen-Hatsushiba**, *Breathing is Free: 12, 756. 3*: Image courtesy of the artist

Pg 355 – 357: **Jun Nguyen-Hatsushiba**, *Memorial Project Nha Trang, Vietnam: Towards the Complex – For the Courageous, the Curious and the Cowards*: Image courtesy of the artist

Pg 359: **Tung Mai**, *Racing Forward*: Image courtesy of the artist

Pg 362: **Richard Streitmatter-Tran**, *The Jungle Book*: Images courtesy of the artist

Pg 363: **Tran Luong**, *Red Scarf/Welt*: Image courtesy of the artist

Pg 372 – 373: **Chi Peng**, *Apollo in Transit*: Image courtesy of the artist

Pg 374 – 375: **Gao Lei**, *Cabinet*: Images courtesy of the artist

Pg 378 – 381: **Miao Xiaochun**, *Microcosm, Microcosm: Garden of Heavenly Delights & The Last Judgement in Cyberspace*: Images courtesy of the artist and Art Seasons

Pg 386 – 387: **Sun Yuan & Peng Yu**, *Hong Kong Intervention*: Images courtesy of the artist and Art Seasons

Pg 394: **Vibha Galhotra**, *Neo-Camouflage*: Image courtesy of the artist

Pg 397: **Ranbir Kaleka**, *He Was A Good Man*: Image courtesy of the artist

Pg 398 – 399: **Jitish Kallat**, *Annexation*: Image courtesy of ARNDT Gallery

Pg 400 – 401: **Nalini Malani**, *Unity in Diversity*: Images courtesy of the artist

Pg 402 – 403: **Nalini Malani**, *Hamletmachine*: Images courtesy of the artist and Arario Gallery

Pg 411: **Osang Gwon**, *BluRay_B*: Images courtesy of the artist and Arario Gallery

Pg 420 – 421: **Tracey Moffatt**, *Artist, DOOMED, Love, Lip, Mother, Other & Revolution*: Images courtesy of the artist and Roslyn Oxley9 Gallery

All artwork images © the artists